The Experience
of Teaching
General Music

The Experience of Teaching General Music

Betty W. Atterbury
University of Southern Maine

Carol P. Richardson
University of New South Wales

McGRAW-HILL, INC.

New York   St. Louis   San Francisco   Auckland   Bogotá   Caracas   Lisbon
London   Madrid   Mexico City   Milan   Montreal   New Delhi
San Juan   Singapore   Sydney   Tokyo   Toronto

This book was set in Palatino by A-R Editions, Inc.
The editors were Cynthia Ward and John M. Morriss;
the production supervisor was Paula Keller.
The cover was designed by Joan Greenfield.
Project supervision was done by The Total Book.
R. R. Donnelley & Sons Company was printer and binder.

THE EXPERIENCE OF TEACHING GENERAL MUSIC

 This book is printed on recycled, acid-free paper containing 10%
postconsumer waste.

1 2 3 4 5 6 7 8 9 0 DOH DOH 9 0 9 8 7 6 5 4

ISBN 0-07-002859-1

Library of Congress Cataloging-in-Publication Data

Atterbury, Betty Wilson.
    The experience of teaching general music / Betty W. Atterbury,
Carol P. Richardson.
        p.   cm.
    Includes bibliographical references, discography, and index.
    ISBN 0-07-002859-1
    1. School music—Instruction and study.   I. Richardson, Carol P.
II. Title.
MT1.A88   1995
372.87'044—dc20   94-33946

About the Authors

BETTY W. ATTERBURY is Professor of Music at the University of Southern Maine. She received her Ph.D. in Music Education from Northwestern University after many years of public school teaching experience. Professor Atterbury is the author of *Mainstreaming Exceptional Learners in Music* (Englewood Cliffs, NJ: Prentice-Hall, 1990) and of "Research on the Teaching of Elementary General Music" in *Handbook of Research on Music Teaching and Learning* (Edited by Richard Colwell, New York: Schirmer/MENC,1992). She edited *Elementary General Music: The Best of MEJ* (Reston: Music Educators National Conference, 1992) and has published numerous articles in all the major music education journals. Professor Atterbury has served the profession as Chair of the *Music Educators Journal* Editorial Committee and as President of the Maine Music Educators Association.

CAROL P. RICHARDSON is Associate Lecturer in the School of Music and Music Education at the University of New South Wales, in Sydney, Australia. She received her Ed.D. in Music Education from the University of Illinois after nine years as a general music teacher at both the elementary and secondary levels. Professor Richardson is the coauthor of "Critical Thinking and Music Education" in *Handbook of Research on Music Teaching and Learning* (Edited by Richard Colwell, New York: Schirmer/MENC, 1992) and has published articles in *Music Educators Journal, Bulletin of the Council for Research in Music Education,* and *Arts Education Policy Review.* Professor Richardson has served as a member of the Editorial Committee of *Music Educators Journal* and is a member of the Editorial Committee of the *Bulletin of the Council for Research in Music Education.* She is a National Academy of Education 1994–1995 Spencer Postdoctoral fellow.

This book is dedicated to our loves:
Bob Atterbury
and
Ian, Julia, and Gregory Richardson

Contents

3. Experiencing Music Through Singing: Primary   32

4. Experiencing Music Through Singing: Intermediate   60

5. Experiencing Music Through Listening: Primary   93

6. Experiencing Music Through Listening: Intermediate   112

7. Experiencing Music Through Moving: Primary and Intermediate   133

Preface

We are experiencing a renewed interest in public education in our country. Social changes in our society and an increased political interest at the federal and state levels are influencing changes in education in all sections of the United States. *Restructuring* and *site-based management* are terms that portray two attempts of public education to accommodate the immense pressures and demands now placed upon public schools. These changes mandate a reconsideration of traditional approaches in music teacher preparation.

The Experience of Teaching General Music represents a vision for the preparation of both elementary and middle school general music teachers that is radically different from anything else that has been published. The text is not constructed to be read and put away after each assignment; rather, it is a resource for experiencing what it means to be a general music teacher. Through the use of case studies, cooperative group experiences, and teaching scripts, students will immediately become involved in the challenging realities and joys of teaching general music. This text reflects the present realities of American education and introduces prospective music teachers to cooperative learning, creative and critical thinking, mainstreaming, gender issues, integrated learning, multicultural classrooms, and whole language approaches.

The power of the musical experience lies in its transcendent quality that allows the individual to gain personal musical insights and understandings that are unavailable elsewhere. The focus of this text is the way in which general music teachers can structure learning to emphasize the affective importance of music. In order to provide children with valid musical encounters, prospective general music teachers need to learn ways to enable children to experience the power of music. This text provides explicit instruction in approaches that will enable children to reflect on musical experiences. It also fosters the integration of a variety of knowledge bases required of the preservice teacher: learning theory and developmental psychology, the structure of music, and procedural knowledge about planning and executing effective music instruction.

Although individual chapters primarily describe single musical behaviors, through the use of introductory and concluding teaching scripts prospective teachers experience an ever-widening spiral of model lessons that incorporates the musical behaviors discussed in each successive chapter. The teaching scripts show preservice teachers that many avenues to musical understanding should be offered within a single music lesson. These scripts also provide models of lesson planning as well as effective questioning.

Case studies form an integral part of this text, as they are a powerful and effective way to experience the delights and dilemmas of the day-to-day professional life of the general music teacher. Each chapter begins with a case study portraying a beginning general music teacher who meets a dilemma related to the chapter content. The case study is followed by cooperative learning tasks that give undergraduates an opportunity to reflect on the experiences of Miss Davis, our novice teacher. Cooperative learning experiences are essential in contemporary teacher preparation if undergraduates are to become comfortable and familiar with this important instructional strategy.

Following each initial chapter case study and teaching script, an introductory section offers a rationale for the chapter topic. The authors of this text believe that preservice teachers should not only practice the art of teaching but should develop an understanding of the nature and value of music education. Each of these rationale sections presents this important aspect of elementary music teacher preparation. Successive sections contain descriptive text delineating specific methods and offering a variety of materials relating to a specific musical behavior. At the end of each chapter are additional teaching scripts that students can use for further practice, along with activities that can be assigned to individuals, partners, or small groups.

Chapter 1 takes the reader into the life of a general music teacher through a series of case studies and snapshots of a typical workday with Mrs. Lockner, a mythical exemplary experienced teacher. The initial case study provides students with an understanding of the complexity of general music teaching and the simple but effective rewards for teachers that children share as they experience music. Other case studies in this chapter expose prospective teachers to important issues in general music teaching, including lesson pacing, the importance of age-appropriate instruction, the realities of mainstreaming, collegial relationships, questioning techniques, and the importance of a philosophy that can be articulated "on the spot."

Chapter 2 introduces the concept of evaluating music teaching based on student learning and provides a rationale for including evaluation in every lesson plan. The chapter outlines suggestions for age-appropriate ways to evaluate students' learning in the areas of singing, listening, moving, playing, and creating. Issues such as portfolio evaluation, formulating letter grades, evaluating social skills, and long-term planning are also explored in this chapter.

The next eight chapters present effective ways to engage children in the musical experiences of singing, listening, moving, playing, reading, and composing. Chapters 3 and 4 focus on the teaching of singing to primary and intermediate students, with content on concept formation, the Kodály approach, and three modes of thinking: convergent, divergent, and critical.

Also covered in these chapters are the learning theories of Piaget and Bruner, integrated learning, and gender issues. Chapters 5 and 6 describe effective means for teaching music listening at the primary and intermediate levels. Included in these chapters are ways to apply Bloom's taxonomy, lists of listening materials and sources, and a variety of charts and maps to focus students' listening.

Chapter 7 delineates ways to involve primary and intermediate children in the musical experience through movement. Such important concepts as types of movement, movement and classroom management, and the Dalcroze approach are included in this chapter.

Chapter 8 focuses on effective ways to involve children in the experience of playing instruments as well as ways to reinforce specific musical learnings through instrumental playing. Content in this chapter includes descriptions of a wide variety of classroom instruments and the approach of Carl Orff.

Chapter 9 introduces composition as a valid mode of musical experience in both the primary and intermediate general music class. Chapter content includes musical problem solving, invented notation, electronic media, and ways to foster creativity in group composition.

Chapter 10 outlines the importance of teaching music reading in the general music curriculum and offers effective ways to achieve this goal at both primary and intermediate levels. Concepts introduced in this chapter include teaching rhythm and pitch notation in both the primary and intermediate grades. Readers are also introduced to the work of Edwin Gordon. The teaching scripts in this chapter offer an opportunity for students to prepare for the realities of student teaching, where they will have to plan complete lessons.

Chapter 11, "Real Teachers in Real Worlds," completes the text by returning to the context of the classroom through a series of short case studies focusing on professional relationships that general music teachers experience: teacher/administrator, teacher/teacher, teacher/student, and teacher/parent. This chapter also contains four role-playing activities that will further enhance students' understanding of the complexity of a music teacher's life. This chapter concludes with a restatement of a rationale for music education based on the value of music itself.

Because of the many innovative teaching approaches found in this text, it can serve a wide variety of students. The case studies, teaching scripts, and role-playing activities will work equally well in courses for elementary and middle school music teachers and in courses that prepare elementary teachers to incorporate music into their curriculum. In addition, because of the innovative approach of this text, it will serve as an excellent resource for graduate music education courses. The Instructor's Manual contains a summary of relevant research for each chapter as well as chapter quiz questions and additional student assignments. *The Experience of Teaching General Music* will prepare students to function as teachers in the schools of the twenty-first century.

ACKNOWLEDGMENTS

The authors wish to thank the following people for their assistance, contribution to, or influence upon this book:

Our students Susan Bolanis, Rob Dunn, Maud Hickey, and Betty Anne Younker of Northwestern University, who contributed so much to the development of this text, and members of the Elementary General Music Methods Course in 1993 at the University of Southern Maine who served as the pilot class for this text and contributed to Appendix B, which lists listening resources: Michael Davis, Brian Gagnon, Martha Grover, Kate Huntington, Mark Ranger, Scott Thurston, and Laurie Turley. We also wish to thank the reviewers, whose comments on our manuscript were of great help to us as we refined the book.

All ideas and innovations in music teaching are a complex amalgam of many influences. However, the authors wish to recognize two teachers who have had a profound impact on their thinking and teaching: Bennett Reimer and Mary Hoffman.

One important part of this text is the illustrations, which provide future teachers with an understanding of the many ways in which children can be brought to experience music. We appreciate the many hours that our artist, Bob Atterbury, spent preparing these illustrations. Without his help the book would not have been complete.

Many thanks to Marion O'Connell and Pam Ave Maria, who graciously allowed us to teach and photograph their students.

Finally, we acknowledge all the children we have met in general music classrooms who taught us all that we really know about teaching.

Betty W. Atterbury
Carol P. Richardson

CHAPTER 1

How Does It Feel to Be a Music Teacher?

INTRODUCTION

The materials in this chapter are designed to give you a glimpse of the day-to-day professional life of an experienced general music teacher and help you to understand some of the unique challenges and delights inherent in this career. The case studies that open this and following chapters put you in the general music classroom and let you in on a music teacher's thinking while she is engaged in the teaching act. The "snapshots" that follow take you through the experienced teacher's encounters with colleagues that are an important part of professional life. The authors of this text expect that you will have an engaging time working your way through this enculturation process, as you move from the role of student to teacher.

Case Study

It is October, and Mrs. Lockner approaches the door of Elm Street School, where she has taught for seven years. As she walks into the office, she greets the secretary and waits her turn to sign in at the counter. After reading an announcement about a meeting scheduled for that afternoon at 3 P.M., she walks to her music room, smiling and greeting teachers and greeting every student by name. When she reaches her room, she begins to prepare for the three Kindergarten classes she will teach this morning.

She takes a set of animal pictures, places them on a music stand, and walks over to the record cabinet to find two tapes she will need. Then she finds her alligator puppet and puts it on the floor next to the stand. She scans her lesson plan one more time. As the voice on the loudspeaker tells the children to stand for the Pledge of Allegiance, Mrs. Lockner puts her three class notebooks where she will be able to reach them easily. She walks to the door to wait for the first Kindergarten class.

When the class is in the hallway moving toward her door, Mrs. Lockner begins to tap her two index fingers together, and as the children see her motion, they begin to imitate her. She smiles at them and says, "As you walk in to music this

beat [handwritten annotation with underline under "tap her two index fingers together"] morning to this steady beat, will you walk as quietly as possible and find a place to sit on the floor? Be sure you make a good choice about where you sit." The children tiptoe softly to the front of the room and sit down. Once they are seated, they notice the alligator puppet, and several children independently begin to warm up their voices with glissandos in the head register.

Mrs. Lockner follows the last child in and picks up the puppet, saying to the children, "Wilbur had a wonderful weekend. He and his mother went to a park and they saw lots of animals and birds. Wilbur wants to share the sounds he heard with you today." Mrs. Lockner then has the children imitate her puppet sounds of birds, chicks, kittens, and puppies. After each sound, she asks the children to identify the animal.

She then picks up her recorder and begins to play the tune of "Old MacDonald Had a Farm," and the children listen intently. By the time she has begun the second phrase, almost every hand is waving and the children cannot contain themselves. Several volunteer the name of the song before she has a chance to ask, so she says, "Who would like to choose the first animal?" As they begin to sing about chicks, she puts down her recorder and begins to pat her knees softly to the pulse. The children immediately follow her motion and continue to sing. After several verses, Mrs. Lockner says, "We are going to learn another song about animals today. I want you to listen very carefully and see if you can remember the names of all the animals I sing about." She sings the first three verses of "Bought Me a Cat."

When she finishes, she asks the children, "Who can tell me the names of the animals?" She calls on three different children and then tells the children to listen again and watch her music stand. As she sings each verse, she turns over the pictures of the cat, hen, and duck. "Now I want you to sing this song with me, children." She sings the words "Ready, sing" on the initial pitch, and the class watches the music stand and sings the song.

Mrs. Lockner smiles and exclaims enthusiastically, "That was really fine singing, and you changed the name of the animal each time. This song is a really neat one because we can make up the names of other animals to sing about also. Who can think of a good animal to add to this song?" Mandy raises her hand and offers, "Pig!" The class tries that verse, and then Mrs. Lockner suggests they add movement to their song. "I want everyone to stand in their own space and look at me by the time I count to three." The children move quickly and Mrs. Lockner counts quietly. "Now let's try out a song with the three verses we already know and the pig verse. As we sing the sound the animal makes, I want you to move like that animal." The children do a good job of being cats and hens, ducks and pigs.

Mrs. Lockner says, "We can add only one more animal today. What will it be?" Julia raises her hand and says, "Can we sing about snakes?" Mrs. Lockner smiles and looks at the class. "Well, what kind of sound will we make?" The children all hiss at her. They begin the song again, and when they get to the snake verse, the children are all on their bellies in an instant and begin wiggling all over the floor. As Mrs. Lockner finishes singing the song alone, she looks at the children, who are still wiggling with pleasure all around the music room. But not one child is singing—they are all too busy moving like snakes! She wonders, with a slight amount of panic, "How are we going to get back on track?" She stops singing and claps her hands three times, and almost all the children stop moving. "Time to come back to our singing places, children." Most of the children stop moving, stand up, and begin to move back to where they were sitting. Four children are still flat on the floor. Mrs. Lockner touches each one lightly on the head and says, "The magic wand has changed all the snakes back into children." The stragglers get up and move to join the class.

"Now I want to see if we can remember how to sing our new song, because we forgot it when we got to the snake verse. I'm going to leave the three pictures on the stand. As we sing these verses together, let's all find the steady beat in this song." Mrs. Lockner starts the class singing with the correct pitch and immediately begins to model the pulse by patting her knees. The children all try to model her movements, and she notes with pleasure that only three children, Samantha, Kim U, and T.J., are not yet keeping the pulse. While she is singing the third verse, she stands and as she ✓ moves toward the tape recorder, she stops and notes this information in her class book.

As the song ends, she says, "You are all doing a very fine job of keeping the steady beat in our music class today. I have two different pieces of music for us to listen to together. As soon as you think you feel the beat, tap it softly with one finger in the palm of your other hand. Let's just practice what we're going to do first." She models the movement and the children imitate her. She then asks the class to close their eyes, and she plays a 45-second excerpt from "The Washington Post March." She observes the class carefully and notes ✓ that the same three children are having difficulty in this part of the lesson also. "You were very good listeners during that music, class. Let's try the second piece. Listen very carefully as the music starts, and try to find the steady beat." She plays less than a minute of "Winter" from Vivaldi's *Four Seasons*. As she watches the class, she realizes that Samantha is ✓ moving her arm to the flowing sound while the rest of the class is softly tapping the steady pulse.

"How do you think these two pieces were different, children?" The children's responses include comments about parades, ballgames, TV shows, and dancing. Mrs. Lockner looks at the clock in the back of the room and says, "Our music time is almost over for today. Let's all put a steady beat in our fingertips and put them on our shoulders. Would the line leader walk to the door with our steady beat?" When T.J. begins to move, she says, "Anyone who is wearing blue may line up next." She continues to keep the beat and line up the children until the entire class is standing at the door. As the class begins to follow their teacher down the hall, Samantha runs over to Mrs. Lockner, hugs her legs, and says, "I love you!" Mrs. Lockner responds, "Thank you, Samantha, I think you are great, too! See you next week."

WHAT DID SAMANTHA MEAN?

Teaching music to groups of young children is a very rewarding endeavor because of the pleasure that all human beings are able to experience when they are involved in music. Becoming a teacher of music means that you can select lesson content that will provide continual opportunities for students to experience these innumerable and indescribable feelings, often called an aesthetic reaction. Although it is important that a lesson be organized and focused, as Mrs. Lockner's lesson was, it is also important that children have an opportunity to feel the power of music. In this lesson, the teacher stressed the feeling of steady pulse. For young primary children, this concept is often a difficult one to master, but in this class, Mrs. Lockner has noted only three children who are not able to show the pulse, and one of them is Samantha.

Clearly, during this music class, Samantha felt the power of music, and even though she could not yet demonstrate a feeling of pulse, she had a musical reaction that she could not contain. But because Samantha is only 5 years old, she associates this joy and delight with the person who makes it possible, Mrs. Lockner. Samantha loved singing, moving like different animals, and listening to contrasting pieces of music. Indeed, she showed a movement response to the Vivaldi piece that no other child demonstrated. And because Mrs. Lockner has been teaching for many years, she understands how Samantha feels. She doesn't tell the child that she needs to work on her steady beat feeling before next week, and she does not point out her different reaction after the Vivaldi listening. She makes a note of these facets of Samantha's musical life, responds to the immediate feelings of a child, and enjoys the moment before preparing for the next class.

YOUR COOPERATIVE TASK

With a partner or in a small group, discuss the following questions. One member of the group should be the designated recorder who will write down individual responses for a later class discussion.

1. When was the last time you can remember having a feeling like Samantha's? Were you able to share it as this 5-year-old did?
2. Do you think these types of feelings are necessary in education?
3. Write down the sequence of events in this lesson. How are they all related? How do you think the children felt during each part of the lesson? How do you think Mrs. Lockner felt?

Thirty Minutes Can Really Be Thirty Minutes

As the fifth grade class enters the room, Mrs. Lockner is standing at the door, saying, "Come in, sit down in your assigned seats, and look at the board." The children file past her, find their assigned seats quickly, and begin reading the day's directions on the board as soon as they sit down. On the board are these words: "Please take your book from under your seat and open it to page 43. When you have your book open to the correct page, hold it open in your lap and look at Mrs. Lockner." As soon as the last student files past her, Mrs. Lockner moves to the front of the room. Several students have already followed the directions on the board and are smiling at her. She acknowledges them with a little wink and smile and says, "Some of you really moved quickly today and are ready for the next direction. Let's give everyone another half minute to catch up. I'll look for your smiling faces." Within ten seconds all eyes are on Mrs. Lockner, and she says, "I'd like each of you to look at the board and study this rhythmic pattern. See if you can hear it in your head, and then try to clap it silently. In thirty seconds I'll ask for a volunteer to demonstrate it for the class." In about ten seconds several students raise their hands and begin to wave them enthusiastically, waiting for Mrs. Lockner's signal to demonstrate the rhythm pattern. When she notices an entire row with their hands up, Mrs. Lockner says, "Let's hear how each person in row 2 thinks this pattern should sound. I'll give you a steady beat and then each of you will clap the pattern in turn without missing a beat." She starts the rhythm clapping for row 2 by saying, "One, two, ready, clap." Each person claps the four-beat pattern in turn correctly, and Mrs. Lockner says, "Well, row 2, your clapping was exactly right, and you really know how to read a rhythm pattern now!" Students in row 2 turn to each other and give "high fives" to their neighbors. Mrs. Lockner then says, "Let's look at the song on page 43 now and see how many times our rhythm pattern occurs. When you know, put your pointer finger on your chin." Within fifteen seconds most of the children have their pointer fingers on their chins, so Mrs. Lockner says, "Most of you are ready with an answer. Instead of telling it to me, turn to the person on your right and discuss your number with them. When you've had enough time to discuss, we'll take a vote to see what you thought." Within thirty seconds most of the pairs have reached a conclusion, so Mrs. Lockner says, "Who would like to volunteer an answer for us?" She calls on a pair of girls in the back row who had engaged in a heated discussion, and one of the pair says, "Well, I thought the pattern happened six times, but Tina showed me the tie that happens the last time and it makes the rhythm different. The right answer is five." Mrs. Lockner says, "Let's take a vote. How many of you thought it appears five times?" Most of the hands in the room go up. Mrs. Lockner says, "Great! Now let's do something with this pattern. I'd like each of you to move to your own space as I beat this hand drum, and when I stop beating the drum, I want you to be in your own space. Remember what 'your own space' means? It means a spot where you can stand and take one turn around with your arms extended without touching anyone or anything. Ready, move!" Students move quickly to

[handwritten margin note: collaborative activity]

[handwritten margin note: clear directions]

their own spaces, and as the drumbeat stops, Mrs. Lockner says, "You all seemed to be listening carefully as you moved, and your stop was precise. Now, let's see if you can sit down in your own space in one count. Ready, one!" Students drop enthusiastically to the floor and sit with their legs folded in front of them. Mrs. Lockner asks them to show the rhythm pattern each time it occurs in the listening example they are about to hear. She restricts their realizations of the rhythm to movements they can make with their hands, arms, head, and torso while staying seated. She instructs them to close their eyes and reminds them that listening takes a lot of concentration. The music plays and the class seems absorbed in the music, with many students simply listening intently and not moving at all during the first two realizations of the pattern. By the third appearance of the pattern, most of the students are showing the pattern in a variety of ways, some percussive, some more flowing, but all are involved and concentrating. When the music ends, she asks, "Can someone tell me how you figured out where the pattern was happening in the listening example? It was so different from the song we sang that I wonder how you could find the pattern without singing it." Several students offer answers, and much discussion ensues, covering such topics as the difference between listening in your head and moving your body around the room. Mrs. Lockner then asks, "How would you describe the difference between the first time you clapped the pattern and this last time when you moved around the room? Did the pattern feel any different to you either time? What effect did the orchestral timbres have on the way the pattern sounded?" The discussion proceeds with students raising hands and waiting their turns, while Mrs. Lockner takes great care to be sure that no one is allowed to dominate the discussion. She notices that the period is over and says, "Rows 1 and 2 may return to their seats and put their books under their chairs." When they are all put away, she says, "Rows 1 and 2 may line up, and rows 3 and 4 may put their books under their chairs." When they are put away, she says, "Rows 3 and 4 may line up, and thank you all for a great lesson. See you on Thursday."

General Music Is Not Theory 101

Mrs. Lockner is teaching a fourth grade class the concept of triad formation. She opens a set of resonator bells and asks the class, "Who would like to try to find three bells that will sound pleasing when we play them at the same time?" Tomas raises his hand, and he comes up and chooses the C, D, and E bells. After he puts them on a desk and picks up the mallets to play them, Mrs. Lockner tells the class to listen carefully and raise their hands if the set of three sounds is pleasing. Tomas plays the bells and looks at the class, but only his best friend has his hand up. "Well, we need another experimenter. Who could try another set of bells?" Marcy raises her hand, comes to the front, and chooses C, D, and F. Mrs. Lockner gives the same direction and the results are almost the same, except that Marcy has three supporters. The class continues to experiment until they discover that a group that skips every other bell makes a pleasing sound. Then Mrs. Lockner shows the class how to write a triad on the staff and writes the C triad and the D triad. She then says, "Has anyone discovered the pattern we use when we write these sounds? Who

Triads

thinks they could write a triad that begins on this note?" (She draws a whole note in the first space of the staff.) "After we discover several other triads, we are going to play them with some songs we already know."

Everybody's in the Fold

Mrs. Lockner is preparing for the next two classes she will teach. They are both third grades, but in each class there are children who need different materials and some special consideration each week so they will be successful in music. In the first class there is Kendra, who is developmentally delayed and can read only single words with her special teacher. Mrs. Lockner looks through the materials she had the aide prepare for her last Friday and finds the set of pictures she will use as cues for Kendra when she teaches the new song. In the same class there is Mike, who is legally blind. She finds his set of picture cues, which are large like Kendra's but also have pipe cleaners glued to the pages to outline the pictures. This addition will make it possible for Mike to feel the shape of each object. His tutor has added the Braille name for each picture in the upper right-hand corner as well.

In the second class there is only one mainstreamed child, Anna, who comes to music in a wheelchair because she has cerebral palsy. She sings beautifully, however, and can read just like her classmates. She does need help when it comes to holding objects, and Mrs. Lockner walks over to the instrument cabinet to find Anna's special mallet. At the end of the mallet handle, there is a special large handgrip made out of many layers of masking tape. The grip makes it easier for Anna to hold the mallet, and she is always delighted when she can play an instrument like everyone else.

China on My Mind

Mrs. Lockner is standing in the teachers' room waiting for the water to boil for her instant soup when one of the new second grade teachers in the building, Miss Douglas, comes over and says, "Oh, Mrs. Lockner, I wanted to see you last week but I just ran out of time. All of us in second grade are starting a new unit on China today, and we'd like you to teach the children some music from China this week and next." Mrs. Lockner looks at Miss Douglas and says very calmly, "This week in second grade we are learning the concept of melodic rhythm, and my plans have been made since last fall. I wish I could change them right now, but we're planning to share what we learn in this unit at the PTA meeting this month. I would be glad to collect some materials on China that all of you could use. I bought a wonderful new video at the last conference I went to, and two of my books with songs from other countries also have cassettes. What would be a good time for us to meet?"

Asking Good Questions

The third grade class has just learned a new song, and Mrs. Lockner is ready to have the children refine their performance. She says, "Who can tell us something about the last time we sang the song? Did you notice anything about our singing that you think we could improve?" Several hands shoot up, and Mrs. Lockner calls on James, who says, "I think we did a nice job on the vowel sounds. They sounded really round, especially the 'ooo.'" Many children nod their heads in agreement, and Mrs. Lockner says, "I agree, James. This class pays a lot of attention to vowel sounds, and it makes the song sound really lovely. Can someone tell us something else about what they heard?" Many more hands are up this time, and Mrs. Lockner calls on Robin, who says, "I think our pitch wasn't very good all the way through the song. On the high part in the middle we had trouble staying on pitch, and our notes were sour." Mrs. Lockner notes that many children seem to be in agreement with this evaluation, and she asks for a show of hands to confirm this. Most of the children raise their hands, and Mrs. Lockner says, "You all seemed to hear the problem. Now what do you think we could do about it? Let's take a few minutes and have you turn to the neighbor on your left to discuss it. When you come to an agreement, face the front and we'll make a quick report of our findings. You may begin." Pairs discuss alternatives, and Mrs. Lockner calls them back to attention in three minutes. One person of each pair reports alternatives, and Mrs. Lockner writes these on the board. When each pair has reported, she draws the children's attention to the list and says, "We have come up with several ideas that we should try. Let's go down the list and see which one should come first." They decide to try the posture exercises first, then the siren exercise, and then throwing a ball into the air and following its movement with voices. Finally, they decide that a much better-supported breath would probably help the most, and they practice the song several times using a better-supported breath as well as a poorly supported breath. Mrs. Lockner then leads the class through the song, and when finished says, "That was fine singing, third graders! Now, let's talk about how it was different from the last attempt, and which one we liked better. Remember, you may give your opinion as long as you have information to support it." A lively discussion follows, with many children giving both positive and negative comments about the most recent performance, and a general feeling of improvement is expressed. Mrs. Lockner thanks the children for their good listening and thinking. She asks the green-eyed children to line up first, followed by the brown-eyed and then the blue-eyed children.

Collaborative learning [handwritten annotation in margin]

Stand Up and Be Counted

The local school district is holding public hearings before making a decision about how to eliminate the major budget deficit projected for the coming school year. Because only 30 percent of the taxpayers in the district have children in the schools, and because the new state mandate for instruction does not mention the arts, the school board has drafted a proposal to eliminate the general music program from the school day, replacing it with a new grant-funded computer literacy program. The computer literacy program will cost the district nothing but will bring high visibility because the company that provided the funding is a nationally known supporter of exemplary schools, and the company has already begun to make further offers of support in science and math.

The first ten persons who stand at the microphone support the computer literacy program and tell their reasons for wanting the school board to accept more financial support from the outside source. The next person moves to the microphone and says, "Well, if you really want to know what I think we should do, I have to tell you that the last thing I want to see happen is the elimination of the general music program. You see, I am the parent of a student whose only success in school each week happens during the two 30-minute general music classes. My child is not a particularly adept performer; otherwise she would be in the band or orchestra. But she is completely turned on by what happens in class, and she loves to listen to music and talks about her music teacher all the time. I wish I could tell you that she is equally excited about the rest of the school week, but I am not that fortunate. My child is struggling to learn many of the things that others her age have already mastered, and she is also a behavior problem in her regular classroom. But in music class, she is transformed into a successful singing, playing, and moving musician who just can't get enough of whatever it is the music teacher does. Please do not take away this child's only academic success. She is only 9 years old."

Mrs. Lockner takes the microphone next and says, "I'm here tonight to verify what the previous speaker has told you. Her child is not the only one in our district who finds her sole success in music class. There are so many children for whom the experience in general music is the best thing that happens to them each week, but they are not here to defend their rights to success. They are at home, either asleep or working on their homework. What I am here to tell you is that all the children in this district are entitled to be educated as complete human beings. This means that we must not only prepare them to be good citizens and productive learners who can support themselves, but we must educate them in what it means to be human beings with feelings and dreams and joy in their hearts. The things that happen in music class are meant to open their ears and minds to one of the most joyous activities humankind has ever engaged in: the art of making, listening to, and wondering about music. Sure, we put on good shows for you and community members who don't know what goes on in music class. But your children are learning to understand what goes on in music in ways that you probably weren't taught when you were a child. Maybe this won't get them an edge in the competitive world of work. But it *will* give them access to one of humankind's most amazing achievements: an art form that moves them. Please do not forget these children when you make your decision."

WHAT IS GOOD MUSIC TEACHING?

Each of the scenarios included in this chapter presents typical scenes from the life of the general music teacher. What you read took you along with Mrs. Lockner as she carried out planned lessons, interacted with her colleagues, and spoke at a school board hearing. What you were not able to read into these scenarios was the wide range of emotion that this teacher experienced while engaged in the activities described above. The eloquence with which Mrs. Lockner was able to speak at the school board hearing sprang from countless hours of thinking about, worrying about, planning for, and actively engaging hundreds of children in musical experiences. The seemingly effortless movement from one task to another, as described in the scenarios, is the result of both hard work and plenty of experience—and is a skill that you will begin to develop during this course. The aspects of teaching that these scenarios do not let us into are the affective levels, the great variety and intensity of feeling that the general music teacher experiences during the typical day. You do not read, for example, the elation that Mrs. Lockner felt as her fifth graders intelligently discussed their singing. You also do not read the dismay that she felt when a new teacher asked her to change her plans on a moment's notice.

What you must remember is that these scenarios all focus on an exemplary teacher who perfected her classroom performance over a period of many years, and for whom the frustrations of beginning teaching are mere memories. Learning to be a performer has taken you a long time, and learning to be an effective general music teacher is an equally arduous task, full of difficulties and challenges as well as sublime moments when it all falls into place and you marvel that someone is actually paying you to do this. The scenarios in this chapter have led you through some of the basic principles of effective general music teaching, and the following discussion will elaborate on each of these aspects. What is the inner story behind each of these snapshots that will help you become as good a music teacher as Mrs. Lockner?

Thirty Minutes Can Really Be Thirty Minutes

Effective music teachers keep the children actively engaged in musical activities from the moment they arrive at the music room door. You must regard every minute of teaching time as a precious commodity, and give plenty of thought to the kinds of directions that will keep children moving while still learning. Knowing exactly what you will say to move the children from point A to point B will keep you focused and will give them the security of knowing that you really know what will happen next. You can review classroom rules easily, without taking a lot of teaching time, by including them in your directions. Giving the class time limits for completing specific discussion tasks is another way to focus students' attention. It is particularly important for beginning teachers, for whom leading class discussion seems to be an especially troublesome area. Organizing the classroom space into a manageable and comfortable configuration is another means to using every teaching minute wisely. Placing books under chairs and having directions on the board gave Mrs. Lockner time to greet the children and focus their attention on the day's lesson instead of simply chatting informally with them as they entered the room. Although all these suggestions are rather small pieces of the much larger whole, each one contributes to maintaining the focus of the children's attention on the musical task at hand and gives the teacher a better chance of fulfilling the goals for the day.

General Music Is Not Theory 101

Throughout this text you will learn how the elements of music (melody, rhythm, harmony, timbre, form) are taught to young children in age-appropriate ways. Your background in music theory is an important part of your personal musicianship because it enables you to understand the ways in which composers have formed great music. This understanding, in turn, makes it possible for you to interpret printed notation and share your own musical ideas. Your musical performance is a demonstration of high-level formalized thinking, synthesis, and evaluation.

It has been suggested that adults experience a "wipe-out" phenomenon regarding childhood thinking. All of us changed the way we think about the world as we grew older. When we were infants and toddlers, we related to what we could see and hold. As we grew older, we understood that parents and toys might be out of sight but that they would return. We could form a mental image and save the idea. Each of these stages, and more, have been named and described by theorists such as Jean Piaget and Jerome Bruner, and their ideas are referred to often in this text. But it is impossible for adults to revert to these types of childhood thinking: we have *wiped* them from our minds.

You cannot expect youngsters to think as you do about music. And in addition, there are important differences between the ways children in primary grades and those in intermediate grades structure and remember their inner reality.

It is important, therefore, to realize that although much of your undergraduate preparation made you a competent, feeling, and fine musician, the content of your courses is not easily transformed into the content of elementary music classrooms. Your knowledge about chord structure, voice leading, and pivot chords may never be part of your explicit teaching in an elementary music class. When you are teaching timbre, for example, you may want to share everything you ever learned about your major instrument. But very young children can differentiate only between instruments with wide register contrasts, such as the flute and the bass violin, while older children may be able to hear the differences between the violin and the bass violin or the flute and the bassoon. What is important for children is that they be exposed to listening to these instruments in structured ways, beginning with wide contrasts and then, with extreme care, narrowing the ranges and families they hear. The history and technique of the instrument are unimportant! Understanding how children learn about music and structuring your musical content in age-appropriate ways are important parts of becoming a good music teacher.

Everybody's in the Fold

Elementary music teaching is a difficult task because most instruction is given with groups of children, but the groups are often not homogeneous in nature. The individual differences may be fairly slight in some groups while in others there may be a wide spectrum of individual contrasts in mental and/or physical abilities. Groups of human beings always include individuals who have different talents and abilities (think of your own classmates!); public school classes often include children with incredible contrasts in ability. These differences are due to the fact that public schools exist for every child and in our democratic society, every child deserves an equal opportunity to an education.

Since the passage of Public Law 94-142 (the Education for All Handicapped Children Act) in 1975, more and more children with severe learning and physical problems have been included (or *mainstreamed*) in public school settings. And you will meet them and need to teach them in your music classes also. If you have had no experiences with exceptional learners, some of these children may cause you fear and concern. They may look different, sometimes act different, and often need some extra time and help in order to succeed in music. However, every child in our country has the same right to a public school music education, and every single child is able to enjoy and respond to the wonderful feelings music provides. Part of your job, therefore, is to make music education accessible and possible for every child you teach.

The challenge you will face as a music teacher will be to find ways in a short amount of time to help these individual learners. Often you will need special materials and help from teacher's aides. You may need to spend time reading the individual files of some children and spend even more time conferring with classroom, resource, and special education teachers. When you realize that 5 to 10 percent of a school population (the average size of elementary schools is between 500 and 700 children) may have been defined as "exceptional," you understand that learning how best to provide a music education for each of these children within a larger group of typical learners will be an ongoing and challenging part of your job.

This text will provide you with many different approaches and suggestions for mainstreamed learners. However, you will greatly enhance your preparation as an elementary music teacher by taking a separate course where you learn about the many types of special learners and how music instruction can be adapted for different disabilities. In addition, any opportunity you can find to work with exceptional children will augment your preparation as an elementary music teacher. Even a day or two volunteering for Special Olympics will provide you with some exposure to the vast contrasts possible in different exceptional populations. Such experiences will enable you to understand that each exceptional learner is an individual, not a member of a category such as "developmentally delayed" or "hearing impaired." And in addition, you will have an opportunity to see these students respond with the same emotions and feelings as you do!

China on My Mind

Music teachers often are perceived as being on the periphery of elementary education because they teach in more than one building and have short amounts of time with each class of children. In addition, as described in the above snapshot, some teachers (usually new to the building!) believe that music class content can instantly be adapted to supplement their social studies content. It is important to support and work closely with every classroom teacher in an elementary building. The way to avert last-minute demands and resulting bad feelings is to help your peers understand that you have content to teach through the structured and sequenced curriculum you are following. You need to share what you are doing with your colleagues. Suggest to them that if you have advance notice, you may be able to use content that will integrate with their classroom teaching. In addition, you will want to be a cooperative member of the faculty; offering materials, tapes, and recordings is one way to enhance your colleagues' lessons and build your reputation as a team player.

Good elementary music teaching depends upon good planning and preparation. There are two kinds of planning that you will need to consider as you begin the experience of becoming a music teacher: long-term and short-term. Long-term planning must occur first, since it is the basis or foundation for everything that happens in your classroom. And the most basic decision involves what you want children to know about music when they leave elementary school. If you believe that every child should be musically literate, then you will have to teach literacy in every lesson. If you believe that every child should know great works of music, then your lesson content must reflect this belief. If you think it is more important that children have a good time in music class, then this belief will also guide what and how you teach.

A compelling approach is to consider the structure of the discipline as the organizing focus for your curriculum. The structure of our discipline, music, is based on the various elements, such as rhythm, melody, harmony, form, and timbre. You will want to consider each of the elements of music as your organizers and decide what you want your oldest students to know about melody, rhythm, harmony, and so on when they leave your class for the last time. This approach is supported by our understanding of the sequence in which these aspects of music can be learned by children and will be explained in further detail in this text. The term *spiral curriculum* defines this approach to music teaching and implies that children encounter each of the musical elements continually and in gradually more complex ways throughout their music education.

Once this decision about your final goal is made, you can move to the next level, planning for each grade level. In this level of planning, you decide which elements you will focus on and for how long (how many units) throughout the year. This decision should take into account the length of each class period and the number of times per week that you teach each class. For example, you may decide that in Kindergarten classes, you will spend six weeks on steady beat and six weeks on melodic register and direction. Then you may want to spend three weeks each on form, timbre, dynamics, and tempo. And you may wish to return to the units on rhythm and melody at the end of the year. In fifth grade, your focus may not be on individual elements but rather on how they all contribute to expressivity in music. So your first unit may last four weeks and focus on this idea. Then your next unit may last four weeks also and stress how rhythm has been used in complex ways such as syncopation in jazz or polyrhythms in the music of other cultures. Before the school year begins, you should have formulated a structure or framework for your music teaching in each grade level.

At this time, you can begin to organize your lesson plans for each successive week. Good music teachers know that the length of individual activities must be monitored carefully and that children learn music best through the various musical behaviors or skills, such as singing, listening, moving, playing and reading, and creating. Each lesson plan therefore incorporates this knowledge in conjunction with age-appropriate and appealing musical content.

As you now understand, all of this planning preceded Mrs. Lockner's discussion with the new second grade teacher and is the reason why music class could not suddenly become a place to learn music of a particular country. Music of other cultures is valid and important content to use, and experiences with multicultural musics provide all youngsters with a validation of their own cultural heritage and an understanding and appreciation of the many other musics that exist in the world. However, the inclusion of this content must not become an end in itself but rather a part of careful and conscientious planning and preparation.

Asking Good Questions

The music teacher in this case study may seem to be abdicating her responsibility by asking the children to make decisions about improving their performance. After all, Mrs. Lockner is the expert in the class and is perfectly capable of telling the children what to do. The point is that she is not only an expert musician who knows how to improve children's singing, but she is also an expert teacher who knows how to draw children into making their own musical decisions. She does this through carefully conceived questions that do not lead to single-word, right/wrong answers. The teacher who wants children to *think* gives them open-ended questions that focus their thinking and allow them to draw on what they already know to arrive at a new solution. These types of questions require more than a simple parroting of the "right" answer; they force the children to use what they understand to formulate a possible solution. The right questions also give the children a sense that they do know a lot by letting them draw on all their previous musical experiences to formulate an answer. The disposition to try new ideas and old ideas in new ways is one of the positive results of good questioning, and this attitude opens up the role of the teacher from keeper of knowledge to more of a partner or coach in the discovery of knowledge. Questioning, and the way you handle the answers your questions elicit, are important aspects of successful general music teaching, and you can begin today to build competence in this area.

Stand Up and Be Counted

If you haven't yet had to articulate your philosophy of music education, you should begin to do so today. One of the most important tasks the public school music teacher must face is defending the school music program. You may be asked to explain your philosophy of music education in a job interview, to a parent who believes that music is a waste of time, or even in a public hearing. What you say, and the way in which you say it, are both important to you professionally and personally. This philosophical statement may simply be a list of beliefs you hold about the importance of music in your life. However, it is one of the most important beliefs you have, and it needs to be strong enough to sustain you in a career that can be physically draining as well as continually exciting.

Your personal philosophy must be based on the nature and value of music to the children that you teach. Although many "extramusical" benefits result from musical experiences, such as working together in a group, creating a sense of school pride, and improving public relations in the community, these benefits can also result from an athletic team or a spelling bee. You want to be sure that your philosophical beliefs and your defense of music education are based on the uniqueness of music (and all art) in our lives.

INTRODUCTION TO FOLLOWING CHAPTERS

The following chapters will lead you through a variety of materials that introduce you to the skills involved in teaching children to sing, listen, move, play instruments, compose, and read music. Each chapter begins with a case study that helps you understand the role of the general music teacher. The case study is followed by suggestions for cooperative in-class activities. One or more teaching scripts are provided in each chapter for you to practice with your peers and roommates and with children. Next you will find a rationale section that explains reasons for including the various types of musical learning in the general music class. Each chapter also contains sections that explain the methods and materials appropriate for teaching each musical behavior. Finally, more teaching scripts of actual lessons are included in each chapter so that you can study lesson construction and try teaching already formulated lessons appropriate for different levels.

As you can see from this brief description, in your role as learner you will be actively involved in discussion, cooperative activities, practice teaching using scripted lessons, and self-evaluation. As in this introductory chapter, you will be expected to jump into the role of general music teacher through both role playing and actual teaching episodes, and each chapter will give you the kinds of information and procedural help that can make this one of the most engrossing classes of your college career.

PLANNING YOUR PRACTICE TEACHING

not applicable

As you plan your practice teaching for this semester or quarter, keep in mind that the scripted lessons are cumulative: song materials presented in earlier scripts often reappear in successive scripts to teach a different musical concept. The musical learnings from earlier chapters at both the primary (K–3) and intermediate (4–6) levels are built on in successive chapters to give you a sense of the way learning really happens over time. For this reason it is essential that you plan your teaching so that you can work with the same primary and intermediate groups throughout the course. Table 1.1 lists chapters, teaching script numbers, grade levels, and musical materials that can aid you in your planning.

Chapter	Script	Grade	Musical Materials
3	1	K/1	"Birdie, Birdie, Where Is Your Nest"
	2	1/2	"One Elephant"
	3	1/2	"Daa, Daa Kente"
5	1	1	"Fanfare for the Common Man"
	2	1/2	"One Elephant" and a nonwestern listening example
	3	K/1	"Birdie, Birdie" and Haydn's Symphony No. 94, third movement
7	1	3	"Hanukkah Song"
	3	K/1	"Bird Songs"
8	1	1/2	"Daa, Daa Kente"
	3	1/2	"One Elephant" and "Taffy"
9	1	1/2	Story and music composition
	3	2	"The Flea Song" and picture prompts
10	1	1/2	"Taffy" a Telemann suite, and "The Flea Song"
	3	1	"Hello There"

INTERMEDIATE TEACHING SCRIPTS

Chapter	Script	Grade	Musical Materials
4	1	5/6	"John Henry"
	2	5/6	"Emma"
	3	4/5	"The Monster Song"
6	1	5/6	"Emma," "Fanfare for the Common Man," and Haydn's Symphony No. 94
	2	5/6	"The Monster Song" and "Under African Skies"
	3	5/6	"Emma" and "Voices of Africa"
7	2	6	"Daa, Daa Kente" and "Turtle Shoes"
	4	5/6	"Voices of Africa"
8	2	5/6	"Emma"
	4	4/5	"The Monster Song" and "Welcome Here"
9	2	5	Theme and variations using your own original composition
	4	5/6	"Eldorado"
10	2	5	"Erie Canal"
	4	5/6	"Rhythm score to Bach's Minuet"

STUDENT ASSIGNMENTS

1. Reread the initial section titled "Thirty Minutes Can Really Be Thirty Minutes" (p. 4) and list each direction the teacher uses. Categorize each item on this list according to headings you think reflect classroom management: transitions, positive reinforcement, moving children from point to point, and so on.

2. With a partner, discuss the feelings you have experienced in the role of a teacher. Decide whether your experiences correspond to those of the general music teacher described in the chapter, and be prepared to share your conclusions with the class.

CHAPTER 2

Evaluating Music Teaching

Case Study 1

It is the beginning of November, and Miss Davis is doing really well in her first year of teaching. She has organized her lesson plans for the year, has learned the names of almost all of the 650 children she teaches each week, and has already had positive evaluations following observations by the building principals at each of the three schools where she teaches. During a casual conversation with a school secretary, however, Miss Davis learns that she must provide letter grades for each child in School A and submit them to each of the classroom teachers by the end of the following week. She calls the principal at School B and learns that she must give the grades to the classroom teachers four days before report cards are to go out, which means that Miss Davis has only three days to formulate grade sheets and hand them out to classroom teachers. In a phone conversation with the principal at School C, Miss Davis learns that, in addition to giving an overall letter grade, she must also give each child an effort grade and a skills grade and write prose commen-

tary on each report card. These grades need to be turned in to the secretary of School C as soon as possible because School C uses a computerized format and the secretary needs a lot of lead time to print all the report cards and get them back to the teachers for the addition of prose commentary.

YOUR COOPERATIVE TASK

1. What should Miss Davis do next? ("Buy a gun" is not an option!)
2. What kinds of information can Miss Davis draw on in formulating grades for each child?
3. Discuss the advantages of each of the four kinds of evaluative information (overall letter grades, effort grades, skills grades, and prose commentary) described in the scenario.
4. Describe and discuss the feelings that this scenario evoked in you as you read about Miss Davis's plight. Relate these feelings to an actual experience you have had in which you were expected to do the impossible, and describe the outcome.

Why Is Evaluation Necessary and Important?

Evaluation is an important aspect of teaching any subject. As you begin your introduction to the complex task of teaching music to groups of children, you need to understand the possible ways to incorporate this vital step in the teaching-learning process. If you think carefully about any of the instruction in which you have ever participated, whether it was a private lesson or a lecture class with hundreds of students, you will realize that in order for you to learn anything, the teacher needed to discover what you already knew or could demonstrate. Similarly, for you to be an effective teacher, you must first be able to determine what children already know and then determine what they learn during your music class.

Evaluation of learning is difficult to observe as an undergraduate because music teachers are evaluating children's learning as they teach, and the process is not overt or obvious. Pencil-and-paper tests are seldom used, nor are they appropriate. All music majors are participants in performance settings where conductors continually evaluate what they hear and make rehearsal decisions based upon this evaluation. In addition, you may have been a participant in a secondary-level performing organization where the evaluation was a playing test or a written test on music fundamentals or style. Groups of young children, however, often seem to be so involved in "making" music that it is unclear to the drop-in observer how the teacher is evaluating learning during the lesson.

Elementary music teachers continually evaluate the teaching-learning process that unfolds in their classrooms, just as performance conductors do. Before a lesson is ever taught, the planning process involves three steps. First, the teacher decides what the focus of the lesson will be; next, the teacher determines how the children will become involved in a singular aspect (or several aspects) of music; and finally, the teacher chooses the method of evaluation.

These steps can be combined in a short statement called an *instructional objective*.[1] In some areas, the term *objective* is no longer used but has been replaced with such terms as *learning outcomes* or *results*. Carefully constructed objectives begin with an introductory phrase such as "The learner will be able to . . ." followed by a clear description of what the student will be expected to do. You must be precise when you select the verb that follows this phrase because it must describe an observable behavior, one that you can really evaluate. For example, if your objective states, "The learner will understand . . . or know . . . or feel . . .," you have selected behaviors that are difficult, if not impossible, to evaluate. Some useful verbs for musical objectives are *sing, play, move, create, read, order, arrange, choose,* and *discuss*. These verbs describe what children will actually do in music and what you should be able to see as a result of your teaching.

One of the best reasons to evaluate student learning regularly is that the process can guide your next steps in lesson planning. Unless you know what

[1] R. F. Mager (1962). *Preparing Instructional Objectives.* Palo Alto, CA: Fearon Publishers, p. 3.

your students have learned, you won't know if you should proceed with introducing new ideas or continue to reinforce previous learnings with further examples. Evaluation lets you determine whether your students learned what you taught them and whether what you *thought* you taught matches what they actually learned.

For example, you may think that the lesson you just taught went perfectly: you stuck to your plan, handled questions with ease, and even disciplined a child without losing your train of thought. This perspective on what transpired during the music lesson leaves out the most important element: the learner. To know whether your lesson objectives were met by your teaching, you must set aside your opinion of what happened during *your performance as teacher* and give the students an opportunity to show you what effect your teaching had on them and their understanding of music.

Music instruction for elementary children does not receive the same amount of curriculum time as other subjects. In North America, there is a vast disparity in the amount of time children spend in music; some children have music class every day, while others have class once a week. This short amount of instructional time requires you to plan lessons and evaluate learning with utmost care and attention. There is no time to spare or waste in any elementary music class, and effective evaluation in each lesson will direct your teaching in the most positive and efficient way possible.

The best evaluation gives data on student and teacher and allows you to step back from the act of teaching to find out what happened on the other side of the desk. This kind of evaluation, which happens during and after each teaching episode, is called *formative evaluation*. It includes those observable behaviors that you should notice as your lesson progresses. (Are students moving the way the melody moves? Can they show the accented beats? Are all groups staying on task? Are their glazed looks telling you that these directions are too long and complicated?) Formative evaluation also includes follow-up tasks that lead children to apply their understanding to a new situation. Your understanding of how well you are doing as a teacher is greatly enhanced when you make formative evaluation part of each lesson plan.

An important part of this evaluative process is reflection upon your own actions. You must continually compare what you are observing about learners to what you observe about yourself as teacher. (Is your pacing quick enough or too quick? Are your questions and instructions clear to your students? Is the content of your lessons appealing and interesting? Does your feedback to students give them the information they need to stay on task? Is your praise specific to a situation, or is it vague and diffuse?) Each of these factors has a tremendous impact upon classroom climate and learning, and reflection enables you to be accurate in your assessment of what students are actually learning when you teach.

As described in the case study in this chapter, even though children are only in the music class for a short time each week, the music teacher is still expected to provide information to parents that informs them of their child's progress. How you determine these grades and how you inform the community about your curriculum will certainly become an important aspect of how both you and music education are perceived by the parents in your community. When parents understand that you have a carefully planned curriculum and that you evaluate student learning and progress constantly, you are perceived as a "real" teacher.

How you evaluate students also shapes your colleagues' opinions about the value of your subject. If your music teaching appears to be a series of mindless yet enjoyable musical activities, a type of extracurricular hobby time within the school day, you will be perceived solely as a "break time" provider. In order to be perceived as a "real" teacher, an equal member of a faculty, you must be doing what every other faculty member does—planning, teaching, and evaluating.

Expanding Your Concept of Evaluation

The traditional forms of evaluation that you have experienced as an undergraduate music major have probably focused on two distinct areas: performance and understanding. You are accustomed to performance auditions and end-of-term juries in your principal instrument, in which your musicality, memorization skills, and technical ability are evaluated and grades are assigned. The means of evaluating your musical understanding have probably included a wide variety of written quizzes, papers, projects, and examinations covering either part or all of the course content for each class. These methods of evaluation give your instructors some information about your skills and understandings, but because they occur so infrequently they may not allow you to fully demonstrate your musical learning (you have a memory lapse during your jury, or you do not do well on the final exam). Your instructors decide how much you have learned and what you are capable of as a performer on the basis of academic traditions that have been handed down from generation to generation. These traditional methods of evaluating students' learning serve a purpose; however, they are appropriate only for adult learners who are experienced participants in two complex symbol systems, English and musical notation, and should not serve as a model for you as a general music teacher working with children between the ages of 5 and 12.

Young children need to be evaluated by means that allow them to show you what they know, and written testing of musical understanding is usually inappropriate. The best guideline for evaluating children's musical learning is to use musical tasks that let children show you what they have learned. It is essential that musical learning be "tested" in a musical way through any of the five musical behaviors: singing, listening, moving, playing and reading, or creating. By including a musical evaluation in each lesson you plan, you can collect a wide variety of data on each student during the course of a marking period. You will then be assured of having a much more accurate picture of each student's musical learning than if you gave, for example, a single test at the end of the grading period.

Portfolio Evaluation

A current trend in evaluation is to compile a portfolio of each student's work during the course of a grading period, during an academic year, or even over several years. Portfolios can include a wide variety of materials that document the student's learning:

1. Audiotapes of singing, individual and group compositions, or small group performances
2. Written examples of student-created notation for individual or group compositions
3. Student-created listening maps
4. Teacher-created check sheets that list specific skills in singing, listening, moving, and reading and playing
5. Other appropriate written documentation, such as worksheets or teacher-created listening guides
6. Students' own reflections on musical experiences, both in and out of the music classroom
7. Students' evaluations of their own learning

Portfolios can be of four types, classified by their function:[2]

1. **A presentation/product portfolio** is meant to be the culminating document of a student's learning at a particular level and to serve as evidence that the student should be admitted to the next level, such as being promoted to the next grade.
2. **A product/performance portfolio** provides the teacher with a look at the same product from each child in a class or grade level at the same point. This type of portfolio can be used to assign grades or to sort students into groups on the basis of ability or achievement.
3. **A program portfolio** is a collection of the finest work of selected students from a grade level, school, or district. Program portfolios could be used by a teacher as supporting evidence for a request to increase funding for a music program or as documentation of the teacher's success in the classroom.
4. **A process portfolio** is a collection of a student's work that documents the individual's learning process. Included in this type of portfolio are tapes of the student's singing at particular points in time, early and more developed versions of the same composition, several versions of the same listening map, or several versions of the invented notation of a piece of music. An essential component of the process portfolio is the student's own commentary on the process. This commentary may take the form of written reflections, or it may be a tape-recorded conversation between the student and teacher in which the teacher asks the student about the portfolio.

Portfolio assessment is an exciting way to document each child's growth in musical understanding, and your task is to develop your own system of managing the large amounts of data required by the portfolio. This may seem to be an impossible task if you see 600 children in 23 classes twice each week, but there are ways to streamline your recordkeeping and minimize the

[2]R. Miller (1993). "In New York State: Assessment and A New Compact for Learning," *Special Research Interest Group in Measurement and Evaluation, 15,* 2.

amount of time you'll need to record information. For example, you may want to keep a separate notebook for each of your classes, organized by sections for skills checklists, group participation comments, singing voice descriptions and improvement, and other areas as you need them. With two dozen separate notebooks instead of one cramped grade book, you can record your weekly or biweekly data and comments relatively easily and then refer to them at the end of a marking period when you must create a letter grade for each student. Similarly, you can keep a box of labeled audiotapes for each class with a numbered student list attached. Label the tapes with the children's numbers so you can easily find a specific tape.

Preparing Grades

The issue of turning the rich data gleaned from the portfolio into a letter grade for a report card is one you must handle from your first day on the job. To assign a letter grade to a child's musical learning may strike you as distasteful, and you may want to give all your students an A, particularly if they are cooperative and attentive and respond well to you in the classroom. Although some school districts ask you to formulate an effort or citizenship grade that directly addresses classroom behavior, the written letter grade should reflect the student's *musical learning*, not behavior in the music room. The letter grade should take the student's improvement into consideration and should reflect the student's actual musical achievement in both skills and understanding.

School districts often have printed guidelines that give teachers specific directions they must use to generate grades for each student. These guidelines usually instruct teachers to convert numerical data from written test results to a letter grade, so they are not very useful to the general music teacher who has relied on a wide variety of observable musical behaviors instead of written tests. The most useful letter grades in music indicate two things about each child: skills and understandings. Musical skills might include singing on pitch or playing a barred instrument; musical understandings included following a peer's expressive indication while singing or creating an ostinato to accompany a particular song. If you can have an impact on the report card format, request that you be allowed to give two letter grades for each student. If you must give a single letter grade, you can use your own formula for each student's improvement in the areas of skills and understandings.

You will never be caught in the same situation as Miss Davis if you ask for your district's grading policy statement and report card schedule *at your first meeting with your building principal after you're hired.* Ask for a copy of the report card you are to use, and ask for a schedule of deadlines for submitting grades. Ascertain whether there are special procedures for "special teachers" (art, music, physical education) to follow in recording their grades. For example, in some schools the classroom teachers put letter grades on report cards first, then route them to the art, physical education, and music teachers so each can put their own grades on the set. Finally, be sure to find out whether prose commentary is required. If it is, you will have a rich set of comments about each child's musical skills and understandings on which to draw, and your comments will be meaningful for the classroom teacher as well as the child's parents.

Evaluating Singing Skills

Each child in your general music class will come with a particular set of singing skills in place, and your task is to document the child's improvement in use of the singing voice. Using the notebook, as suggested above, you can create a checklist of each child's specific singing skills, including which pitches that child can match, the vocal range, a description of tone quality, and a comment on musicality. You can update this information from week to week by keeping the notebook open during singing activities and jotting additional information immediately after class or as soon as you notice a new note in a child's range or pitch-matching repertoire. Your initial entry for each child may include the letter names of those pitches the child can match and whether the tone quality is focused or breathy. Each week you can add more information, and over the course of a grading period (usually nine to twelve weeks) the trend in the child's singing skills improvement will be easy to see. It will be much easier for you to sense global singing improvement, such as for an entire class; the sound of children singing together is very easy to characterize. Unless you provide many opportunities for children to sing individually, you will not be able to gather important data about their singing skills, and they will not develop as independent singers. By keeping your notebook entries current you will have an accurate picture of each child's singing development.

Another fine source of information about children's singing skills is an audiotape of each child's singing. Whenever a child offers to sing a solo part in class, make an audiotape on a cassette labeled with the child's number from the class list. Hundred's of tapes may initially sound like an expensive venture but such a purchase is easily defended as an important part of your equipment budget. Tapes to use in this manner are similar to workbooks and standardized tests which are purchased for many other subjects. Your tapes, of course, will be used year after year.

To facilitate this, keep the set of tapes from each class in numerical order in a separate box, and arrange them so that the number labels are visible at a glance. Each time a child sings alone and is taped, place a check next to his or her name on the class list and record the date *on the tape* as well as on the class list. Over a period of a few months, you can record each child several times, placing a check next to his or her name on the class list each time. You can then use these individual audiotapes as a source of information about each child's singing improvement when you need to formulate grades. The tapes, then, combined with your anecdotal notes in the class notebooks, will provide you with all the data you need to arrive at an accurate singing grade for each child.

Evaluating Listening Skills

Evaluating students' listening skills is a continual and ongoing process in all music teaching. In formal listening portions of a primary (K–3) music class, you may choose to focus childrens' listening on a single musical element, such as pulse or melodic direction. Your focus broadens and deepens during intermediate grades (4–6) to encompass several elements occurring simultaneously, such as melodic direction, dynamics, and timbre. In Chapters 5 and 6, you will read about many approaches to teaching focused listening.

not simultaneous

Once you have selected what you want children to hear, your next task is to determine how you will know whether they hear what you planned as the focus of your lesson. You must carefully create an evaluation method for your students that provides data based on musical learning instead of reading level, inability to follow directions, or difficulty in writing.

One of the simplest ways to evaluate listening is to have young children point to pictures of what they hear. When you use a pointing response, you provide students with a set of possible correct answers; they must identify and match what they hear with what they see, but they do not have to generate the answers. Even if you are sure that you are no artist, you can buy children's coloring books and picture books that will provide models to trace. More difficult pointing responses for intermediate children might include a set of dynamic symbols or the names of several instruments from which they can select the correct response. Pointing evaluations can be further refined by giving only two choices for each section of a paper, thereby forcing the listener to choose between a correct and an incorrect response. Most important, your evaluation must include a way for you to keep track of who is successful and who is not. The simplest way is to use the class notebook and make columns to use as checklists during evaluation time.

Another fairly simple listening evaluation involves movement responses. In Chapter 7 you will learn many approaches to teaching movement and music. Movement is an ideal type of evaluation because it is a way for every child to participate, using a natural response to music. Simple movements can be teacher- or student-generated and can accompany many different aspects of music, such as pulse, meter, melodic direction, and phrasing. One way to track primary children's development in feeling a steady pulse might be to place dots on your checklist next to the names of the children who cannot move to a steady pulse. A quick scan of this section of your checklist will help you decide how many future lessons must be devoted to this important musical concept.

Manipulative materials can also be prepared to use as evaluative tools during listening portions of lessons. They can be simple, such as a laminated card with an outline picture of a violin which the child holds up every time the violin plays or a set of small shapes the child must arrange to show various musical forms. Other useful manipulatives include sets of dynamic symbols, pictures of instruments, and icons or words. Manipulatives should be laminated, paper-clipped together, and kept in individual small envelopes so that you do not spend time organizing materials between classes. Each time you use a set of manipulative materials to evaluate student learning, you should record individual learning. It will be easier to keep accurate records of individual students' learning if after each evaluative activity you place a circle or a minus sign next to the names of those children who were unable to complete the task successfully.

As students become more mature, you can use more complex evaluations of listening. Students can draw their own contours, notations, or charts and maps of entire pieces and share their drawings with their peers. Knowing that they are going to share their maps with each other motivates children to be very careful listeners and recorders of what they hear. Indeed, the map sharing can initially be done with a partner and perhaps later with a group, or even in a type of round-robin with the entire class. Your directions to students should focus their attention on a particular feature of the music. If you want students to draw dynamic changes in addition to a single sforzando, you must tell the class to focus on this particular aspect of the music. If your directions are clear, the resulting maps will show you which students heard the various dynamic levels and which ones did not.

There are many other methods of evaluation that can be used with inter-mediate-age children, but your selection must always consider the response mode. In other words, if you ask students to write an answer or a description, is every child capable of the writing task? If not, your evaluation of musical learning will be not be an accurate one but will be confounded by the child's writing ability. Call charts, described in Chapter 6, are a type of written evaluation that require students to listen and circle an answer or fill in a blank when you call a number. Other forms of written evaluation appropriate for interme-diate students can include true-false, multiple-choice, and matching-item questions.

Evaluating Moving Skills

In Chapter 7, you will learn how to include the important aspect of movement in music instruction. Children do not begin school with equal amounts of movement experience, and some children appear to be very well coordinated while others demonstrate difficulty in such a simple task as jumping. As with each of the skills that you will evaluate, your initial task is to determine what each child can do. You may wish to make up your own categories for the ease with which children move to music, such as "stiff" and "less stiff" or "coordi-nated" and "less coordinated." These categories can also be used to describe such locomotor movements as walking, jumping, hopping, and skipping. A single lesson might include many kinds of movements, and your job will be to note which children need more experiences in moving in certain ways.

It is especially important to evaluate movement carefully in very young children and discuss what you notice with other professionals in your school. Some children you observe who have severe motor deficits may be in adaptive physical education classes where they receive individual instruction to improve their motor skills. An understanding of the specific skills these chil-dren are working on will assist your evaluation of how they move in your music class.

In later elementary grades, you will want to assess whether or not the chil-dren you teach are able to further refine their movements to what they hear in music. You will need to note the ability to respond to music that is smooth, jagged, quick, or jumpy, and keep careful track of children's progress in these areas. In addition, you will want to document the progress of children in improvising movements and expanding their movement repertoire.

Evaluating Playing Skills

Many different types of instrument-playing experiences are included in ele-mentary music instruction, and you will quickly discover that all children love to play unpitched and pitched instruments. In addition to providing enjoyment, these experiences should be structured carefully so that you are able to determine whether or not children make progress in this skill area. All evaluation in elementary music should be based on what you planned to teach and how well the children learned what you taught. However, when you begin to assess playing skills, you will again be faced with the fact that some children have better motor abilities than others.

This difference in motor abilities is dealt with in the same manner as the assessment of singing skills. It is important that you determine what each child can do and then keep track of the progress that is the result of your teaching. As simple a task as hitting two wooden sticks together may be difficult or impossible for some children who have problems with eye-hand coordination. You need to note on your checklist which children have difficulty with each type of skill—hitting, shaking, strumming, and so on. If you keep tape-recorded examples of each child's instrumental playing, you can easily note his or her progress.

Evaluating Creating Skills

In Chapter 9 you will learn about many different ways children can become involved in creating and composing in general music class. Because of the elusive nature of creativity, it is often thought that this aspect of musical learning cannot be assessed. However, important aspects of this component of musicality can be used as a basis for evaluation. They are grounded in the definition of divergent thinking. Many authorities in creativity believe that the thinking of creative individuals is accented by the ability to think divergently.[3] Divergent thinking implies using given information and generating new or varied outputs which are then evaluated in terms of fluency or extensiveness (quantity), flexibility (different approaches used), originality (uniqueness), and syntax (using musical ideas in an ordered or harmonious manner). When children set about composing or creating, you should discuss the importance of these four ideas so they will understand that divergent thinking is acceptable in your music class.

The parameters you establish for creative encounters reflect the methods you use to evaluate children's creativity. If you have individuals or groups create a short composition to illustrate the contrast possible with different dynamics or tempi, you might use a five-point Likert-type scale. (Draw a horizontal line, put the numeral 1 at one end and 5 at the other, and designate one end with a term such as *little* and the other end with a term such as *great deal*). Use this scale with only one aspect of creativity at a time—extensiveness, flexibility, originality, or syntax. Then as you listen to each composition, you can quickly put a check on the line to indicate your evaluation.

Your evaluation will initially be more effective and accurate if you focus on evaluating one aspect of creativity in a particular lesson. The number of dynamic or tempi contrasts in the composition (extensiveness) can be recorded with a simple number, as can the number of unusual or inventive ways in

[3]J. W. Getzels and P. W. Jackson (1962). *Creativity and Intelligence.* London: Wiley. E. P. Torrence (1963). *Education and the Creative Potential.* Minneapolis: University of Minnesota Press.

which children used instruments to attain the musical effects. As with all evaluation, your initial task is to determine what aspect of composition you will evaluate and how you will do so. Be consistent and keep careful records so you can evaluate progress in this important musical skill.

One music education researcher, Peter Webster, has developed a test of creativity for children from ages 6 to 9, titled *Measures of Creative Thinking in Music*.[4] The test contains eighteen tasks designed to stimulate young children's musical imagination, focusing on pitch, tempo, and dynamics. The test requires a Nerf ball; a microphone with an amplifier, speakers, and a small reverberation unit; a piano; and a set of temple blocks. Testing sessions are videotaped and scored for musical extensiveness, flexibility, originality, and syntax.

Evaluating Social Skills

One important aspect of elementary education is the development of each child's social skills. You will spend a large portion of your teaching time planning and organizing activities in which children learn to work together in pairs, in small groups, and as an entire class. Fostering social development is part of your job as a teacher, and you will need to help each child in each class get along with others in many different contexts. As a performer, each child will learn to work with others to produce and communicate musical ideas. As a listener, the child will learn how to show respect for the composer and performer through focusing attention. As a creator, each child will learn to express ideas in ways that others can understand and share, as well as to manipulate and modify ideas through collaboration. As a mover, each child will learn to share space with others and to move in ways that show respect for others' personal space.

Because of the wide variety of roles that children take on in the general music class, you, the music teacher, will see many examples of their social skills developing or needing attention. You can keep a log of both positive and negative social skills development data by using a section of the class notebook to regularly record what you notice about each child. You won't need to go out of your way to notice that Susan is kind to her neighbors or that Jack has an especially gentle way of giving criticism to his peers. You will need to record these observations, however, so that they are right at your fingertips at report card time.

You can also formulate a checklist of the social requirements for each assignment. If, for example, the class was split into composition groups, each group could be rated on its process abilities: time spent on task, level of involvement of each individual, and the degree to which divergent views were incorporated into the process. These process categories could be evaluated by the teacher, or the students in the group could evaluate themselves in each area. Teaching students to be accurate, honest, and tactful in their evaluations of themselves and others is an important aspect of socialization that happens often in the context of the general music class.

[4]The test is unpublished, but it can be obtained from Professor Peter Webster at Northwestern University, School of Music, Evanston, Illinois.

The Grading Dilemma

In the opening case study of this chapter, Miss Davis is faced with preparing grades for hundreds of children. You too will encounter the same situation, probably at the end of each ten weeks of teaching. If you are aware of this fact from the very first day of school, you will be prepared to collect the evaluative information you have on each child and translate it into an appropriate grade. The grade may be a letter, a number, a set of checks, or a written statement. Whatever system is used, you must decide how you are going to determine grades for your students in a manner that is consistent and fair.

First, at each grade level you must decide how many bits of data (grades, checks, dots, etc.) will be included in each child's grade. Then you must decide whether each bit of data should receive equal weight or not. Are you going to give equal weight to musical skills (singing, listening, moving, playing and reading, creating) and musical understandings (pulse, melodic direction, meter), or are you going to choose just a few as the basis for a grade? To make your evaluation fair, whatever you choose should have been the primary focus of your ten weeks of instruction.

The next step is to determine grades based on the same criteria for every child in a grade level. If you evaluate children on their ability to sing a song you have taught, but the class includes only three children who could sing on pitch at the beginning of the grading period, is it appropriate to give each of those children an A and all the others a lower grade? The authors of this text hope you will agree that this would be unfair and that any evaluation should be based on the individual learner's progress.

It is very important that you make evaluation and grading decisions carefully because at some time in your teaching career you will be asked to explain why an individual child received a particular grade. If you have followed the above suggestions, you will be able to open a grade book and describe what was taught during a particular grading period and how your grades for the entire class were determined. All teachers, not just music teachers, must be prepared for such an occurrence because report cards are the accepted form of communication between teachers and parents.

Standardized Tests

At times during your elementary teaching you may be asked to evaluate the musical ability of the children you teach using measures other than the grades you derive from their progress and achievement. You may be asked to use a standardized test that will enable you to compare individuals to a very large sample of other children. For example, in order to determine which first graders are gifted and talented in music, you may wish to use the *Primary Measures of Music Audiation* (PMMA) by Edwin Gordon (Chicago: G.I.A. Publications, 1979) as one of your screening measures. Gordon believes that the ability to "audiate" (that is, to hear musical sounds that are not present) is measured by this test and that the test is a way to determine developmental musical aptitude (the potential to learn music). The PMMA can be used with children from ages 5 through 8 and contains a tonal section and a rhythmic section, each with 40 pairs of patterns that are the same or different. The tonal test uses electronically synthesized tones of equal length, and the rhythm test examples are on one frequency. Children are required to circle a set of similar or dissimilar faces to indicate what they have heard in the test. In addition, to make the test accessible for primary grades, the successive examples are not numbered but are identified by pictures, such as a boat, a cup, or a tree. A second test, similar to the PPMA in content and response form, titled *Intermediate Measures of Music Audiation* (Chicago: G.I.A. Publications, 1982), has been developed by Gordon for use with children from ages 6 through 9.

Summary

Throughout this chapter you have been given many examples of valid ways to evaluate children's musical skills and understandings. As this course progresses, return to this chapter for suggestions about actual techniques for evaluating each type of musical learning. The following statement needs to become part of your store of professional knowledge and should guide your actions in the classroom from the first time you step in front of a group of children:

Whatever musical learning you evaluate must be evaluated in the same mode in which it was taught.

For example, if you are teaching children the feeling of different meters by singing songs in different meters, you *should not* evaluate their understanding of different meters by having them point to choices while listening to orchestral examples of different meters. The orchestral timbres become the focus of their attention and meter moves to the background, making your test one of listening skills rather than of their understanding of different meters. You *should* use other songs they can sing as the method of evaluation. When the mode in which the idea was presented matches the mode of the evaluation, you get an accurate picture of what the child understands. So evaluate singing by having the child sing songs similar in range and difficulty to the ones practiced, and evaluate listening by having the child listen to music of similar style, genre, and timbre. Match your teaching examples to your evaluative examples, and you will have the easiest access to what your students really know.

Planning and Evaluation

Good music teachers decide in advance what is important for children to learn and when the material will be taught as well as how they will evaluate whether learning has occurred. Since you will be teaching many different grades, you need to understand that there are several levels of effective planning and all are important for good music teaching. Your initial decision is the hardest one, but it will influence all of your teaching. What do you want children to know about music after you have taught them for five or six or seven years? The answers to this critical question will determine your planning at successive levels because of the underlying fact that elementary music teaching results in cumulative learning. Sources that may help you make some reasonable decisions include the introductions and prefaces of music series textbooks, the *National Standards for Education in the Arts* published by Music Educators National Conference, and state and local curriculum documents.

The next level of planning should be more specific and should reflect the differences in how children learn in primary and intermediate grades. As you will read in later chapters, young children learn best through concrete experiences with music (singing, playing, moving, and so on), and while older children continue to expand their musical behaviors, they are also able to learn abstract musical vocabulary and notational symbols for what they have experienced. Fifth and sixth graders need to experience the complexity of music and should be taught to recognize and transfer the understanding of musical elements that you presented in earlier grades.

Musical elements (see Appendix A) are one way of organizing your focus at the next level of planning. You should make clear decisions regarding what you will teach about each element (rhythm, melody, harmony, and so on) in Kindergarten through second grade, in third and fourth grades, and in fifth grade (and sixth grade if you do not have a middle school). You can then break down this level of planning into yearly goals for each grade level, asking yourself, "What do I want Kindergartners (first graders, and so on) to learn about rhythm?"

The final level of planning begins with a determination of how many instructional periods actually exist during a school year. Experienced teachers know that some weeks are not "prime" time for music instruction, such as the week of Halloween, the week prior to Christmas vacation, and standardized or achievement test week. For example, if you see each class once each week, you may have 35 teaching periods in the school year. How many of these time slots will you use for each musical element? Some elements, such as tempo or dynamics, need much less time for an effective unit, while the amount of time for melody or rhythm may need to be much longer, depending upon the grade level.

N. B.

This type of planning enables you to establish clear relationships between your individual lessons and between successive years of music learning. In addition, such planning makes it possible for students to recognize that the time they spend in your music class is valuable and that the connection between past lessons and the present one enables them to become more musically knowledgeable. Through such planning you maximize your short amount of weekly instructional time and emphasize the real importance of a musical education.

Case Study 2

Miss Davis is waiting at her door for the next third grade class to come to the music room. As they enter, she begins to beat a metrical pulse of three softly on her drum. Without any spoken direction, the children begin to move toward their seats in time to the pulse, bending their knees on each strong pulse.

This movement activity was the culmination of the previous lesson. This morning Miss Davis sees that three students, Antonio, Juan, and Tania, still are not responding to the stronger pulse. As she reaches for her recorder, she says to the class, "That was a really good beginning to our music class, children. Who can remember why we moved like that in the last lesson?" Tracy raises her hand and tells Miss Davis that the movement was showing the steady pulse in sets of threes.

"Now, I want you to listen to a song you know, and as soon as you can find the pulse, I want to you pat it softly on your knees. After you begin patting, I want you to try to decide where the strongest pulse is and clap that pulse." Miss Davis begins to play "My Hat" (Figure 3.5, p. 48). The entire class begins patting the pulse by the second measure, and by the beginning of the second phrase all but two children are clapping the initial pulse of each measure. Miss Davis continues to play the entire song and then has the class sing with her. They all pat the pulse and clap the initial beat throughout the song. "I want to know if all of you understand how many beats there are in each set when we sing 'My Hat.' Listen to me sing the song, decide if you will put up two or three fingers, and when I finish, close your eyes and show me your answer."

Next, Miss Davis begins to teach a new song, "All Night, All Day" (Figure 3.7, p. 51). "Children, as I sing our new song today, I want you to listen carefully for the pulse of the song. The words are very easy for third graders, so you can really focus on the pulse. When you can pat it softly with two fingers, please do so." She sings the song and watches the class response. "As I sing the song the second time, I want you to find a way to show the stronger pulse in this song. You can touch another body part, or clap very softly, or whatever you wish, but your strong pulse must be different." Miss Davis again sings the song, and monitors the class response. As she has the class sing with her, she models a movement to show the duple meter, and almost every member of the class sings and moves the meter correctly.

"Today we are going to use our shape envelopes. Would the end person on each row count the number of children in the row and get the correct number of envelopes from the shelf?" Miss Davis softly plays "My Hat" and "All Night" while the children count and pass out the materials. When every child has an envelope she says, "Each row needs to move out of the chairs and find floor space to use. Row 1, please move quietly. When they are all seated, row 2 may move." After the entire class is seated on the floor, she directs the children to take out their sets of light- and dark-colored rectangles so they can construct an icon for each meter.

YOUR COOPERATIVE TASK
1. At this point in the lesson, how can Miss Davis evaluate the children's understanding of meter?
2. At what other points in the lesson could Miss Davis have formally evaluated the individuals in the class? How could she record these evaluations and still keep the pace of her lesson?
3. Brainstorm two other ways in which Miss Davis could evaluate these children before the lesson concludes.
4. Make a list of the prior knowledge that these children needed in order to participate in this lesson. *def of pulse* *Keep steady pulse* *1 st pulse*

Very challenging   Case Study 3

Miss Davis is standing at the door when the sixth grade class arrives. She directs them to sit in a circle on the floor, then divides the class into four groups by putting the list of names in each group on the overhead. The students move to their assigned areas in the room, which Miss Davis has labeled with big poster-size numbers. When they have settled, she gives the assignment. Each group has different sound sources: group 1 has metals, group 2 has woods, group 3 has membranophones, and group 4 is to use body percussion. They are to create a rhythmic ostinato for a song they already know, using one rhythm for the verse and a different one for the refrain. After they create the two different ostinatos, they are to notate them in any way they choose, and these notations will be put on the overhead for the rest of the class to learn and play.

YOUR COOPERATIVE TASK

1. With a partner or in small groups, decide h[ow]
Miss Davis will evaluate the group efforts. [Dis]cuss the various categories that could be used [to]
determine a group grade, and determine h[ow]
the categories will be weighted to arrive a[t a]
group grade.
2. Miss Davis looks in her grade book and reali[zes]
that she needs to have some more individu[al]
grades for everyone. Develop a checklist s[he]
can use to evaluate the individual participati[on]
and performance of each member of the com[-]
position groups.

ss Davis can incorporate the
[peer] evaluation into this composi-
[tion? Wh]at other means of documenta-
[tion could she inc]lude?
[Meet each composition group]
[and eval]uate the products of the other
[Discuss th]e ways in which Miss Davis
[m]eets to arrive at letter grades.
[Discuss w]hich Miss Davis can use the
notation as a way to evaluate

10/27
focus
on
Case
Study
3

Objectives—

Case Study 2
Children will accurately identify, perform
and diagram meter patterns
of 3 & 4.
Concept: rhythm

Case Study 3
Children will create rhythmic ostinatos
that correctly match the meter
and form of a known composition.
Concept: rhythm, form

31

CHAPTER 3

Experiencing Music Through Singing:

PRIMARY

Case Study

It is January, and Miss Davis is in her first year as the general music teacher at Fifth Street School. She teaches all three sections of each grade level once a week for 40 minutes and has finally learned almost all the names of the 650 children she meets each week. As the second graders come into the music room, Stevie stops beside Miss Davis and says to her, "I learned a song from my grandma this weekend—may I share it with the class?" Miss Davis leans over the says, "Stevie, that would be wonderful. I'll save some time at the end of the period. What is the name of the song?" Stevie replies, "'Wait Till the Sun Shines, Nellie,' only my grandma uses my name instead."

Miss Davis is delighted that Stevie has volunteered to sing to the class, as he has seemed withdrawn so far this year in music. After concluding the lesson she tells the class that Stevie has a song to share before they leave. As Stevie sings the song, the class is quiet and attentive, and when he finishes, they applaud enthusiastically. Stevie beams, and Miss Davis turns to the classroom teacher, who has just entered the room. "Did you hear Stevie's song that he shared with us? Today is the first time he has ever sung a solo in music!" Both teachers are now looking at a class of waving arms as every child volunteers to sing. Miss Davis says, "Next week when we have music, we will save time for more sharing."

The following week, Miss Davis has a difficult time selecting children to sing solos—every child wants to sing alone. The second singer she selects is Nancy. As the child begins her song, the class is quiet. But as she continues, some children begin poking each other and looking at Miss Davis. Nancy is not singing in tune. In fact, Nancy is droning on only one pitch.

YOUR COOPERATIVE TASK

With a partner or in a small group, discuss the following questions. One member of the group should be the designated recorder who will write down individual responses for a later class discussion.

1. How might Miss Davis bring closure to the class? As a group, create a script of her closing remarks and directions.
2. Make a list of the positive and negative aspects of allowing everyone to sing a solo in class.
3. What are some different ways Miss Davis might have handled the initial request to sing solos?
4. Do any factors in this case study make you uncomfortable?
5. What additional information would you need to make your group decision?
6. Develop a list of ways to use solo singing by primary children as teaching opportunities.

Introduction

You have spent many years practicing scales and études and preparing music for rehearsals and performances. These behaviors have enabled you to become a musician. The skills you have attained as a musician are the important foundation for becoming a music teacher. In this elementary methods course you must begin another type of preparation, because the art of teaching requires an equal amount of sustained and focused practice. In each chapter of this textbook, you will find three or more teaching scripts. These scripts will enable you to practice small segments of a lesson and become familiar with appropriate methods and materials for different grade levels. The contents of these scripts will be referred to in successive chapters as further steps are added. In the scripts in Chapter 10, you will need to add sections to a partially created lesson. In this way you will create an entire lesson based on what you have learned in previous chapters.

Script 1

Practice the technique of teaching a song by rote (singing it line by line and having the students echo you) to another adult who is not taking this class, such as your roommate, a friend, or your spouse. If possible, practice the script next with a primary child or a group of children. Use the rote method described in the following script.

GRADE LEVEL: Kindergarten/Grade One

MUSICAL CONCEPT: Dynamics

SPECIFIC ELEMENT: Dynamic contrasts in different phrases

LESSON OBJECTIVE: Students will be able to demonstrate an ability to perform dynamic contrasts through singing.

MATERIALS: "Birdie, Birdie, Where Is Your Nest" (Figure 3.1); a piece of string or long piece of grass; a recorder or another melody instrument (resonator bells, Orff xylophone, etc.)

STEP ONE

Warm up singing voices; review a familiar song; demonstrate steady beat via patschen *(patting thighs).*

STEP TWO

Teach the new song as follows:

When I went out in my yard yesterday after school, I saw a bird that had something in its mouth—it looked like a piece of string or a long piece of grass. What do you think that bird was doing?

Solicit answers from the class.

After I saw the bird, I remembered this song, and I want to share it with you. Kindergartners, I want you to listen very carefully to the new song and when I am finished, I want you to tell me what or who the song is about.

Birdie, Birdie, Where Is Your Nest?

Folk song

FIGURE 3.1.

(Another possible way to introduce this song is to use the book No Roses for Harry *by H. A. Ray, a children's book about a dog who so disliked the sweater that Grandma knitted for him that he let a bird unravel it and use the yarn to build a nest.)*

Sing the song in a clear, centered, and well-supported tone with minimal vibrato but with musical expression and musical phrasing.

Raise your hand if you can tell me who the song is about.

Call on one child, then continue:

I want you to listen to the song again, using your best listening ears, and when I have finished singing, I want you to tell me where the birdie built her nest.

Sing the entire song.

Raise your hand if you can remember where the bird built her nest. I want to sing the song to you one more time, because it will help you learn it much more easily. While I sing it this time, I want you to softly tap the beat with one finger just as I do.

Sing the song and model tapping the beat with one finger in the palm.

Now we're going to learn the song together. I will sing one part and when I finish, I want you to sing it with me.

Sing the first two measures. Then indicate to the class that they are to sing by singing "Ready, sing" on the initial pitch and motioning for the class to join in. Sing two measures with the class.

Now I want you to listen to the next part of the song.

Sing the next two measures with contrasting dynamic level. Indicate to the class that they are to sing by singing "Ready, sing" on the initial pitch of the third measure and motioning for the class to join in.

Now we're going to sing both parts together.

Sing "ready, sing" on initial pitch and sing both phrases together.

Now listen to the third part of the song.

Sing third phrase.

Does this part sound like you already know it? I want you to sing that part with me.

Sing "ready, sing" on initial pitch of fifth measure and motion class to begin.

Now we're going to sing all three parts of the song from the beginning.

Sing "ready, sing" on initial pitch and motion to begin.

Raise your hand if you can remember where the bird built her nest. That part of the song sounds like this:

(Sing the last phrase.)

Now you sing that part with me.

Sing "ready, sing" on the initial pitch and motion to begin.

Let's use our best singing voices and sing the first verse.

That was a really nice sound. I'm going to do something different with my voice as I sing it again, and I'd like you to tell me how I'm changing how the music sounds this time.

Sing, exaggerating change in dynamic levels.

Who can tell me how the music was different this time? How did I do that with my voice? See if you can tell me how it feels when you make your voice do that. Let's try it now.

Lead, beginning with "Ready, sing."

How did it sound when you sang it that way? Is there another way we can change the loudness or softness while we're singing it?

Take suggestions and try them. After each trial, ask:

How did this change the music?

After final trial, ask:

Which one did you like the best? Why?

Allow for class discussion and try to come to a consensus.

Why Do We Teach Young Children to Sing?

All schools have several types of curricula. One curriculum is the printed document for each subject area—and another curriculum has often been called the *hidden curriculum*. The hidden curriculum encompasses many aspects of school life, including the amount of instruction time in each subject area. Because music instruction for children in elementary schools is rarely equal in length to the amounts of time devoted to reading or math or science, our subject is sometimes considered less important.

In order to cope successfully with this reality, music teachers must not only know *how* to teach as efficiently and effectively as possible, but they must know *why* they teach music. The art of music has existed throughout human history because an involved feelingful interaction can occur between human beings and musical sound. All good music education, therefore, must enable children to encounter the wealth of unnamed feelings and emotions that music elicits.

Elementary music instruction is most effective when children are actively engaged in music making. To other teachers this continual involvement looks like "fun" or "a break from real work," and some elementary classroom teachers even use participation in music class as a reward for completing work or withhold it as a punishment for not completing classwork. For young children, the development of cognitive processes depends upon concrete experiences; musical *participation* is the only way for them to learn. Primary teachers do understand the importance of having young children use Cuisenaire rods and other manipulative materials to learn about mathematics. But it is not as clear to them why musical learning requires direct experiences with the materials of music. In order to establish your subject as a valid component of the educational process, you must be able to inform others why learning in music involves *making* music.

An important part of your explanation will be based on your understanding of the various learning theories that you have met in other college courses. Valid elementary music instruction is grounded in the cognitive constructionist approach, which is derived from the work of Jean Piaget, Jerome Bruner, and presently, the thinking and research of Howard Gardner and others at Project Zero. These theorists suggest that children's thinking changes in qualitative ways as they mature. Music instruction must provide children with opportunities to construct musical meaning within the scope of their present cognitive abilities. For primary learners, the emphasis must be on concrete or enactive (action) experiences with music. In other words, *doing* music is how young children learn music.

There is an implicit expectation in American elementary schools that the music teacher will include group singing experiences in all classes. This expectation is sometimes verbalized by administrators and other teachers or is implied by the surprised expressions of these same peers when they observe children engaged in composing or moving or listening to music. Beginning elementary music teachers need to be aware that this expectation is based not only on past practice but on the historical beginnings of music education in our country.

The colonial singing schools offered the first organized music instruction in America. These schools were initiated in order to improve the singing and music-reading ability of church choirs and congregations. In the late eighteenth and early nineteenth centuries, these private schools flourished and were the foundation for the later successful attempts to incorporate music into the public school curriculum.[1] This historical precedent explains both the current expectation that singing will be part of the curriculum and the dual curricular focus on music reading and singing.

There are other reasons, of course, why singing is an important part of elementary music teaching. The one instrument that all humans possess is the vocal instrument. Normally developing infants produce a variety of vocalizations that are not only the beginnings of learning to speak but also of learning to sing. Parents who imitate and reinforce these beginning musical attempts provide a basis for later singing expertise in their children.

Just as all children differ in their abilities and strengths, so do parents. The music teacher of any Kindergarten class meets some children who possess well-developed singing instruments and many others whose vocal imitation has been limited to television commercials or cartoon accompaniments. These children will probably be nonsingers or presingers. One challenge in teaching primary children is instructing every child to sing tunefully and expressively.

Singing is a spontaneous form of expression for young children. Toddlers and preschoolers often improvise their own song fragments or whole songs to accompany play. These beginning compositions are effortless and natural expressions of enjoyment. Beginning music instruction must continue to reinforce the joyfulness and pleasure of this basic human ability.

Singing is the one way that all human beings can experience music as performers. Adult performers not only produce musical sounds but are constantly monitoring and reacting to what they hear. In primary music classes, singing is not only an activity and a means of teaching for musical understanding; it is the most effective and important way of providing youngsters with opportunities to perform music. These performance opportunities must be musically valid and must provide children with opportunities to perceive and react to the affective power of music.

Choosing Repertoire

Many factors enter into a enter into a teacher's choice of which songs to include in each lesson. However, the most important factor is that the songs selected must be *worth* learning. The songs must be musically valid (see Table 3.1 for examples). Teachers should carefully examine the melodic, rhythmic, and harmonic construction of any song to be taught to young children in the same manner they would examine a piece to be learned by a performance group. The musical construction and expressive features contribute to the presence of tension and release in music. Music that contains this tension and release is music that provides an affective musical experience. In addition to the musical considerations, the text of each song needs careful scrutiny. The

[1]E. B. Birge (1937). *History of Public School Music in the United States*, 2d ed. Boston: Oliver Ditson. (Reprinted in 1966 by Music Educators National Conference, Washington, DC.)

TABLE 3.1. Suggested Song Literature

Kindergarten	Grade One
"Twinkle, Twinkle"	"Blue Bird, Blue Bird"
"Bought Me a Cat"	"Five Little Pumpkins"
"This Little Light of Mine"	"Eensy Weensy Spider"
"Dipidu"	"Five Angels"
"Hush Little Baby"	"Chatter with the Angels"
"Kum Ba Yah"	"Little Rabbit in the Wood"
"The Old Gray Cat"	"Sally Go Round the Sun"
"Mary Had a Baby"	"You Can't Make a Turtle Come Out"
"Jan Ken Pon"	"Mary Mack"
"Riding in a Buggy"	"Six Little Ducks"
"Five Fat Turkeys Are We"	

Grade Two	Grade Three
"All Night, All Day"	"Little Liza Jane"
"Michael Finnegan"	"Sarrasponda"
"Aiken Drum"	"Polly Wolly Doodle"
"Mi Chacra"	"Sakura"
"Michael Row the Boat"	"Old Joe Clark"
"She'll Be Comin' 'Round the Mountain"	"Oh, How Lovely Is the Evening"
"Shoo Fly"	"Alouette"
"Frère Jacques"	"El Rorro"
"Lavender's Blue"	"Suo Gan"
"A la Puerta del Cielo"	"Down in the Valley"

text should stand alone as poetry appropriate for young children. It should be rich in imagery, have content which children find humorous or enjoyable, and be enhanced by and wedded to the music. Folk music is one genre that often meets both the musical and textual criteria outlined here, and beginning teachers will find it a rich source of repertoire. Because children receive a limited time in music instruction, you must select songs that are truly worth learning and remembering, or you risk wasting the children's time. It is also important that you, the teacher, like the song. You will be singing it many times with each class, and if you are heartily sick and tired of a song after teaching it to one class, the song is not worth your time or the students' effort.

There are some important musical considerations to keep in mind when choosing song literature for young children. Songs for beginning singers should be fairly short and should contain repetition of text and/or melody. If a class includes many children who are unable to move to head register, begin teaching them songs with a very limited range. A fine source is *Sing It Yourself*, a collection of 220 pentatonic American folk songs by Louise Larkins Bradford. (Van Nuys, CA: Alfred, 1978).

Concept Formation: Experience before Symbol

Can you remember your early development as a musician? Your private instrumental instructor probably introduced the term *dynamics* to you fairly early in your study by saying something like, "Can you play that part louder next time?" Perhaps the instructor said nothing at all about dynamics, but you learned that playing softer and louder were ways to make the music sound better. Can you remember when you realized that there were many gradations of dynamic levels and that in some music, greater contrasts in dynamic level were more appropriate? Since you began studying music, your *concept* of dynamics has changed, and you have acquired an elaborate knowledge of both procedural skill (what physical manipulations are required to change dynamic levels) and contextual skill (when to use the various levels, how gradually or abruptly to change levels, how to follow a conductor's indication of such changes). Your ideas about and understanding of dynamics have become broader as you've gained experience as a musician.

Each of your individual musical experiences was a small component of a body that gradually accumulated and coalesced into your understanding of what, in this case, makes up dynamics. At the same time, you developed concepts of melody, rhythm, harmony, form, and so on. It is important to understand that a musical concept is an abstraction based on cumulative perceptions; a concept becomes reality for learners only after many, many experiences.

The important principle in organizing music instruction for children is the actual structure of the discipline of music, the elements of music. Children do not form the musical concept of pulse in one lesson, nor do they acquire the concept of melodic direction after learning one song with a scalewise pattern. Even though your students can label a musical event, they still may not actually have formed the concept. Musical concepts are formed through many experiences, and you must be aware that children often use musical terminology without understanding how the words relate to sound.

The taxonomy of musical concepts found in Table 3.2 on p. 40, is organized in a hierarchical fashion. This listing implies that children need to have many experiences with the simpler elements, those found at the beginning of each list, before they can be expected to begin to understand the more difficult concepts. Primary children, therefore, need to have multiple encounters in successive grades with steady beat and subdivision before the abstraction of meter can eventually be introduced. Similarly, young children need to first master the concept of register and melodic contour before the introduction of intervals or melodic sequence.

As explained in Chapter 1, your curriculum and lesson planning should be based on the elements found in Table 3.2. Good teachers carefully organize their instruction in order to provide the many experiences young children need to develop their individual understanding of each of these concepts. These experiences must be based on the premise that children gradually develop their awareness and knowledge of each musical concept by *doing* music, not through verbal description.

All the concepts that children have formed in their first five years of living serve as the foundation for learning to read the language they speak. The process of learning to read usually begins in Kindergarten and first grade. Therefore, music instruction at this level cannot be based on the printed word. The rote method is the most effective method to use in teaching songs to young children, as outlined in Script 1. The rote technique helps children remember short segments of text and melody and provides the practice necessary to learn the whole song. This process can be described in Piagetian terms

TABLE 3.2. Musical Concept Taxonomy *See Appendix A*

Rhythm

1. Awareness of beat and no beat
2. Beat subdivision (rhythm patterns)
3. Duration
4. Meter
5. Uneven beat subdivision (dotted, syncopated, fermata)

Melody

1. Register
2. Direction
3. Contour
4. Duration
5. Phrases
6. Tonal centers
7. Intervals
8. Sequence

Harmony

1. Presence/absence
2. Contrasts of texture (homophonic, polyphonic, monophonic)
3. Polyphonic (descants, canons, rounds)

Timbre

1. Difference between voices and instruments
2. Contrasts of high and low instruments
3. Contrasts of instrument families

Form

1. Phrases
2. Song sections
3. Introduction, coda
4. AB, ABA
5. Rondo, theme and variations, fugue

---

as an opportunity for children to assimilate and accommodate new information (see Chapter 4). Rote teaching allows young children to become competent with the building blocks that are the foundation for forming musical concepts and mastering musical symbolism.

Once children become competent beginning readers, music textbooks can be introduced. Some music teachers prefer not to use any books until third grade while others begin using books in second grade. An effective way to introduce music books is to begin with songs the children already know. The presence of familiar text makes it easier to teach "how" to read a song in a book. Pretextbook reading experiences can also be introduced on charts, similar to the "experience charts" that primary teachers use for reading. Music series textbook companies publish "big books" just for this purpose.

Singing is a valid way of experiencing and learning music, and it is one of the activities or behaviors *through* which children are actively involved in learning the various elements (melody, rhythm, harmony, etc.) found in music. Songs chosen for primary lessons should not only fit the criteria described above but should clearly illustrate the musical element being taught in a particular lesson. Almost all songs, of course, can illustrate steady beat, a musical concept that must be stressed in early primary teaching (see Table 3.2). When a song is selected to provide an experience with a particular musical element, the song must provide a clear illustration. For example, the song "Where Is Thumbkin?" contains initial phrases that begin with ascending direction, but only three tones are really insufficient to help young children to understand upward direction. A better example is "The Flea Song" (Figure 3.2), in which the ascending (and descending) phrase encompasses the entire scale.

Teaching Children to Sing

A Contemporary Approach: Kodály

The Kodály approach in present-day American music education is an offshoot of the work of the Hungarian composer Zoltan Kodály. Kodály believed that the outcome of music education should be a musically literate population. He was very concerned with the music used in schools in his country and advocated the inclusion of authentic Hungarian folk music and well-composed art music. An important philosophical part of his approach was the belief that the historical development of music from primitive beginnings to developed art music is recapitulated in the way that children develop

FIGURE 3.2. *From* Music for Very Little People *by John Fierabend.*
©*Copyright 1986 by Boosey & Hawkes, Inc. Reprinted by permission.*

musically. For this reason, he believed the initial music used with young children should be short, simple, and based on the pentatonic scale.

In its emphasis on providing the desired musical literacy, the Kodály approach differs considerably from other approaches to music education. Children are taught to sing and read the notation of short patterns and short songs using Curwen hand signs (see Figure 3.3), a simplified notational approach using stem notation and rhythmic syllables, and the "movable do" system. When adapting this approach, teachers should select authentic folk music consisting of songs and singing games as the basic repertoire in primary grades. Musical concepts are taught via singing, moving, and the use of simplified musical notation.

Kodály-based music curricula are less common in elementary schools in the United States than in Canada and Australia. A Kodály-based curriculum has a very specific set of objectives in rhythmic, melodic, and listening skills for each week of instruction and involves children in a set sequence of unaccompanied folk singing throughout the elementary grades. The Kodály emphasis on indigenous folk songs as the proper musical materials for children has been somewhat problematic to implement in our musical culture, as much of what is considered American folk song material is not naturally in the

FIGURE 3.3. Curwen hand signs

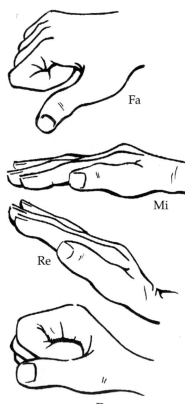
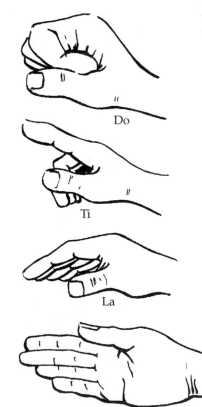

pentatonic mode. Kodály's emphasis on using only the works of "great composers" is also difficult to implement because much of the song material found in music series textbooks is from a wide variety of sources outside the "great composer" genre.

In most elementary music classes you will find some use of Curwen hand signs for solfège learning, along with an adherence to the Kodály-inspired sequence of interval introduction (as described on p. 46). You may also find a fairly wide use of the Kodály rhythmic syllables (ta, ti, etc.). In addition, you may find some teachers who are using "Thresholds to Music" charts, which were compiled by Mary Helen Richards after she visited Hungary briefly in the 1960s. These charts are not accepted as valid expressions of the Kodály method, but they do represent a sequential approach to introducing rhythmic and pitch notation to young children via a singing approach.

Prospective teachers who are interested in this method will find a wealth of information in the text *The Kodály Method* second edition, by Lois Choksy (Englewood Cliffs, NJ: Prentice-Hall, 1988). Summer workshops offering Kodály certification are offered at various universities in the United States and Canada.

Contrasts in Voices

In a single class of young children, teachers will find vast contrasts in singing ability. Some singers will demonstrate the unique child vocal quality that can be described as "light" or "clear," and others may have a heavy, forced sound. These contrasts are the result of the vocal models that children have imitated during their preschool singing experiences. Children who are hearing-impaired or developmentally delayed may also have speaking and singing voices that show very little contrast in inflection. In any one class, some children will sing on pitch and in a wide range, some will sing within a restricted range of only a few notes, and others will sing or chant on one or two pitches. Still others may not be singing at all but only speaking song texts. Despite the wide contrasts of mental and singing ability evident in primary classes, it is the job of the music teacher to teach all children *how* to sing.

Introducing Head Register

Young children often use their speaking voice (chest) register for singing. There are a number of ways to help each child move out of this restricted register and sing in an unforced manner with a wide range. The first step in the process must be to differentiate the four different ways in which voices can be used—speaking, singing, whispering, and shouting.

Teachers should model the different ways of using the voice and have beginning singers identify and vocally imitate the contrasts. One simple way is to use familiar nursery rhymes and begin by speaking the rhyme, changing to another voice in the middle of a line, using all four possible voices. Next, children can be asked to speak a familiar rhyme and at a signal from the teacher, change from speaking to singing and vice versa. This activity can be extended by having individual class members do the activity and instructing the other children to raise their hands when a change is made. A second signal could easily be added to this activity, such as touching the lips to indicate singing.

Initiating musical conversations is another way of providing a singing and speaking contrast. The teacher can sing questions about the class, the school, an approaching holiday, children's pets, or any other topic of current interest. If children try to answer using their speaking voices, the teacher must continue to sing the question and sing directions to answer; the manner in which this is done can motivate the child to continue.

Each time a child attempts to match your pitch, it is up to you to let her or him know whether the sound produced was correct, close to, or far away from your pitch. Instead of saying "That was much better!" you can tell the child that her or his sound was higher or lower than your pitch (or ask other class members to respond) and ask the child to try again. The next try is likely to be closer in pitch than the previous try (a *successive approximation* of the desired pitch) and your continued very specific information can serve as a motivator in a way that simply praising the child cannot.

Once children are able to distinguish vocal contrasts, the teacher needs to move to activities that enable them to experience head voice. Imitating fire sirens and engines, train or factory whistles, birdcalls, or (at Halloween) ghosts are some of the ways to help children to move their voices into the head register. These activities should not be used in isolation, however, but should be linked directly to singing. They should be used prior to every singing experience as a means of warming up the singing voice and "turning on" singing just as children turn on the TV or radio.

A useful device is a teacher-held hand puppet used to tell improvised song stories. Any hand puppet with a movable mouth, such as a parrot or a crocodile, will focus children's attention. You can easily turn a green mitten into a singing frog by adding two eyes (either buttons or the fancier plastic eyes with movable irises). Song stories can focus on weekly puppet adventures that include opportunities for the children to join in using head voice sounds. Children can also be challenged to create their own singing stories.

Teachers may wish to use stories that are already familiar to the class. A number of "Curious George" books lend themselves nicely to adaptation for head voice practice, as do books by Dr. Seuss (such as *Horton Hears a Who* and others). Well-known European folktales such as "Goldilocks and The Three Bears" or "Three Billy Goats Gruff" can also be told with vocal additions. To expand the horizons of all your students, include folktales from other cultures also. You can find these easily by searching in the juvenile book section of your public library. If your student population includes children from other cultures, be sure to include tales from their cultures as well. Have the children decide on an appropriate sound for each animal or character or event, and as you read the book or tell the story, they can add each head voice sound where it fits the story.

Some children may also be able to experience head voice register more easily if they do not use text. The importance of using melody without text is documented in a careful research study by Mary Goetze.[2] You can incorporate this idea in song stories or when you use published books or folktales by having the children add sounds without words. If you have taught the song as

[2]M. Goetze (1985). "Factors Affecting Accuracy in Children's Singing." Unpublished doctoral dissertation, University of Colorado, Boulder.

outlined in Script 1 on page 33, in the next lesson you might begin by warming up with an imitation of an environmental sound to move into head voice, then sing the song on a neutral syllable such as "loo."

Matching Pitch and Tonal Memory

Pitch Matching

Although very few children are true monotones, many of the children you teach will be unable to sing all the pitches of your song in tune. These are uncertain singers, and their skills will develop through sequenced instruction in two other important aspects of singing: pitch matching and extending tonal memory. One effective way to include pitch matching in each lesson is to begin each class with a roll call activity. Sing the name of each child and have the child respond with "Here" or "Here I am," echoing the interval or pitch pattern you presented. Begin this activity by using a descending minor third; gradually expand the range, and also vary the intervals used and the length of the pattern.

There may be some children whose pitch-matching skills seem quite well established when they sing their names back to you at the beginning of class, but whose voices seem to wander while singing in the larger group. Some who sing at a consistent interval above or below the correct pitch in group singing may match perfectly when you work with them individually. There may also be some children whose voices seem to slide from random pitch to random pitch, matching only occasional pitches. While it may sound as if the class is producing tone clusters instead of "Eensy Weensy Spider," instances of sliding and wandering are normal occurrences, and you should anticipate them when teaching young children to sing in groups. Your task is help them to improve their unison singing ability, but before you can tackle this job, you must focus on your own listening ability.

One challenging part of the general music teacher's job is to listen to both the overall group sound and the individual voices within the group. Your conducting class and ensemble experiences have provided opportunities to analyze what is happening in a particular performance. This skill now needs to be refined so that you can listen to an entire group and hear the individual vocal idiosyncrasies of each child. In order to effectively accomplish this task you need to focus simultaneously on several possible categories of beginning singers:

1. Those who sing above and below pitch
2. The children who are strong pitch matchers
3. Those who are using talking voices
4. The children who may not be producing any sound at all

One technique that will enable you to diagnose the singing ability of individuals within the group is to have small groups echo together. You can ask a single row of children, or even pairs of children, to echo you as you sing a phrase or line of the song you are teaching. You may want to isolate a two- or three-note pattern in the phrase and use it for the exercise, moving to another pair or row when it is sung correctly by the previous group. You will begin to discover the extent of each child's vocal development this way, and you can chart each child's progress by writing the letter names of matched pitches in your class notebook.

It is important that you discuss the singing development of individuals as well as the entire class while you are teaching. A class where the teacher continually emphasizes the fact that different children acquire the skill of singing at different rates provides a supportive environment for vocal experimentation and learning. You know from your study of Piaget, Bruner, and others that although all children progress through similar stages of development, these stages are fluid and cannot be defined by age or grade level. Young children need to be reassured that their singing progress need not be identical to that of their classmates.

You might begin by focusing on the group sound and then move to a row or a set of partners. In this way you will enable the children to become discriminating listeners, an important part of good singing. For example, discuss with them the different ways their voices sounded, some higher than the song, some lower. Explain to them that singing is something that everyone can do and is a learned skill. Young children can readily relate to a discussion of the difficulty of learning how to catch a ball or jump rope, and they can understand that singing is an ability that they will have to practice in order to acquire competence. Another useful analogy for the earliest grades is that just as some students have already begun to lose their baby teeth and others haven't, some of them have already found their singing voices and others haven't. Children need to know that singing will be taught in your music class and that every child can learn to sing.

A useful tool for helping children match pitch involves the teaching of hand signs (see Figure 3.3) that were initially developed in England by John Curwen. As noted above, they were later incorporated into the Kodály approach to music education. The physical action accompanying sound production reinforces, for some children, the meaning and relationships of the sounds they are singing. The hand signs are also a concrete expression of the relationships of intervals and register and provide a valid conceptual framework for the eventual teaching of music notation. An accepted sequence of introducing the hand signs and intervals is as follows:

sol-mi

sol-mi-la

mi-do

mi-re-do

sol-fa-mi-re-do

sol-la-ti-do

As with all singing activities, the model teacher voice for pitch matching must be as light, clear, centered, and well supported as possible, with a minimum of vibrato. Male elementary teachers must be aware that uncertain singers may try to imitate the male octave difference. In addition to explaining vocal differences, male teachers may need to give initial pitches using falsetto until the children are secure with their own singing voices.

Other pitch-matching activities can be included when teaching songs. For example, "John the Rabbit" (Figure 3.4) has a repeated refrain of "Oh, yes" on a single pitch. Songs with repeated patterns, such as "Frère Jacques" or "Three Blind Mice," also lend themselves to teacher and class echo and provide experiences in focused listening and pitch reproduction.

Beginning singers need very careful pitch preparation before they reproduce a phrase or a song. In the teaching script on page 55, you will use the words "Ready, sing" on the beginning pitch of each phrase. Experienced singers find the pitch from tonality and musical context, but young children do not have these abilities. You must be sure that the children have ample opportunity to hear and even reproduce the starting pitch before they are expected to sing any song.

John the Rabbit

American folk song

FIGURE 3.4.

In Script 1, which outlined the rote song method, we saw how young children learn an extended song when it is broken into segments or "chunks" that can more easily be remembered. Once the class has learned a song, tonal memory can be reinforced through an activity where parts of the song are sung internally. The teacher could begin by teaching "Bingo" or "My Hat" (Figure 3.5), songs in which children must initially think one letter or word internally and then, in successive repetitions, omit additional letters or words. Another method of extending tonal memory is to choose a short segment in the song and provide a cue for students to stop singing and begin singing aloud again. Later experiences should extend the length and number of phrases that children sing "in their heads."

The way a song is taught also provides a means of extending tonal memory. As children mature, they will be able to move to learning whole songs instead of segments. Whole song learning should be reinforced initially with movements or visual cues that will enable the children to remember the text sequence. Songs such as "Eensy Weensy Spider" or "Little Cabin in the Woods" (see Figure 3.6) can be learned as wholes by primary singers because the hand motions that accompany the song provide clues to the text sequence.

Another technique for extending melodic memory can be incorporated into every lesson. Instead of announcing which familiar song the class will sing, play the melody of the song on a soprano recorder, tone bells, or a xylophone. It will not take many lessons before the hands start to shoot up after only a few notes. This activity is an easy way to encourage focused musical listening.

My Hat

German folk song

My hat it has three cor - ners; ____

__ three cor - ners has my hat; _____

__ And had it not three cor - ners, __

__ it would not be my hat. _____

FIGURE 3.5.

All facets of singing instruction with primary children will be more successful if the use of the piano is limited or even avoided. The piano does not produce a good model for young singers. Indeed, the heavy sound, especially if chords or harmonic accompaniment is included, may deter children from hearing their own voices and the voices around them. Including accompaniment may also make it impossible for young children to aurally distinguish the musical feature that is most important in learning a song—the melody.

A similar problem exists with commercial recordings, even those produced by music textbook companies. Often these "tools" do not provide a

FIGURE 3.6. *"Little Cabin in the Woods" from* Exploring Music I: Teacher's Reference Book *by Eunice Boardman and Beth Landis, copyright © 1975 by Holt, Rinehart and Winston, Inc., reprinted by permission of the publisher.*

good model of the child singing voice, although it has become the norm to use children instead of having adults try to sing like children. The extensive accompaniments used in textbook recordings mask the vocal line, and some recordings rely so heavily on synthesized timbres that children rarely hear themselves accompanied by a recognizable acoustic instrument. Although synthesized sounds are often funny and enjoyable for kids to hear, the heavy reliance on these timbres as a motivator for young singers is musically deplorable.

Young children do not readily sort the two competing stimuli of melody and accompaniment. A song presented with a heavy piano accompaniment confuses their ears, and they try very hard to drown out the accompaniment by singing louder. While we don't know exactly what they do hear and how they process it, children eventually need to be helped to focus their attention on a competing melodic line or accompaniment while at the same time continuing to sing the melody. An easy way to begin this process in second grade is to occasionally have them listen to you play a melody on soprano recorder, which you then use to accompany them while they sing a song they know very well. Make sure the melodic contour of your accompaniment contrasts the melodic contour of the song, and have them trace the melodic contour with their arms as you play. Then have them trace the contour of their song as they sing. When you perform the two melodies together, have half the class listen to you play and trace the contour while the other half sings and traces their own contour. Then have them switch parts. An example is given in Figure 3.7 using "All Night, All Day."

Warming Up the Child's Instrument

The child voice is a musical instrument that deserves careful attention to its development, and we are all aware that warming up any instrument before it is used is an important musicianly behavior. The children need to be taught that during this activity they are actually warming up their bodies as well as their singing voices. It is a time of synthesis of all that they understand about posture and breathing, and yet it need take only a minute or two of class time.

This short amount of time needs to be planned very carefully. If the class contains many children who are not using head voice, you may want to begin with a short activity that enables the entire class to produce the head register. For primary children, an unaccompanied four- or five-note descending and ascending scale sung on "ooo," beginning on F or G and moving up diatonically one or two steps, is an effective transition from talking voice to singing voice. It will also get their ears accustomed to the round vowel sounds that you want them to produce and will help you to put the "ooo" back into the sound when the vowels start to spread. Then you will want to connect the remainder of the warm-up to your lesson content. The best warm-ups for young voices are those that have some connection to the songs they will be singing in class that day. You can create an unaccompanied warm-up out of any melodic or rhythmic motive and have the class echo it. Your lead question, as you begin to teach the song, can then focus on the warm-up motive: "How many times does this pattern happen in this song? Listen and be ready to tell me after I sing the entire song."

All Night, All Day

Spiritual

FIGURE 3.7A.

FIGURE 3.7B. "All Night, All Day" descant

Teaching Singers to Listen

Class Management

In order for young children to focus on their own singing voices, they must be in a class setting where careful listening can occur. During the first music class with your primary students you must establish your behavioral expectations, creating a positive learning environment in addition to beginning to teach correct singing posture and breathing techniques. You must tell them what they need to do in your class. Do you want them to come in and sit in a circle on the carpet, or in rows of chairs? How do you want them to file into the rows? Randomly? In the order in which their classroom teacher lined them up? Are there materials and equipment in the room that they should avoid until instructed differently by you? Music room procedures and expectations should be explained and modeled for the students in the simplest terms during the first class. Try to limit yourself to three or four rules that you believe essential, and focus on these during the first few lessons. Areas to consider are

1. Entering the room
2. Finding a seat

3. Playing instruments
4. Touching neighbors
5. Talking to the teacher
6. Talking to neighbors

As you teach a song to young children, you are also teaching them what a musician in action looks like. They notice and imitate all that you do the first time through, like it or not. They learn correct singing posture, breath support, facial expression, intonation, phrasing, and dynamics each time you sing something for them to echo. It is essential that you know your song inside out before you try to teach it to a group of young children, for they will learn it exactly as you present it to them the first time, every word and note.

During the first class singing session, you need to teach your students to listen and watch for your signals for classroom procedures as well as singing. In teaching good singing posture, you might ask them to roll their shoulders up and back. To prepare to sing, you might ask them to take a sip of cold air through a straw. "Shoulders up and back" and "Cold air sip" become your signals for correct singing posture and preparatory breath. In teaching a rote song, for example, you can avoid all "teacher talk" by simply pointing to yourself while you sing and to them when they should echo. You don't need to stop and tell them what was wrong or right because you can just continue to sing, repeating whatever line was difficult or incorrect and pointing to them to echo until it is corrected.

Listening to Their Own Voices

Primary children will vary in their ability to hear themselves while singing, both in a group and individually. It is important for teachers to include activities that will enable children to improve in this important aspect of singing. One very effective activity is the "cupped hands" exercise. Have each child cup a hand around the back of each ear while singing alone first, then in the group. Discuss how the two ways sounded different. Ask them to consider why it is easier to hear their own voices with their hands in place. Then ask them to try to hear their own voices without using their hands to help.

Another way to help young singers focus on their own voices is through a partner exercise. Have the children stand in a circle, then turn to face each other in pairs. Go around the circle, giving each pair a pitch to match. Have them take turns singing the pitch and telling each other if they were matching exactly or singing higher or lower than the pitch. Reinforce the correct pitch by playing it on a recorder. As their singing and listening skills grow, try this activity in quartets, eventually including the entire class.

A third way to focus on this important ability and yet provide variety in your lessons is through an activity called "stringing the beads." Have the first child in a row echo a word, line, or phrase sung by you. Ask the child if it was correct, and if it was not, ask which part was a problem. Then have the child try again and ask for volunteers to tell if it was correct. When it is sung correctly, have the second child in the row sing along with the first child, adding children and repeating the questioning until the entire class or row is singing correctly.

The goal of all music instruction is to enhance the inherent musicality of each child. Your job is to enable each child in your class to make musical decisions and judgments based on what they know and what they feel, and these skills must be taught explicitly. Attainment of musical concepts is an important outcome, but it is only a means to the end of enhanced musical perception and reaction. Unless children are asked to use their musical knowledge and understandings to find their own meanings in what they heard or performed, music instruction becomes indoctrination into a symbol system rather than an enriching human experience. The difference between teaching for musical concept formation and teaching for enhanced musical perception and reaction lies in the types of questions posed by the teacher.

There is a direct relationship between the kinds of questions that the music teacher asks and the amount and kinds of thinking the students engage in. While there are infinite possibilities for teacher questions, there are three kinds of thinking that questions can stimulate in the music class: convergent thinking, divergent thinking, and critical thinking. The musical thinking that you can stimulate in your students is an amalgam of these three. You are there to lead the child to music literacy, but you are also there to make the child aware of how the music does what it does to us, as listeners and participants. Your keen interest in how the music affects each of them needs to be expressed in your questions, facial expression, and body language.

Convergent Thinking

When teaching musical concepts, the teacher asks students for convergent thinking, prompting them to give the single, correct answer to a question. Such questions tap only the lowest level of cognition, which includes remembering or recalling specific terms, symbols, facts, or classifications.[3] Examples of convergent thinking include labeling two melodies as same, different, or similar; using arm movements to illustrate louder and softer sounds in a piece of music; and raising both hands in the air when many voices sing, as opposed to raising one finger in the air when once voice sings. Whether the convergent response is verbal or gestural, it is important that you accept children's terminology and reasoning as a valid way of explaining their answers to your question.

Divergent Thinking

When you ask a question that has no right or wrong answer, you are asking children to engage in divergent thinking. Questions such as these lead to divergent responses: "What could we do when we sing this song to make it sound better?" "When we sing the song this time, can you show me how its sound is different from the previous time by moving your whole body?" "How could we change the way we sing it so that it is easier to understand the words we're singing?" You can list all the verbal responses to divergent

[3]See Benjamin Bloom, Ed. *Taxonomy of Educational Objectives: The Classification of Educational Goals. Handbook I: Cognitive Domain* (New York: McKay, 1956).

questions on the chalkboard and show the class that although each response is different, each one is valid. Although divergent thinking is prized as the source of inventions and marvels of modern science, divergence is not valued highly in our society. It seems that teachers, who have been trained to expect the right answer, often don't know what to do with responses that differ from the norm. Encouraging divergent responses to music is one of the easiest ways to help children engage the feelings that we know are a necessary and important part of any musical reaction. This type of discussion highlights and validates this important and often neglected aspect of music teaching.

Critical Thinking

Critical thinking is a term that has a variety of definitions and applications in education. In some schools students are taught critical thinking skills and are shown how to apply them in each area of the curriculum. Critical thinking in math, for example, requires the student to reason as a mathematician would, using the terminology and concepts of mathematics to solve problems. Thinking poetically requires students to think as a poet would, using terminology and concepts of poetry to construct or discuss a poem. Critical thinking skills are practiced in the context of solving a problem in a particular content area, and the skills involved are related to logic: presenting well-reasoned arguments supported by ample evidence and based on valid assumptions.

Critical thinking experiences in music enable children to make decisions and judgments about music in the same way the musician and music critic make decisions and judgments. Children engaged in critical thinking in music class use their knowledge and skills, musical imagination, and individual internal response to the music in arriving at decisions. Although the level of musical sophistication that the primary child will achieve will not approach that of the adult musician and music critic, young children can still engage in musical thinking as young connoisseurs, *given the right questions.*

Questions that focus on skill issues can easily lead children to draw on their musical knowledge to make musical decisions: "How can we improve the sound of the phrase we just sang?" "How can we make the rhythms clearer?" "How can we make sure the last notes are heard?" Questions that focus on the musical expressiveness of the performance can lead to a rich discussion: "How did this way of singing change the way the song made you feel?" "What things can we try to make it sound more musical?" "Which of the two ways we just tried sounded better? Why?"

It is important that teachers give children the opportunity to engage in convergent, divergent, and critical thinking in each lesson. Through the inclusion of carefully constructed and differentiated questions in all parts of the lesson, young children are started on the path to becoming musical thinkers.

TEACHING SCRIPTS

The following teaching scripts focus on only one part of a lesson—teaching a new song. Script 2 illustrates teaching a song via the rote method; Script 3 illustrates teaching a song via the whole method. It is highly recommended that you practice each of the following teaching scripts at least twice—with a small group of your peers and then with children. If you are able to practice the scripts several times with young children, you will be able to focus on listening to the children's actual vocal reproduction and also further refine your group management skills.

Script 2

GRADE LEVEL: Grades One and Two
MUSICAL CONCEPT: Rhythm
SPECIFIC ELEMENT: Steady beat
LESSON OBJECTIVE: Students will be able to demonstrate the ability to perform a steady beat through movement and playing instruments.
MATERIALS: "One Elephant" (Figure 3.8); a picture of an elephant or a toy elephant; a recorder or another melody instrument (resonator bells, Orff xylophone, etc.); rhythm instruments; an elephant chart with four elephants per line, eight lines total.

STEP ONE

Warm up singing voices; review a familiar song; demonstrate steady beat via patschen.

STEP TWO

Teach the new song:

Today's song is about this elephant. I want you to listen carefully and tell me what this elephant did.

Sing the song and then ask the class to respond to your question.

After you listen carefully this time, I will ask you what kind of day it was.

Sing the song and then ask the class the question again.

One Elephant

American folk song

FIGURE 3.8.

The third time I sing the song, I want you to tell me why the elephant called for another elephant.

Sing the song and then ask the class the question again.

Before we learn the song, does anyone know what the word *enormous* means?

If there is no response, describe some other enormous objects and have the class deduce the meaning.

Teach the song: Sing the first phrase; give the beginning pitch by singing the words "Ready, sing"; the class sings the first phrase.

Sing the second phrase; give the beginning pitch; the class sings the second phrase.

Sing the first two phrases; give the beginning pitch; the class sings the first two phrases.

Sing the third phrase; give the beginning pitch; the class sings the third phrase.

Sing the first three phrases; give the beginning pitch; the class sings the first three phrases.

Sing the fourth phrase; give the beginning pitch; the class sings the fourth phrase.

Sing the entire song. The class sings the entire song.

As we sing it again, let's see if we can find the steady beat of the song. Find the steady beat and pat your legs with the steady beat as we sing just the first line.

Who could find the steady beat? Can you tell us how you found it? Can you explain how it felt when you patted it and sang it at the same time?

Let's all try to find our own personal steady beat this time. You each have a steady beat that goes on all the time, and it's your heartbeat. Find your heartbeat and show it by tapping your finger in the air. Now let's jump up and down five times and find it again. How did it change? In our song, the steady beat doesn't change, does it? So a steady beat in music is steadier than your heartbeat, isn't it?

Let's figure out how to make this song sound better. What instruments could we add to remind us of the steady beat? What could we add to make it sound more interesting?

Analyze the kinds of instruments chosen, asking how they make sound and what the children think each will contribute. Try each suggestion; discuss the effect. Keep incorporating new ideas. Remind them that silence adds interest as well. Show them how to add silence to whatever instrument part they've suggested; then try it and discuss the result.

As a visual aid, you could use one of these charts:

1. *A picture of a single elephant*
2. *A single row of four elephants*
3. *Eight rows of four elephants each*
4. *A row of four elephants across the top and seven successive lines with four stick "ta" signs*

Script 3

GRADE LEVEL: Grades One and Two
MUSICAL CONCEPT: Rhythm
SPECIFIC ELEMENT: Duration
LESSON OBJECTIVE: Students will be able to demonstrate an ability to perform contrasting durations through movement.
MATERIALS: Copy of "Daa, Daa Kente" (Figure 3.9). Note: the text of this song is written phonetically. The *a* and *e* vowels should be short (ah and eh) and the *o* long (oh), while the *i* should sound like ee. The title means "always in kente" (a brightly colored woven cloth that is made only in Ghana and is usually made into skullcaps for men or scarves and shawls for women). One can go about proudly and feel well dressed in this beautiful cloth.

STEP ONE

Warm up singing voices; review a familiar song; demonstrate contrasting durations in the song with hand motions.

STEP TWO

Teach the new song:

The song I am going to sing is from the African country of Ghana. See if you can hear the words of a language that is different from English.

Sing the whole song once.

Daa, Daa Kente

Ghanian folk song

rhythmically complex

FIGURE 3.9.

These words are really different. I want to sing the song to you again, and I want you to also watch my hand carefully.

Sing the whole song again, showing relative pitch levels with your hand.

Now we're going to practice saying the words so we'll all be able to sing the song together.

Say the words of the song. The class listens, then says the words with the teacher.

When I sing the song again, I want you to *think* the words and show how the melody moves in the song.

Sing the song again, modeling pitch levels.

Now it is time for you to sing this folk song from Ghana.

Sing the song together with the children.

You made a really nice clear "ah" sound in your words that time, first graders! Good job! *(Use if appropriate.)* **When we sing it this time, I'd like you to tap your pointer fingers together each time you sing a sound. When we're finished singing, see if you can tell me which sounds took the longest. Ready, sing.**

(Sing these last two words on the first pitch of the song.) Let the class answer, taking many suggested answers.

Let's sing it again to check and see which answer is right, only this time we'll step the quick sounds as we sing them, and we'll crouch when we sing a long sound. Find your own space in the room now. Remember that your own space is somewhere you can stand with your arms out, take one turn around, and not touch anyone or anything. Have each of you found your own space? Good. Ready, sing.

(Sing on the beginning pitch.)

We found the long sounds that time, didn't we? But it was pretty hard to crouch and sing the long sounds. Can you think of another way we could show the difference between the long and short sounds? Let's think of two different kinds of movement we could use that would be easy for everyone to do.

Take suggestions and have children try out at least three. Let the class decide which one to use.

Do you think we could make up another movement to show the difference between the two kinds of short sounds? What words have the shortest sounds, the sounds that move the quickest?

Take class answers.

Let's use our three different movements this time to show how the sounds move in this song.

Sing the song with the class as the children move.

Which of the different ways of moving to the music helped you feel the sounds the best?

Allow time for children to respond.

STUDENT ASSIGNMENTS

1. Teach one of these scripts to real children while being videotaped. Write a reflection paper on the experience, outlining your reactions, learnings, and insights.
2. Teach a script to real children with peer(s) doing the evaluation. Your partner(s) should use the following evaluation checklist:
   1. The teacher motivated the class. The children were interested in the song.   __ yes __ no
   2. The teacher used directed listening questions that focused the children's listening three times.   __ yes __ no
   3. The teacher taught the song phrase by phrase and "chunked" the phrases successively.   __ yes __ no
   4. The teacher gave the correct beginning pitch for each phrase or section of the song.   __ yes __ no
   5. The teacher's voice was light, clear, and well supported, with a minimum of vibrato.   __ yes __ no
   6. The teacher was at ease with the children.   __ yes __ no
   7. The teacher sang the song correctly each time, word for word, note for note.   __ yes __ no
   8. The teacher listened to the class and corrected errors.   __ yes __ no
   9. The teacher sang with dynamic changes and musicality.   __ yes __ no
   10. The teacher made continual eye contact with the children.   __ yes __ no
   11. The teacher moved around the room to hear individual voices within the group.   __ yes __ no
   12. The teacher's directions were clear upon first hearing.   __ yes __ no
   13. The teacher gave the children specific positive reinforcement _____ times.   __ yes __ no
3. Rewrite one of the three scripts in this chapter in order to teach one of the following musical concepts: register, repeated phrases, or duple meter.
4. *Cooperative or partner assignment*: Find songs appropriate for primary children and describe how each could be used to teach about music. Include complete citations of your sources.
5. Develop a checklist that you could use to evaluate children's progress in singing skills.

Experiencing Music Through Singing:

INTERMEDIATE

Case Study

It is the third week of October, and Miss Davis, the new music teacher at Fifth Street School, is teaching her first fifth grade class of the week. The students come into her room and seat themselves on the rug in an informal way. Most of the children are sitting near their friends, and the children are obviously grouped by gender.

The class begins by listening to the recording of the song they learned last week, "The Wabash Cannonball" (Figure 4.1). After the class discusses the meaning and effect of the diminuendo at the end of the song, Miss Davis asks for volunteers to play the recorder ostinato. Several girls wave their arms enthusiastically and are chosen by the

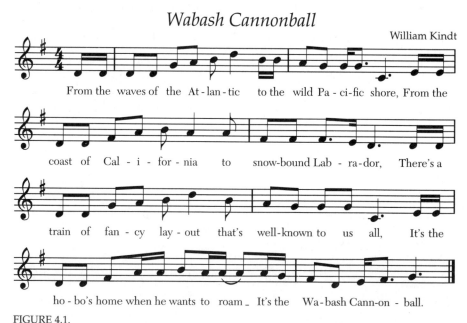

FIGURE 4.1.
Words adapted by Merrill Staton and used by permission.

teacher. As the class performs the song, Miss Davis conducts the diminuendo and the children approximate the dynamic change they heard on the recording.

Miss Davis then has the class turn to another song in the same unit, "Billy, Billy" (Figure 4.2). She uses the suggested question in the teacher's manual, which focuses the children's listening on the tonal center of the song. As she sings the song and plays her guitar, she notices that several boys sitting together are not looking at their books. They are nudging each other with their elbows and smiling at each other. Miss Davis stands up with her guitar and continues to sing as she walks through the class. As she pauses by the off-task group, they appear to become very attentive to the textbooks in front of them.

After she has sung the first verse of the song, she again follows the suggestion in the teacher's manual and asks the class to pat their knees when they hear the tonal center. She sings the first verse again, and the same boys make an excessive amount of patting noise. Again, she begins to casually stroll through the class and the boys seem to become attentive when she stands near them.

Finally, she asks the class to sing the first verse with her. As she sits in front of the class, she realizes that the boys in the same group are not actually singing. Their lips are moving, but she can see that there is no vibration in their throats. As she listens carefully, she realizes that no sound is coming from that section of the class.

YOUR COOPERATIVE TASK

1. Create a script of the next actions and remarks that Miss Davis should follow in this class.

2. What steps might Miss Davis have taken earlier in the lesson to prevent this scenario?
3. What types of songs do *you* think will appeal to intermediate-age students?
4. How could a music teacher use this situation to teach careful listening or discrimination skills to the class?
5. A model of motivation researched in mathematics describes the subjective reasoning of students as they decide whether or not to pursue an activity. One factor in the process is described as task value and includes three parts:
   - Attainment value: how students perceive that doing the task will support self-perception (including "correct" gender roles)
   - Intrinsic value: the inherent enjoyment of the activity
   - Utility value: how the activity will help the students attain another goal

   Discuss how each of these three components might explain the off-task behavior of this group of children.
6. In pairs, work on the following role-playing exercise: One of you take the role of a vocally talented fifth grade boy and discuss the effects of singing in front of other boys in the class. The partner should then take the role of a fifth grade girl and tell what she thinks about singing in front of others in music class.
   - Describe some of the cultural expectations we have of males and females in regard to singing.
   - Brainstorm a list of important ideas to remember when planning singing activities with an intermediate class, taking into consideration the different views about singing held by males and females.

Billy, Billy

Texas folk song

Here's the way we Bil - ly, Bil - ly, Bil - ly, Bil - ly, Bil - ly, Bil - ly,

Here's the way we Bil - ly, Bil - ly, all night long.

FIGURE 4.2.

61

PRACTICE TEACHING SCRIPT FOR WHOLE SONG

The whole song script that follows represents only one small segment of an entire lesson. Use this script to practice the technique of teaching a whole song to another adult who is not in this class, such as your roommate, a friend, or your spouse. If possible, then practice the script with an intermediate-age child or group of children.

Script 1

GRADE LEVEL: Grades Five and Six

MUSICAL CONCEPT: Rhythm

SPECIFIC ELEMENT: Syncopation

LESSON OBJECTIVE: Students will be able to demonstrate an ability to identify and sing syncopated rhythm patterns.

MATERIALS: "John Henry" (Figure 4.3); accompaniment instrument (guitar, autoharp, or piano)

STEP ONE

Warm up singing voices; review a familiar song that contains syncopation (check with the regular music teacher for suggestions prior to teaching this lesson).

STEP TWO

Teach the new song as follows:

Do you know any songs that tell a complete story? Many songs and poems were written just to tell a particular story—they are called ballads. The song that I am going to sing to you tells the story of an African-American man named John Henry who worked on building the railroad. I am going to sing the entire song to you, and after I sing it, I want you to be ready to tell me the story that is described in the song.

(An alternative way to introduce the song would be to lead a discussion of the types and purposes of work songs—sea chanteys, cowboy songs, railroad songs, and so on—focusing on the particular songs that the students already have learned, how they were used in actual work, and where each fits into this genre.) Sing the entire song expressively, changing dynamics and playing accompaniment on guitar, autoharp, or piano.

Can you tell me what the story is in this song?

Solicit answers.

Why do you think the "boss" wanted to use a machine? What does the song say happened to John Henry? We know that John Henry actually died during the construction of a railroad tunnel in West Virginia. The song, however, makes a real person into a legend—someone who is larger than life. Are there other people you have heard about who also seem to be legends?

Children may mention Casey Jones, Calamity Jane, Paul Bunyan, and other folk heroes and heroines.

John Henry

CHAPTER 4
Experiencing Music
Through Singing:
Intermediate

FIGURE 4.3.

Now I want you to sing the entire song with me.

Give the starting pitch by singing the words "Ready, sing" on the pitch. Have the class sing all verses of the song with you, with accompaniment.

There are some places in this song where the rhythm changes from even sounds to uneven sounds. I want to sing the first verse only, and I want you to silently tap the steady beat with two fingers and see if you can find those places where the rhythm changes.

(It changes in measures 1 and 5.)

text

Who can tell me which line has the first uneven rhythm? Which words go with this uneven rhythm? Where is the other similar rhythm? We call these *syncopated rhythms*. **We can't tap our fingers on the four beats of the measure and have the melody sounds fit each beat—they are "off" the beat. Why do you think a composer of a song or any music would use such a rhythm?**

> *Solicit answers.*

Now I want you to sing just the first verse with me and clap those rhythms as we sing. How do you think the song would sound if it did not have those syncopated parts?

> *After class discussion, play the song on the piano for the students, but do not include any syncopation. Then have the students sing one verse of this "straight" version with you and discuss how this version was different. Was it easier to sing? Did it have the same kind of emphasis as the syncopated version? Which way of singing made it sound more like a folk song? What kind of song did it become when you took out the syncopation? How did the syncopated rhythms reinforce the meaning of the text?*

WHAT YOU NEED TO KNOW

Why Intermediate-Age Children Should Sing

The act of vocal expression is as important for intermediate-age children as it is for younger learners. Despite the thin veneer of sophistication that these students assume as a result of watching television, especially if they watch MTV, singing quality music must continue to be an important activity in every music class. The singing role models that children see on the TV screen are exciting and attractive, and music teachers need to be aware of this societal factor. However, it is not in any way possible for children's voices to replicate these carefully engineered recordings or for teachers to replicate the elaborately sampled accompaniments.

What is possible in general music class is the provision of genuinely enjoyable singing experiences where the love of singing and the love of music are carefully nurtured. General music class is one place in the school where intermediate-age children are not sitting quietly and passively listening to a teacher. Rather, they are actively involved in music making, and singing is their prime means of musical production. This important facet of self-expression must continue to be an important way for children to experience the undefined but all-important feelings that musical expression provides.

It is important for all children to understand their unique vocal potential and to gain control of their own singing voices. In primary music class, children learn to sing on pitch and begin to experience the joy and satisfaction of musical unison singing. Vocal instruction does not end in primary grades, however. Older elementary children's voices also will continue to improve with focused instruction.

Intermediate students are physically able to control their voices in a way that makes singing expressively an obtainable goal. They are able to understand and emulate the singing of musical phrases; they can learn to sing harmony; and as their vocal control increases, they can replicate combinations of dynamic changes. All these musical abilities provide intermediate learners with the musical skills needed to participate in very satisfying classroom and public singing performances.

Intermediate music class may be the last organized music instruction many students receive in the public schools. It is imperative that your students become comfortable with their own singing voices and experience the powerful beauty of vocal music if they are to continue to sing as adolescents and adults.

Ways to Nurture Love of Singing in Older Students

By the time they reach third grade, most children have begun to develop a sense of how their own singing ability compares with that of their peers, and they have well-established opinions about singing in music class. In the intermediate grades, as in the earlier grades, you might find a wide range of pitch-matching skills and vocal quality with a particular class. You might hear the occasional wanderer and the slightly-under-pitch singer, as well as the girl who feels more comfortable in chest register because that is where her entire family speaks and sings, or the boy who is trying to hasten the advent of his voice change. In addition, a class may include children who are developmentally disabled or physically impaired. Many of these students continue to sing in their speaking voice register.

However, the same children who, as first graders, would work on finding their head voices with you in class and would sing anything you asked them to with their entire body, heart, and soul are now selective in their singing participation. Although this first bloom of preadolescence may seem unbecoming and difficult to deal with from your perspective as music teacher, it marks the beginning of the child's journey to adulthood and is an important aspect of upper elementary school life. Your task is to maintain your students' interest while continuing to develop and refine their singing skills. You can most easily do this by choosing repertoire that challenges and excites upper elementary students.

Choosing Repertoire

Exciting song literature for fourth, fifth, and sixth graders needs to meet their criteria for what is interesting, both musically and textually. Songs that have more than one voice, a melody with a good mix of steps and skips, fairly complex rhythmic patterns, a quick or changing tempo, and changing dynamic levels are more popular with this age level (see Table 4.1) than songs that have slow-moving melodic rhythm, primarily stepwise melodic motion, and little harmonic variety. Texts that tell an unusual or silly story or require tongue-twisting to pronounce are popular with this age group. See "The Frog in the Well" (Figure 4.4), "Old Dan Tucker" (Figure 4.5), "Fooba, Wooba, John" (Figure 4.6), and "Erie Canal" (Figure 4.7). A good Halloween song that upper elementary students enjoy is "The Monster Song," which is used in Script 3 at the end

TABLE 4.1. Suggested Song Literature

Grade Four	Grade Five	Grade Six
"Rattlin' Bog"	"Dixie"	"Camptown Races"
"Who Built the Ark"	"Battle Hymn of the Republic"	"Scarborough Fair"
"Swing Low, Sweet Chariot"	"This Land Is Your Land"	"Joshua Fit the Battle of Jericho"
"Buffalo Gals"	"Amazing Grace"	"The Golden Vanity"
"Waltzing Matilda"	"Erie Canal"	"Dry Bones"
"Oh, Susanna"	"Casey Jones"	"Ahrirang"
"Git Along, Little Dogies"	"You're a Grand Old Flag"	"This Train"
"Dan Gato"	"Goober Peas"	"Glendy Burke"
"Clementine"	"Roll On, Columbia"	"John B. Sails"
"The Star-Spangled Banner"	"Sweet Betsy from Pike"	"Hava Nagila"
"Sakura"	"La Cucaracha"	"Blow the Man Down"
		"Tzena, Tzena"

The Frog in the Well

Traditional

There was a frog lived in the spring,

Sing song Kit-ty can't you ki-mey O, He was so fat that he

could not swim, Sing song Kit-ty can't you ki-mey O.

Kee-mey O ma ki-mey O ma dir-ey O ma wear, Me hi me ho, me

in come Sal-ly Sin-gle, Some time Pen-ny Win-kle, In stepped nip cat,

Hit him with a brick bat, Sing song Kit-ty can't you ki-mey O.

FIGURE 4.4.

From English Folks Songs from the Southern Appalachians *collected by Cecil J. Sharp, edited by Maud Karpeles. Reproduced by permission of Oxford University Press.*

FIGURE 4.5.

FIGURE 4.6.

Erie Canal

American work song

I got a mule, her name is Sal,

Fif-teen miles on the Er-ie Ca-nal! She's a good old work-er and a

good old pal. Fif-teen miles on the Er-ie Ca-nal! We've

hauled some bar-ges in our day, Filled with lum-ber,

coal, and hay, And we know ev-'ry inch of the way From

Al-ba-ny to Buf-fa-lo.

Refrain

Low bridge, ev-'ry-bo-dy down,

Low bridge, 'cause we're com-ing to a town; And you'll

al-ways know your neigh-bor, you'll al-ways know your pal, If you

ev-er nav-i-ga-ted on the Er-ie Ca-nal.

FIGURE 4.7.

of this chapter (see Figure 4.15 on p. 90). You can take advantage of the upper elementary student's fascination with deciphering and creating code by introducing songs with non-English texts. As with the younger grades, folk songs from around the world can provide a wealth of musical and textual variety and can help older students experience the musical variety present in other cultures. In addition, many settings of Schumann's lieder are challenging and fun for upper elementary students to learn, and they are available with both German and English texts. Three examples are "Were I a Tiny Bird" (Mark Foster octavo MF 854), "Lanliches Lied" (National Music Publishers octavo WHC-56) and "Herbstlied" (National Music Publishers octavo WHC-54). The main point to remember is that the music and the text need to be musically stimulating both for you and the class.

Teaching Students to Sing Harmony

One aspect of singing that clearly differentiates younger and older children is the ability of intermediate-age students to sing harmony. The challenge and satisfaction gained in this type of singing creates intrinsic motivation for continued musical learning as well as aesthetic pleasure. These factors are, of course, the foundations of good music education. A very clear hierarchy of singing experiences exists for part singing instruction and is based on the harmonic content. The easiest type of two-part singing for children who are in third grade or older is the singing of partner songs (see Table 4.2). Any two songs that have the same meter and harmonic structure should first be learned independently. The next step in the process is for the class to sing one song while the teacher sings the other. When these two steps are achieved, the class is divided and challenged to sing both songs simultaneously. Two songs that work well are "All Night, All Day" and "Swing Low, Sweet Chariot" (Figure 4.8). Partner songs are the easiest way for children to learn to sing harmonically because the songs are different both melodically and textually.

TABLE 4.2. Partner Songs

"Now Let Me Fly"	"Ezekiel Saw the Wheel"
"Three Blind Mice"	"Row, Row, Row Your Boat"
"Joshua Fit the Battle of Jericho"	"Go Down Moses"
"When the Saints Go Marchin' In"	"She'll Be Comin' 'Round the Mountain"
"When the Saints Go Marchin' In"	"This Train" / "Good Night Ladies"
"Oh, Dear, What Can the Matter Be"	"Skip to My Lou"
"Vive L'Amour"	"Down the River"
"Dobbin, Dobbin" (verse and refrain)	"Tina Singu" (verse and refrain)
"Zum Gali Gali" (verse and refrain)	"One Bottle of Pop" (contains three equal parts)

Partner Song Example

FIGURE 4.8. "All Night, All Day" and "Swing Low, Sweet Chariot"

Ostinatos for *Swing Low, Sweet Chariot*

FIGURE 4.9.

Clementine

Percy Montrose

In a cav - ern in a

Light she was and like a

can - yon ex - ca - va - ting for a mine Dwelt a

fea - ther and her shoes were num - ber nine Her - ring

min - er for - ty - nin - er and his

box - es with - out top - ses San - dals

daugh - ter Clem - en - tine Oh my

were for Clem - en - tine Oh my

dar - ling oh my dar - ling oh my dar - ling Clem-en - tine You are

lost and gone for - ev - er Dread-ful sor - ry Clem-en - tine.

FIGURE 4.10. Countermelody for "Clementine"

The second step in the harmonic singing progression is the addition of ostinatos or descants that use some of the text found in the song. For example, each of the ostinatos in Figure 4.9 can be learned by the entire class and sung while the teacher sings "Swing Low, Sweet Chariot." Then the class can be divided into two parts, one part singing the melody and one part singing one ostinato. When this step is achieved, the teacher can join in on the second ostinato. Finally, the class can be challenged to sing three parts simultaneously.

Clementine

Percy Montrose

Ooh

ah   ah   ooh   ah   ooh

FIGURE 4.11. Backup vocals for "Clementine"

Older children are delighted with this challenge and respond most positively to successful part singing in class. They are really excited to discover that they do not have to be in a select or special group in order to produce very satisfying musical results.

After intermediate children are successful in singing simple harmonic accompaniments, you can create countermelodies to accompany known songs. Because the second melody is still quite different from the known melody, this type of harmonic singing is the obvious next step in successful two-part singing. It is relatively easy to write such contrasting melodies based on the harmonic structure of the song; your countermelody should provide both a melodic directional contrast and some simple rhythmic difference. Class instruction should follow the same order. The children should first sing the countermelody in unison and with confidence before being expected to sing the known melody and the countermelody simultaneously. (See Figure 4.10.)

Singing rounds should follow as a harmonic experience only after students have successfully sung each of the above types of harmony. Singing "Three Blind Mice" or "Row, Row, Row Your Boat" as a round is not easy for children because they are all singing the same tune and same rhythm. It is common to see children who have not had adequate singing experiences with easier harmonic structures attempting to sing rounds in music class with their hands over ears so they can concentrate. Such a reaction means the children are not yet comfortable or confident in singing harmony and it is too soon to try to include rounds in your instruction.

After a class becomes comfortable with the process of singing rounds, the final step in singing harmony is to sing parallel thirds and sixths. Students can initially be introduced to this type of harmonic structure through singing "backup vocals" for familiar songs, consisting of block triads and inversions for each measure of the song (Figure 4.11). Much of the published treble chorus music for children uses parallel thirds and sixths, and this introduction will help children deal with the more difficult structure (See Figure 4.12). As in all phases in learning harmonic singing, students must be confident as a class or section on each part before ever singing the parts together.[1]

[1]Additional information can be found in publications for directors of children's choirs, such as *Lifeline for Children's Choir Directors* by Jean Ashworth Bartle (Toronto: Gordon V. Thompson, 1988); *Choral Music Education,* a series of five volumes by Doreen Rao (Boosey and Hawkes, 1988–1991); *Teaching the Elementary School Chorus* by Linda Swears (West Nyack, NY: Parker, 1985); and *We Will Sing* by Doreen Rao (NY: Boosey and Hawkes, 1993).

Wake Up, O World

Countee Cullen

Michele Pressley

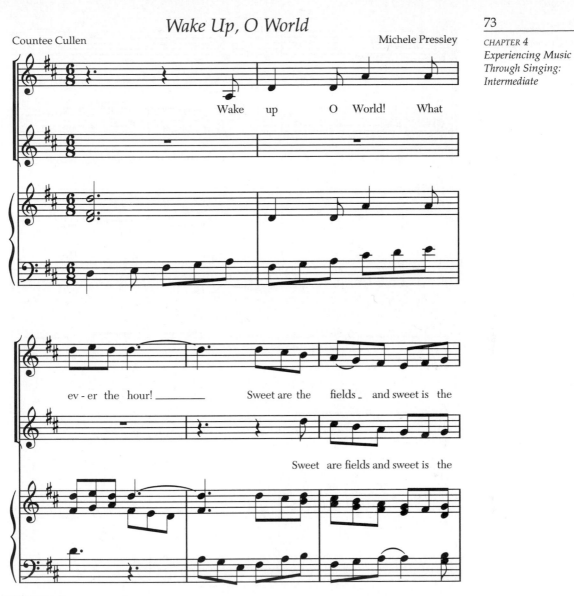

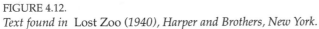

FIGURE 4.12.
Text found in Lost Zoo *(1940), Harper and Brothers, New York.*

FIGURE 4.12. *(Continued)*

FIGURE 4.12. *(Continued)*

Opportunities to Perform

Another way to nurture older students' love of singing is to provide them with a variety of opportunities to perform for each other. Singing solos for peers in class can be part of each lesson. Grade-level assemblies, where students from a single grade perform for each other, are another way to let upper elementary students share their accomplishments. Upper elementary students also enjoy singing for younger students, either in their own school or "on tour" at feeder schools. Performances at assemblies for younger students serve as great short-term goals for improving singing skills, and the promise of going "on tour" to show off their school's music program is an exciting reward for this age group. And in schools with parent organizations, the possibility of performing at a monthly meeting may also exist.

The singing activities that you provide in the general music class may naturally lead to an interest in forming a chorus. One important issue that you need to consider before discussing the idea with your building principal is whether the chorus will be select or nonselect. There are pros and cons to both choices, and you need to think very carefully through these questions:

1. Why do we need to have a chorus?
2. What kinds of musical learnings do I want students to have that they can't get in music class now?
3. Where will these children perform? How many concerts per year? Will these performances be in addition to, or replace, the general music class performances as they occur now?
4. When will this group rehearse? How often? How will this affect their school day? Your workday? Will parents drive the children to school early? Is bus transportation available?
5. How much will it cost? Where will the funds come from?
6. Do you want only the finest singers? Why?
7. Would you take anyone who wants to participate? Why?
8. What kinds of repertoire do you want to perform?
9. How will you recruit students this year? Next year? Do you have a vision of what you'd like the group to be like in three to five years?
10. What is your sense of how the community would support this idea?

Besides offering participation in a chorus, you can renew the singing interest of intermediate-age students by having them perform plays and operas in class as part of general music curriculum. Many commercially available musical plays written especially for children come with recorded accompaniment tapes as well as libretti. They vary in both musical and textual quality. You can request review copies so you can check their suitability for your students before placing an order. Even more appealing to older children is creating their own music to enhance a story that they can act out in class. You can begin with a simple fairy tale or folktale. Have children develop dialogue for characters, then add incidental music. They can further refine their production turning dialogue into recitative and aria text.

In the past few years, the Metropolitan Opera in New York City has sponsored an educational outreach program for elementary music and classroom teachers. The project consists of a team approach: a music teacher and a classroom teacher attend a two-week summer institute and learn how to involve intermediate-age children in writing and producing an opera of their own. The administrator of the sending school where these teachers are employed agrees to support the endeavor during the following school year.

In one setting the entire sixth grade becomes an opera company for a portion of the year. Every student applies for and receives a teacher-assigned job as either a creator of text, lyrics, or music; a designer or producer of scenery, sets, or costumes; a member of the musical performance team—singer, dancer, pit orchestra, or band; or a member of the administrative team, which includes production and business managers, public relations workers, box office workers, and house manager.

The entire group of children is led through an initial brainstorming activity to generate ideas for a plot. In this way, the students establish ownership of the opera, and the themes that emerge are genuine to their immediate lives. One recent plot centered on the feelings of children when their parents are divorcing. Another described the death of a classmate.

A project such as this does not suddenly appear in sixth grade as though springing from infertile ground, however. Preparation for opera composition is established in prior grades as children are gradually introduced to operas such as *Amahl, Hansel and Gretel,* and *The Magic Flute.* Recent video and film productions of these and other operas provide a wonderful resource for music teachers to use. Your local video store of public library video collection is a great resource for this purpose and can provide you with the most current releases.

Integrated Learning

The creation of an opera exemplifies one of the current educational trends, integrated learning, inasmuch as students are incorporating many subject areas and skills throughout the course of the production. Students can create plot, dialogue, and recitative and aria text in their English classes. The areas of production and set costs can be combined to decide on ticket prices in math class. In addition, set construction can initially be approached via mathematics. It is easy to foresee the integration of art into this project, and if the physical education curriculum incorporates a movement emphasis, staging can become integrated in that area as well. In a school where the integrated curriculum approach is stressed, creating an opera provides an opportunity for music to be the focus instead of an accompaniment to other subjects.

Participating in creating an opera also validates musical expression as an important facet of human endeavor to all members of a school faculty as well as to the students. Through creating and producing an opera, students and teachers can become even more aware of the importance of the human singing voice and how feelings are conveyed in music.

Providing Role Models

One of the challenges of maintaining children's interest in singing is the notion that singing in head voice, or in the style of the classically trained Western art song/opera tradition, is an emasculating activity. Because few children spend time singing with their families, their notions about singing come from MTV and rented videotapes rather than family sing-alongs where men and women participate equally. By the time they are in fourth or fifth grade, children have formed the idea that opera singers are shrieking fat ladies and that "real men" (rock stars) do not sing the way the men in the music textbook recordings do.

There are several ways to provide positive musical role models for upper elementary students. One of the most effective ways is to use older students in your school district, either junior high or high school singers. Invite entire ensembles to do miniconcerts for your older students at grade-level assemblies. Ask them to come back in quartets to spend a day doing demonstration rehearsals for your general music classes, and include time for questions in each session. Seek out other role models from your school and community and invite them to perform for your students. Many community choral groups, barbershop quartets, and senior citizens groups welcome such invitations to perform for students. Indeed, in some communities, music teachers have established intergenerational choruses with intermediate-age children and senior citizens.

Your students will have their own role models from a variety of fields, including sports. One way to involve these nonmusic role models in music class is to have your students write letters to ask their favorite sports or political figures about their in-school musical experiences. Publicize the responses in school newspapers or newsletters or on prominent bulletin boards where all the students will see them. Some students may even wish to invite local respondents to their next assembly or evening concert. Tying into the students' "real-life" heroes can be an effective way to maintain and expand interest in singing.

Gender Issues: The Second Curriculum

Very little attention has been given to the topic of gender in elementary school music instruction. However, as noted in the case study that opened this chapter, by fifth grade children tend to demonstrate unspoken but clear sex segregation in their informal choices, such as lunchroom seating and playground games. This whole set of unwritten rules governing male and female behavior has been called "the second curriculum" by one researcher.[2] Music teachers need to be aware of its powerful influence on children's behavior and learning, as well as the subtle ways in which teachers can foster cooperation and interaction between boys and girls in their classes.

As demonstrated in the case study, informal seating arrangements will only support gender segregation. Music teachers need to be aware of the importance of teacher-assigned seats and how such teacher decisions affect classroom management, singing voice instruction, and informal gender interactions. For example, effective cooperative learning experiences depend on the careful construction of groups. Music teachers need to control the mix of students for temperament, learning style, and leadership abilities as well as intellectual achievement and gender. Although elementary teachers often use gender as the basis for classroom management of transitions (moving from one

---

[2]R. Best (1983). *We've All Got Scars. What Boys and Girls Learn in Elementary School*. Bloomington: Indiana University Press.

FIGURE 4.13.
Doonesbury copyright 1993 G.B. Trudeau. Reprinted with permission of Universal Press Syndicate. All rights reserved.

activity to another, taking turns, or moving from classroom to lunchroom), there are other effective ways to divide children into manageable groups. Instead of having boys and girls line up separately, you can use color of eyes, hair, or clothing; shoe type (lace-ups, high-tops, sandals, boots); birthday months; or first letters of names.

Even more important than how you manage groups of children are the behaviors you engage in throughout your instructional day. Researchers have found that teachers treat children differently on the basis of gender. As noted in a major report,

> whether one looks at preschool classrooms or university lecture halls, at female teachers or male teachers, research spanning the past twenty years consistently reveals that males receive more teacher attention than do females. There is also a tendency beginning at the preschool level for schools to choose classroom activities that will appeal more to boys' interests and to select presentation formats in which boys excel or are encouraged more than girls.[3]

As a music teacher, you need to monitor your own actions and expectations regarding girls and boys in your classroom. For example, do you typically call on children of one gender? Do you select activities for your lesson because the girls or the boys will like them? Is the pace kept quick so as not to lose the attention of one group? Is your choice of songs based on content that is most appealing to a particular gender? Do you typically use one gender group to determine whether learning has occurred? Whether you are teaching a segment or an entire lesson, you must be aware of the signals you send to children both in your responses to them and in your lesson planning. Figure 4.13 powerfully illustrates how children receive these signals.

Keeping Older Children Singing

Because of singing examples in the media, it is most challenging to keep older children interested in singing. In many school districts, band and orchestral

---

[3]*How Schools Shortchange Girls: A Study of Major Findings on Girls and Education.* Commissioned by the AAUW Educational Foundation and researched by the Wellesley College Center for Research on Women. Washington, DC: National Education Association, 1992, p. 60.

instrument instruction is offered in fourth or fifth grade, and the appeal of this new form of musical expression makes it acceptable for children to start playing and stop singing. Given the choice between producing a lilting, bell-like head voice and producing the appealing sound of a saxophone, it's easy to understand why so many girls and boys find it easy to stop singing when they start playing an instrument.

Peer pressure is another factor that influences the intermediate-age child's decision about whether to continue singing. The benefits of participation need to outweigh the negative pressures from peers, and your careful attention to repertoire and performance opportunities are the means by which you combat this problem. Providing solo singing opportunities in your class and initially featuring the class leaders will signal to the other children that "singing is cool."

There are several ways you can maintain the interest of these children in continuing to sing. Certainly you should follow the advice given above for how to introduce the challenge of singing harmony in your music classes. In addition, you may want to consider beginning a select chorus to challenge these youngsters. You may want to introduce the idea by playing recordings of the many fine children's choruses that currently exist.[4] Recordings of boy solos, such as the "Pie Jesu" from Andrew Lloyd Webber's *Requiem*, can also spark interest. Children are intrigued to discover that they really cannot tell whether a 12-year-old singer is a girl or a boy.

While your select group will probably start with a few singers, your choice of repertoire and the kinds of performance opportunities you provide will draw more interested singers after your first concert or assembly. You should use the same criteria explained above in choosing repertoire, with the added requirement of further musical challenge. All children thrive on singing solos, so splitting up pieces and providing lots of short solos is also an effective way to keep your oldest students interested in singing in a group.

All children also respond to your interest in their other abilities, whether in a spelling bee, in art class, on the soccer field, or on a basketball court. Attend other school events; offer to help children practice lay-ups (or ask them to teach you how to free-throw). A few minutes outside class can go a long way to showing your interest in your students as people and may help you to know another side of them. Just knowing that you are a regular person who values their other activities may motivate students to continue to participate in singing groups as well.

Changing Voices

Although most children maintain their child singing voices through the upper elementary grades, some do not. Both boys and girls experience vocal changes

---

[4]You can obtain tapes of the Glen Ellyn Children's Chorus, for example, by writing to 501 Hill Avenue, Room 202, Glen Ellyn, Illinois 60137. The *Choral Journal* lists addresses where you can order tapes of choruses that perform at national and regional conventions of the American Choral Directors Association.

with the onset of puberty; some begin to experience the vocal changes associated with adolescence as early as the fifth grade.

Boys whose voices are beginning to change usually experience spurts of growth that give them lengthened limbs, hands, and feet and often make them appear awkward. You may notice that the bridge of the boy's nose is thicker than it was and that his speaking voice has embarrassing breaks and squeaks. You may notice breaks in his singing voice, too, as he descends from head voice to upper chest register. Boys are often reluctant to sing through this awkward time and may suddenly appear to have a range of only a few chest register notes. The best thing you can do for a boy who is experiencing vocal change is to help him maintain his head voice and then bring it down past the "empty spots" to the upper chest register. The clarity and control required to produce head voice can be used to master this new lower voice and will build his confidence that his singing voice is still intact.

The reality of boys' changing voices is that no two boys you teach will proceed through the vocal change in exactly the same manner. It is important that all boys understand what will happen or is happening to their vocal mechanism, and that you think it is exciting and worth noticing each time an incremental change occurs. You can place the most positive focus on this important part of maturation by celebrating each boy's advance into adolescence rather than ignoring it. Keeping a chart of the pitches that boys can sing, adding pitches as their voices lower, and writing special parts for them for class or chorus will contribute to a positive atmosphere and will help boys cope with this natural change.

Although their vocal changes are not as dramatic as those of boys, girls, too, experience changes in their singing voices as they undergo puberty. Their singing voices often become flutelike and airy, and their dynamic capacity may decrease, leaving them with small voices that, at full volume, can produce little more than a focused mezzo forte. This lightening of the voice may be gradual, and the girls themselves may not even be aware that their voices are changing. The middle school or junior high girls' chorus sound is typically much smaller and lighter than the typical elementary classroom chorus. It will help both boys and girls if they hear the junior high sound and discuss the changes they may experience as they grow.

Helping Uncertain Singers

By fourth or fifth grade, children have established habits of vocal production that may or may not be effectively producing the pitch or vocal quality you want. Most students who have had good vocal models from birth and have been sung to as babies will have clear, light singing voices and will match pitch easily. Others will have slipped through, matching pitches occasionally but not really knowing when they were matching pitch or quality. Even in general music classes where students sing often and with gusto, there will be those who are unable to match pitch or even correct their pitch when told they are not on pitch. These children must be helped in the upper grades or they will never learn to sing. One of the challenges you face is to help these uncertain upper elementary singers to improve their skills while keeping them interested in singing.

Since these children will be the exception rather than the majority of each class, it is best not to work on their pitch-matching skills in class. The social stigma attached to remedial work in any subject, including singing, is tremendous, and it is up to you to create a supportive atmosphere in which these uncertain singers are motivated to improve their skills. Explain to the entire class that some children have trouble learning math or writing and need extra help from teachers, while others have trouble learning to sing on pitch. Find a time during the school day to work with small groups of same-age children and invite them to join a special chorus where improving singing skills, not performance, is the goal. Calling it Preparatory Chorus or Beginning Chorus and having a variety of activities planned for each "rehearsal" will go a long way to improving both the self-esteem and pitch-matching skills of these uncertain singers.

Review the activities for pitch-matching found in Chapter 3 and apply them to these upper elementary students. Start by matching their pitches first. Have an individual sing a pitch, sing it back yourself, and then have her or him tell you whether the sound you produced was higher or lower. This activity is an effective way to improve tonal discrimination skills as well as pitch matching. Group students into pairs or trios with similar abilities and have them continue the pitch-matching exercise. Find songs or refrains to songs that have a range of a third or fourth or fifth and use these to reinforce group pitch matching.[5] You can make up a two-note ostinato (do-sol or sol-do) that can be used as accompaniment sung by half the group while the other sings the limited-range song or refrain. Stay away from the piano and use a recorder or your own voice for starting pitches. Best results will occur with frequent limited practice: 10-minute practices three times each week are better than a single 30-minute session. Praise students lavishly each time they attend, and let them know how important their participation is. Expect them to make small gains, and keep a chart of these. It is also important to let them know if there is a skill level they need to attain to join the regular chorus, and let them know how often you will be testing them for admission to chorus. Your genuine concern for their singing improvement, and your continued positive reinforcement for attendance and progress, can motivate these uncertain singers to gain the skills of which they are capable.

Differentiating Primary and Intermediate Learners

You will have noticed that the suggestions in this chapter for enhancing singing with intermediate-age children are quite different from those recommended for primary children in Chapter 3. The reason for this contrast is predicated on the reality that younger and older elementary-age children learn in very different ways. An understanding of how particular child development theories pertain to music teaching and learning is important as you begin to learn how to combine diverse musical behaviors into complete lessons and instruct children at many different age levels.

[5] See *Sing It Yourself* by Louise Larkin Bradford. Van Nuys, CA: Alfred, 1978.

You have probably been exposed to several theories of how children learn if you have taken a child development class. The learning theories discussed in this text have been found to be particularly useful both in explaining how musical learning occurs and in helping music teachers to structure curricula.

According to learning theorists Jean Piaget and Jerome Bruner, who are considered cognitive constructionists, learning is based on the premise than an individual constructs understanding and knowledge of an idea or concept on the basis of experience. For the cognitive constructionist, knowledge is actually built from the interaction of the human being with the environment and is further refined each time the learner encounters a similar situation or problem. Piaget and Bruner have slightly different ways of explaining the development of the process of learning.

Jean Piaget

Jean Piaget, a Swiss biologist, derived his understanding of how children learn by watching his own children and making extensive notes on their cognitive development. His book *Origins of Intelligence in Children* (New York: Norton, 1963) documents the growth and development of thinking in his three children. Piaget postulated that all children pass through several stages in their cognitive development:

1. *Sensory-motor stage (ages 0 to 2).* During this stage, the learner's responses to sensory stimuli evolve from simple reflexes (random vocalizations in response to environmental sounds) to intentional responses (using a higher-than-normal speaking voice and echoing the direction of pitches of a lullaby).

2. *Preoperational stage (ages 2 to 7).* This is the stage during which the learner begins to gain mastery of language as a means of symbolizing real things. The child tends to think egocentrically at this time. One aspect of this stage is called deferred imitation (preschoolers often sing improvisations as they play and incorporate parts of songs they have heard sung to them, such as "E-I-E-I-O" from "Old MacDonald"). At the preoperational stage, the child cannot perform three cognitive operations: transformation (the child does not understand that a pitch that sounds high in one song can be a low pitch in another song), centration (the child can listen for and identify the long duration at the end of each section of "Ballet of the Unhatched Chicks" but cannot simultaneously determine the number of sections in the music), and reversal (the child is not able to understand the idea that a crescendo is the reverse of decrescendo or that two melodies that differ in meter or rhythm may still be somewhat the same). Two important music learning ideas are important to remember about preoperational children. First, they learn best through imitation and active participation rather than through being told information. Second, they have difficulty using correct terminology for the concepts of high/low (pitch) and loud/soft (dynamics). This confusion is understandable when we consider how interchangeably these terms are used in our culture ("Turn it down!").

3. *Concrete operational stage (ages 7 to 11).* During this stage, children are able to concentrate on many aspects of an idea and can now perform the operations they were incapable of at ages 2 to 7. They can also

conserve, which means that they can understand that a musical phrase can be changed slightly (instrumentation, tempo, mode, etc.) yet still be considered somewhat the same as the original phrase. Or they can understand that the G resonator bell can be the root of a G chord and also be a part of a C chord.

4. *Formal operations (age 11 to adulthood).* At this stage, students are capable of abstract reasoning in symbolic systems (language, numbers, musical notation) and can mentally evaluate the effects of possible changes during music composition or performance.

Jerome Bruner

Jerome Bruner also believed that children's cognitive growth changes over time. Bruner's theory is based on the premise that the learner goes through three modes of representation in order to assimilate the information gained from a new experience.

1. *Enactive.* The learner manipulates the environment and gains knowledge of it through sensory contact. (The young singer imitates a siren by swooping up into head voice and then descending to chest register.)
2. *Iconic.* Learners represent the sensory experience to themselves in some form that looks like the experience. This representation could be a gesture, a shape, or a picture. (The singer traces the outline of a melody line while singing.)
3. *Symbolic.* The learner now represents sensory experience in universally understood symbols, such as language, numbers, or musical notation. (The singer uses musical notation to record the actual pitches sung during the siren exercise.)

Despite the differences noted above in the actual number and definition of stages occurring in developmental thinking and maturation, the theories of both Piaget and Bruner have profound implications for elementary music teachers. Most important is an understanding that curricula for younger children must be filled with opportunities to construct meaning from actual music. In other words, primary children must always be *doing music.* Young children must learn about duration of sounds, for example, by singing, moving, and drawing durations rather than by talking about whole, half, and quarter notes in relation to each other or as the equivalents of sections of a pie. And in contrast, older children must be challenged in music class to use their changed ways of thinking and conceptualizing. For example, older students can classify and categorize the songs they have learned in younger grades, and as illustrated in Script 1, they can discuss an abstract idea such as the impact of changing a particular rhythm pattern in a song.

Teaching Children to Sing and Read

Your students need not be restricted for the rest of their lives to learning anything they want to sing via the rote approach. As an elementary music teacher, you will see the same students for a number of years, and your long-term planning must incorporate both readiness for, and the actual process of, singing while reading musical notation. Because of the short amount of time that is normally allotted for music instruction, you must have a clear long-range focus for teaching reading. An understanding of the changes in cognition that occur as children mature must be incorporated into your goals. When you consistently demonstrate the iconic representations of known musical structures, you provide the connection between the enactive or action stage and the symbolic stage of representation as described by Bruner.

Experiences in both pitch and rhythm reading readiness must be part of primary music instruction. Pitch notation readiness is established through the continual inclusion of movement and playing activities that reinforce the singing of contrasting registers, melodic direction, and phrase contour. Curwen hand signs (see Figure 3.3 on p. 42) are also recommended, especially if teachers model clear spatial differentiation when singing and using these signs. Rhythmic readiness evolves from the emphasis of singing, playing, and moving experiences that emphasize pulse, meter, and repeated rhythm patterns. If a solid pitch and rhythm readiness foundation for music reading is provided in primary years, intermediate-age children can easily be taught to sing music from printed notation. Instead of thinking of singing from notation as a "new" skill or something that can be learned only in a particular grade, children will believe that music reading opportunities logically follow from what they have already experienced.

Enhancing Music Thinking Through Singing

Singing activities are an excellent way for upper elementary children to participate in musical recreation and build skills that will lead to a lifetime of musical enjoyment, and they also provide opportunities to nurture students' musical thinking. There are three roles through which students can experience ensemble or solo singing: as the performer, the critic, and the conductor. Each role allows students a different perspective from which to make musical decisions.

Performer

In the role of performer, students can be asked to focus on the visceral and kinesthetic aspects of singing to make thoughtful decisions about what they heard and felt. "What happened in your body?" "How did it feel when you were able to hold the half note for its full value and complete the phrase?" "How did that sound different from the last time we sang it?" "What did you do physically to make that change in sound?" Questions like these allow students to reflect on and take ownership of the workings of their own vocal instruments and the resulting musical product.

Critic

In the role of critic, students can be asked to make reasoned judgments about both the technical and musical aspects of their own and others' performances. One model for this kind of activity is the work of researchers at Harvard's Project Zero, who are dedicated to studying how children develop competence in diverse symbol systems. A method for eliciting student evaluations of performance groups was developed by Lyle Davidson and Larry Scripp in the Arts Propel project in the Pittsburgh schools. During a rehearsal each student fills out a form that questions the quality of the student's own performance, peers' performances, and the group as a whole. Students reflect on what would make the performance better and what they personally would need to do to improve their own performance. The form is then turned in to the teacher, and given back to the student to fill out again at a later date. The series of written comments allows the teacher to monitor students' progress in musical thinking and give the students a record of their musical judgments. While intended for high school performance ensembles, this form could easily be adapted for use at the upper elementary level.

Class discussion is another way to get students to make evaluative statements about their singing. It is an especially useful way to model the kinds of musical judgments you are looking for. Instead of asking, "Did you like the way that sounded?," you can ask, "What did you notice about the way that sounded?" The first question leads to a simple yes or no response, but the second requires the student to draw on tonal memory, musical terminology, and conceptual understanding to make an evaluative statement with supporting evidence. Class discussion is an important way for you to model the components of musical thinking, such as making comparisons of how the music went, how it might have gone, how it should have gone, and what could have been done to make it more effective musically. The questions you ask to stimulate class discussion allow your students to watch you think musically and give them models to emulate as they form their own evaluative statements, based on their limited musical understanding.

Conductor

When making musical decisions in the role of the conductor, students are given the opportunity to apply all the musicianly knowledge that they have (terminology, gesture, and Western musical idiom) as well as their own accumulation of personal experiences with music as they identify and solve musical problems. One way to get an entire class into the role of the conductor is to ask, "How is this piece supposed to sound? What has the composer told us, and what was left out of the directions?" Upper elementary students who are familiar with standard musical interpretive markings and some Italian tempo markings enjoy decoding the composer's intent.

You can take this activity a step further and ask for a volunteer (or pair of volunteers) to act as conductor to lead the group in either a steady tactus beat (a simple up-down pattern) or the appropriate duple or triple pattern, while at the same time showing the changing dynamic levels, staccato and legato notes, and so on. If there are several conductor tasks to accomplish at the same time, pairs or even trios can be used, with each student taking a single task. The follow-up questions that the conductors must answer can range from "Did we sing it the way the composer wanted us to?" to "What would you do to make us sing through the phrase the way the markings indicate?"

Another way to take on the conductor's role is to have everyone listen to and compare several interpretations of a song they're working on, using either recordings, videotapes, or live performances by individual class members. By asking them to explain the differences, similarities, and positive features of each interpretation, you allow students to use musical vocabulary the way musicians do. If, in addition, you ask them to pretend they're going to conduct the same group and decide what they'd tell the group about how they wanted the piece to sound different, you let students experience the thought processes that a conductor engages in while preparing a piece.

This type of experience is genuine, and it affects students more immediately than merely being told that conductors take charge of a performance, keep a pulse, and cue singers and musicians. When followed with the opportunity to hear the class try an individual's interpretation of the piece, the experience becomes one of thinking about and with music: making musical decisions, then hearing the results. Such cognitive exploration of musical ideas enables children to truly think musically.

Evaluating Student Progress in Singing

There are several ways to keep track of your upper elementary students' singing progress. One that was explained in Chapter 2 (see p. 22), charting pitches matched on a weekly basis, is a straightforward way to document progress. You may want to include information on range, vowel clarity, and intonation in your chart. However, this system may be unwieldy if you are teaching 700 students each week. If that is the case, less frequent charting may be more workable. Another way to document progress is to make class audiotapes, with each child singing a short solo part of a single song. If done at the beginning and end of each grading period, it provides information about the child's musicality as well as singing skills. Students accustomed to singing by themselves regularly in class enjoy hearing themselves on audiotape and frequently beg to do it more often. Your written chart of vocal progress and audiotaped individual voices give complementary types of data about each student and serve as the basis for portfolio evaluation.

The term *portfolio evaluation* is derived from the type of evaluation done in visual art, where a collection of each student's work is compiled and surveyed. It relies on the collection of several types of data to document student progress rather than on a single test score or vocal audition. Data in a music portfolio could include your vocal progress chart, the audiotape, and written comments by both you and the student. Students could be asked to keep a journal of their experiences in music class or to write a paragraph or draw a picture at the end of the grading period, explaining what they feel to be the most important musical learning that happened. The wide variety of types of data included in portfolio evaluation make it an especially attractive way for both teachers and students to look at musical learning, for it requires students to reflect on and take ownership of their accomplishments as well as their difficulties. Portfolio evaluation offers music teachers a rich source of data they can use to make judgments about student progress.

TEACHING SCRIPTS

Practice each of the following scripts at least twice, first with a group of your peers and then with children. If you can teach these scripts with several different groups of children, you will be able to refine your pacing and presentation.

Script 2

GRADE LEVEL: Grades Five and Six

MUSICAL CONCEPT: Rhythm

SPECIFIC ELEMENT: Syncopation

LESSON OBJECTIVE: Students will be able to demonstrate an ability to perform syncopated rhythms through clapping, singing, and playing.

MATERIALS: "Emma" (Figure 4.14); a piano or guitar for accompaniment; bongos, guiro, claves, and maracas

FIGURE 4.14.
Used by permission of Dr. J.D. Elder, St. Anns, Trinidad, West Indies.

Have the class echo rhythm patterns as follows: First clap several four-beat patterns that are straight quarters and eighths, and then alternate syncopated patterns with even rhythms. (If the class has had experience with rhythm canons, lead a four-measure canon with alternating even and syncopated four-beat patterns.) After completing this activity, put the notation for even and syncopated rhythms on the board and have the class read and clap the patterns. (Chapter 9 discusses ways to teach musical notation.) Then label the syncopated rhythms with the musical terminology.

STEP TWO

The song I am going to teach you today contains a lot of repetition. As I sing it to you, see if you can find all the repetition.

Sing the song expressively with guitar, autoharp, or piano accompaniment.

Who can tell me where the repetition is in the song?

Take answers.

I want to sing it to you again, and as I sing, you decide where the musical contrast is in this song.

Sing the song again with accompaniment.

What elements in this song provide a musical contrast?

Take answers.

I want to sing it to you one more time—it will be really easy for you to sing then. As I sing, I want you to quietly tap two fingers together on the steady pulse and decide where the syncopated rhythms are in this song.

Sing the song with accompaniment.

First, I want you to sing the song with me, and then we will talk about the rhythm patterns.

Establish the starting pitch for the class by singing "Ready, sing." Accompany the class.

Now, what did you decide when you tapped the steady beat?

You may need to demonstrate by singing the first line of the song and tapping the beat.

Let's sing the song again, and each time a measure begins with a syncopated rhythm, tap the rhythm with your fingertips in the palm of your other hand.

Provide the starting pitch and model with tapping instead of playing accompaniment.

If you look carefully at the song, you will be able to tell what country it came from. When we know that information, we can decide which instruments would be most appropriate to play while we sing "Emma." Trinidad and Tobago are two islands in the Caribbean, and the song is an example of calypso music. Some of the instruments that are used when people sing in those countries are the guiro, bongo, claves, and maracas. We need to decide which sounds will make the song more musical and which patterns each instrument is going to play.

Lead the class in discussion and try out each instrument. Then have the class determine whether even ostinato or syncopated ostinato patterns played on the instruments best suit the style of music. Perform the song again with the class, with harmonic and rhythmic accompaniment.

Script 3

GRADE LEVEL: Grades Four and Five

MUSICAL CONCEPT: Form

SPECIFIC ELEMENT: Phrase structure

LESSON OBJECTIVE: Students will be able to demonstrate an ability to differentiate similar and different phrases through singing and reading musical notation.

MATERIALS: An overhead copy of "The Monster Song" (Figure 4.15); a piano or guitar for accompaniment; contour charts (Figure 4.16)

STEP ONE

Warm up children's singing voices using intervals and rhythms found in "The Monster Song."

STEP TWO

I'm going to teach you a song today that's full of interesting and gruesome

FIGURE 4.15.

©*Copyright 1977 by Galaxy Music Corporation. Reprinted by permission of ECS Publishing, Boston.*

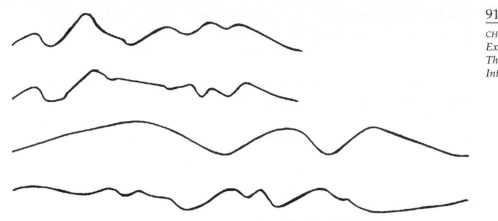

FIGURE 4.16. Contour charts for "The Monster Song" by Condit R. Atkinson

creatures. See if you can listen carefully and learn the melody as I sing the verse.

Sing the verse unaccompanied, with appropriate dynamic changes, phrasing, and diction, while tracing the melodic contour in the air with your hand.

Did you notice how my hand moved up and down as my voice changed pitches? Watch and listen again as I sing and move my hand to trace the contour of the melody.

Sing the verse again as above.

This time, see if you can sing this song with me and trace the melodic contour in the air while you sing. Make sure your hand moves from left to right, tracing each line of the verse.

Start the class by giving the first pitch on "Ready, sing." Sing the song with the class, moving in line from right to left so students can mirror as they follow.

This time, as we sing it I'd like you to try to decide the correct order for these four contour charts on the chalkboard.

Sing the song with the class while students look at the board, drawing the melodic contour with their hands and trying to determine the correct order of the charts. Students offer suggestions for placing the charts in the correct order.

What can you tell me about the four phrases of this song?

(Two are short, two are long.)

Are any of them the same or similar?

(The first and second phrases are the same; the third and fourth are similar in that they are long phrases, but their melodic contour is different.)

Let's look more carefully at how these phrases are built by looking at the actual notation that the composer used when writing the song.

Show four more charts in random order, this time with note heads drawn on the treble staff.

Can you put these in the correct order?

Students arrange phrases in the correct order; ask them to explain how they figured it out.

Musicians like to know how a piece of music is put together so they can learn and remember it more easily. You've already figured out how the

musical phrases of this piece are put together, and now I'd like to show you what musicians would call the form of this piece. If we give the first phrase the letter name a, what should we call the second phrase?

> *Take answers, trying them out to see the reasoning behind each, and asking each student for an explanation of the decision.*

What about the third and fourth phrases?

> *Write aabc on the board.*

Now that you really understand the form of this song, let's sing it again.

> *Sing the song together with the class.*

Now that you can sing this song so well, let's see if you can add some accompaniment that will enhance the mood of this song.

> *Discuss the possibilities with the class, including vocal sounds and pitched and unpitched classroom instruments. The class then experiments and discusses the effects of each choice.*

STUDENT ASSIGNMENTS

1. Teach Scripts 2 or 3 to a group of intermediate children and have a peer or the classroom teacher videotape your lesson. After you view the videotape, write a reflection paper that includes the following sections: description (what you did), information (what happened during the lesson segment), and reconstruction (how you could do it again differently).

2. Teach Script 2 or 3 to a group of intermediate-age children and have a classmate evaluate your teaching using the following checklist:

    1. The teacher motivated the class by using facial expression and voice inflection and by expressing enthusiasm for singing and for the song. ___ yes ___ no
    2. The teacher used directed questions that focused student listening. ___ yes ___ no
    3. The teacher demonstrated the whole song method in teaching. ___ yes ___ no
    4. The teacher gave the correct beginning pitch for the song and for any section that needed repetition or correction. ___ yes ___ no
    5. The teacher provided a good singing voice model. ___ yes ___ no
    6. The teacher sang the song correctly (pitch, rhythm, text). ___ yes ___ no
    7. The teacher listened to the class and corrected errors. ___ yes ___ no
    8. The teacher sang the song expressively. ___ yes ___ no
    9. The teacher made continual eye contact with the class. ___ yes ___ no
    10. The teacher's directions were clear. ___ yes ___ no
    11. The teacher gave specific positive reinforcement _____ times. ___ yes ___ no

3. Rewrite Script 2 or 3 in order to teach another musical element.

4. Working in a small group or with a partner, find five songs appropriate for intermediate children. Include complete citations of your sources.
    - Describe how each song could be used to teach musical elements.
    - Discuss why each song was chosen.

5. With a partner, discuss ways you could involve children in evaluating their own progress in singing skills.

CHAPTER 5

Experiencing Music Through Listening:

PRIMARY

Case Study

Miss Davis is ending the first month of her new teaching position at Fifth Street School, and she is really looking forward to teaching the next class. It will be the first time she has had any primary children listen to a piece of music, and she is excited about beginning to share her love of classical music with first graders. As the class arrives at her door, she moves to greet them. "Good morning, children. Come into the music room with your best listening ears today. We're going to have a special class. Everyone choose a good place to sit on the rug and we'll begin."

She picks up her alligator puppet and sings to the class, "Who can find their singing voice?" The children respond with siren sounds and she begins a vocal warm-up, ending with the intervals found in the familiar song. Miss Davis then walks to the piano and begins to play the melody of "Daa, Daa Kente" (see Figure 3.9 on p. 57). By the time she has played the second measure, many hands are raised and waving. She calls on Jason to name the song. Miss Davis asks at the end of the song, "Who can remember what we learned about the sounds in this song last week?" After Marissa answers correctly that the song has quick and long sounds, Miss Davis leads the class in a review of the movement and singing activity (see Chapter 3, p. 58).

Miss Davis then begins her directions for the next section of the lesson. "The next thing we are going to do is listen to a piece of music that has some very long sounds. The first time we listen we are going to raise our hands when we hear those long sounds. And we're going to do something we have not done in music class this year, and that is close our eyes while we listen. So we have three things to do—close our eyes, listen for long sounds, and raise our hands when we hear the long sounds." Miss Davis looks at the class, waits until all the children have closed their eyes, and then starts the tape. The class begins to listen to "The Ballet of the Unhatched Chicks" from *Pictures at an Exhibition.*

During the initial A section, Miss Davis asks the class, "Do you hear those quick sounds?" As some of the children raise their hands at the end of that section, she says "Good job, boys and girls." During the B section, Miss Davis says, "Here are some more quick sounds." Very soon she says, "Here come more quick sounds." As the final A section begins, she says, "Here are some quick sounds again." In the middle of this final section, she says, "Listen carefully now for the next long sound."

At the end of the piece, she says, "Boys and girls, you were such very good listeners. I am really proud of you because you showed me that you heard the long sounds. Now I want to play the music again, and I am going to show you that two parts of the music are the same. I want you to watch my hands and follow me as soon as you can." She turns on the tape and models quick hand movements that also outline the melodic contour of the A section—and the children immediately begin to imitate her movements. In the middle of the section she says, "Now get ready for the long sound!" At the fermata, she holds up both hands and the children imitate her movement. As the music continues, she praises their response. During the B section, Miss Davis taps her two index fingers together, and the class imitates her actions. Partway through the section she says, "Do you hear all those quick movements?" During the final A section, she repeats the same quick movements outlining the melody that she used initially, and just before the final cadence, she says, "Now listen carefully for another long sound."

"You were such very good listeners during the music, boys and girls. I want each of you to find your own space in the room, and we are going to move to the quick sounds and stand very still for

the long sounds." After the class is standing, she turns on the tape, and during the A section, all the children stand in place, moving their arms. During the B section, one of the boys begins to hop a-round, and he is soon joined by many other children who begin laughing and talking to each other as they hop and sometimes fall.

YOUR COOPERATIVE TASK

1. What is the next thing that Miss Davis should do? As a group, write a script of what she should say.
2. What should Miss Davis have done earlier in the lesson to be sure this situation did not occur?
3. Do any other aspects of this lesson segment bother you? If so, how would you suggest that they be changed?
4. Make a list of the positive and negative reasons for including listening in primary music class.
5. Apply the motivation model described in Chapter 4 (p. 61) to this scenario.
6. Is this music teacher really modeling perceptive listening? Explain your reasons for your answer.
7. Should Miss Davis have told the children the name of the piece of music? Why or why not?

PRACTICE TEACHING SCRIPT

In order to be able to practice teaching this listening lesson segment, you will need three items: a large piece of poster board upon which to copy the listening map illustrated in Figure 5.1; the score of "Fanfare for the Common Man" by Aaron Copland; and a recording, tape, or CD of the music. (When you copy the listening map, the sections correspond to the score as follows: 1, m. 1–5; 2, m. 6–12; 3, m. 13–21; 4, m. 22–23; 5, m. 24–35; 6, m. 36–end.) After you prepare the poster board map, you will need to listen to the music several times and learn which sections of the map and the music correspond. Only after this preparation will you be ready to practice teaching a listening segment of a lesson to another adult not in your class, such as your roommate, a friend, or your spouse. If at all possible, practice the script again with a primary-age child or several children.

Script 1

GRADE LEVEL: Grade One
MUSICAL CONCEPT: Tone color
MUSICAL ELEMENT: Brass and percussion contrasts
LESSON OBJECTIVE: Students will be able to identify contrasting timbres through movement.
MATERIALS: The listening map (Figure 5.1); a tape of "Fanfare for the Common Man"

I have a wonderful piece of music for you to listen to today, and I hope you will enjoy it as much as I do. I especially like this piece because it uses a drum so many times and it is really easy for us to hear when the drum is playing. I want you to practice this motion with me.

Demonstrate tapping one finger in the palm of the opposite hand.

Did I make any sound when I did that? I want all of you to practice that movement, which we will do when we hear the drum.

Now, what can all of you do so that I can tell if everyone hears the drum?

Solicit answers until one child says, "Close our eyes."

Everyone close their eyes during the entire piece, and listen really carefully. Make our motion only when the drum is playing.

Play the entire piece.

You were such good listeners. I could tell that you heard every time that the drum played. Now I want to ask you a question that does not have anything to do with this music. If you were out in the car, sitting on the back seat, and your father was driving and he asked your mother, "I think you had better get out the map?," what would that mean?

Solicit responses; lead a short discussion of what a map represents.

FIGURE 5.1. Listening map for "Fanfare for the Common Man" (primary level)

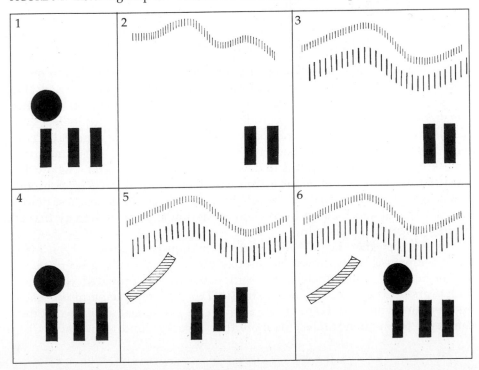

I have a musical map for us to follow. It does not have the names of instruments on it. It shows some circles and lines and other shapes. What I want you to do is to listen to the music and follow my map. When the music is finished, I want you to tell me how my map and the music go together.

Play the piece and point to the circle for the gong; rectangles for the tympani; and lines for trumpets, French horns, and trombones.

You were really following that map well. Who can tell me something about my map?

Solicit answers and get beyond "It tells us where to go" to the idea that different shapes represent different sounds. Solicit as much specificity as possible. First graders can tell after one viewing and listening which shapes represent drums, gong, and "horns."

Now we are going to listen to the music one last time today, and we are going to listen for the drum *and* something else. But I am not going to tell you what it is. Each of you can choose other sounds in the music to hear this time. I am going to leave the map up, and you can follow it if you want or you can close your eyes and listen without a map. The great part about listening to music is that we each can choose what we like best in the music and there is no right or wrong answer.

Play the music; after it is finished, expect a variety of responses. Some children will want to tell you what they noticed while other children will be waiting for you to ask them a question, and still others may look confused and will not be able to verbalize their musical reactions. Responding to the variety of reactions provides sufficient closure for this segment of the lesson.

WHAT YOU NEED TO KNOW

Why Young Children Should Listen to Music

One of the most important skills that young children must develop in music class is the ability to *listen* to music. Listening is the one musical activity that can provide all students with lifelong pleasure both as potential audience members and as consumers of reproduced music. Too many adults feel ill at ease in concert halls and, indeed, many never attend a single concert because they never learned what to listen for in these settings. The most important long-term goal for our subject is to develop a population of adults who value music so highly that they want to continue their musical participation once they leave school. This goal can be achieved if we begin in the earliest grades to foster careful and focused instruction in the single musical activity that all adults participate in—listening.

By the time they begin Kindergarten, children have already been inundated with music in their own homes, day-care centers, malls, grocery stores, and restaurants. Unfortunately, this early exposure has provided youngsters with years of experience in ignoring music. The challenge facing music teachers therefore is twofold: (1) to enhance children's perceptual skills so that they can begin to experience music as more than a background to life, and (2) to enable children to fully experience the power of music. Unless these skills are developed in the earliest grades, students will become adults who cannot focus their attention on anything other than the beat or the lyrics of the most accessible popular tune.

Music and musical activities can both enhance children's skills and open their ears to the richness of our musical heritage. Many children will be exposed to the greatness of the Western art music tradition only in your class. It truly is part of your job to provide all students with an awareness of our common musical culture. In the book *Developing Talent in Young People*, Lauren Sosniak discusses the commonalities in background she discovered in interviews with a number of world-class concert pianists.[1] One of these pianists describes the pivot point in the transformation from a 12-year-old student who was seriously thinking of quitting piano lessons to a dedicated pianist. This turnaround occurred in a general music class when the music teacher played Edvard Grieg's piano concerto. Until that time, the child did not know how glorious a piano could really sound or how wonderful the piano and orchestra were when they played together.

Our American musical culture is grounded in the traditions of Western art music, but there is a much larger musical world that can and should be brought to the young ears of your students. One of the most exciting and creative aspects of teaching music listening to young children is choosing from the wealth of resources. All the music in your own listening collection, from rock to reggae to Rachmaninoff, could be considered for classroom use, along with any recordings in your school's music library. As young children do not yet have firm musical preferences but will listen to and like all styles and genres equally well, your choices from among the myriad available are assured a fresh, unbiased audience of young listeners. Although there is plenty of challenge involved in lesson construction, you can be sure that most primary students will be receptive to the music you choose for them to hear if you are enthusiastic in your presentation and involve them in active listening.

Approaches to Focus Listening

Music Selection

You can simplify the task of finding listening selections that are appropriate examples of the musical concept you wish to teach. Keep several points in mind: First, the piece or excerpt you choose needs to be a very clear and obvious example of the musical concept. For example, if you choose a piece because its bass line is a perfect example of a descending scale but the bass line is obscured by the homophonic texture, primary students will not be able to distinguish the descending sounds. One way to check whether your perception of an example is accurate is to ask an adult nonmusician to listen to it with you and tell you if he or she can easily hear what you hear. If so, you may be able to direct young children to eventually perceive what seems so evident

[1]Lauren Sosniak (1985). "Concert Pianists." In Benjamin Bloom (Ed.), *Developing Talent in Young People*. New York: Ballantine Books.

to you. However, if an adult nonmusician cannot easily identify the concept you're hearing, choose another piece! It is vitally important to remember in your music selection process that children will not hear the foreground and the background of music simultaneously. You must enable them to perceive one musical element; and if they are to do so, that element must be vivid.

Listening examples for young children or beginning listeners in any grade should initially be limited to one minute or less. Children's ability to remain focused on the salient features of the music wanes very quickly. After Kindergartners can focus for that amount of time, you can gradually begin to use slightly longer excerpts or pieces of music, but the length should never exceed three minutes. You need not worry that the students won't have enough music to listen to if the examples are this short, as you will be playing the selection several times in the music lesson and/or in successive lessons.

The selections you choose should accurately portray the wide variety of musical genres, tempi, and timbres found in the world's music. Young children take great delight in all kinds of music, and it is up to you to ensure that they hear every possible type of music in your classes. By presenting them with a wide variety of genres and styles, you open their ears to the possibilities available in the real world. In addition, your teaching is enlivened because you continue to explore and learn about the richness of our musical culture. Proposing one musical style or genre as the best or most worthy of study exemplifies a parochial view of the world that has, in the past, led to a distinction in the minds of children between school music and real music—school music being some strange, isolated, contrived musical idiom that is only heard in music class and real music being the forbidden fruit that music teachers want to keep from their classrooms. When you choose selections that illustrate the commonalities of all music as well as the uniqueness of particular musics, including those with which students are most familiar, you eliminate this false dichotomy in the minds of your students.

Focused Listening

The most effective music listening experiences require an active response from the children involved. You can begin the listening with a question that focuses the students' attention on the music and lets the children know that they must listen carefully.

Initial questions such as "How many different instruments do you hear?" and "Can you tell me how many times the melody is played in this piece?" appear to focus the child's attention and give purpose to the listening task. These questions have clear answers and require only a rudimentary musical vocabulary. But listening for the correct answer to even these two questions can be very confusing to young children. For example, instead of attending to the different timbres to determine how many different instruments were played, a child might focus on the number of times the melody repeated. Or instead of focusing on the recurring melody, the child might pay more attention to the different dynamic levels at which it was played. Such seeming confusions as these are to be expected when teaching young children to listen to and discuss music, and it is your task to construct classroom activities that help children to better focus their attention on the salient features of the music.

A kinesthetic response to each of the previous questions lets the teacher know immediately which children are having difficulty attending to the musical element. For example, the music teacher can direct each child to move in a particular direction while listening and to change direction each time a new instrument begins to play. This activity should not, however, be combined with determining melodic change. Another listening and movement activity should focus on this very different musical idea in another lesson.

At a later time, children can be instructed to move their arms in a "rainbow shape" (an arc) each time the entire melody has been played and to keep count of the number of rainbows they draw. If the children find it too difficult to draw the phrase arcs and keep accurate count, one child should be designated the "rainbow scorekeeper." In both of these examples, the children's kinesthetic response enhances their perception of the musical element in question: the concrete bodily "doing" of the movement serves as a preparatory activity for the more abstract counting up involved in the verbal response. These types of activities not only enable children to focus on a single musical idea; they also provide the teacher with accurate means to evaluate whether children are able to listen perceptively.

In either case, the children need to have many opportunities to hear a single selection. The instructional pattern of synthesis-analysis-synthesis must always be followed when teaching children to listen to music. In this approach, children first listen to the entire piece or excerpt; then they focus on one or more of its component parts (melodic direction, timbre, phrases, dynamics, etc.); and finally they experience it again in its entirety. The final listening experience in this sequence is designed to let the student fully integrate the understandings gained from the analysis portion of the lesson.

One kind of culminating activity that allows for synthesis is to have the students work in pairs to create movement compositions that show each instrument's entrance and reiteration of the melody. The activity draws on understandings each student brings from listening, but it goes beyond the counting and figuring-out exercise to focus on the musical integrity of the whole selection. Thus, the musical import of the piece is allowed to resurface and take the child's full attention. Teaching that puts the child back into the experiential and responsive mode is satisfying, both for teacher and student.

Teacher Modeling

The music teacher engaging children in a listening portion of a lesson must model every disposition she or he wants to see reflected by students: an alert, expectant facial expression; a body poised in concentration and interest; and a firmly closed mouth. The listening selection needs to be introduced clearly and enthusiastically (for example, "I have this really *great* piece of music for *us* to listen to today"), but then the teacher must be silent and attend to the music.

Whenever music is playing, you need to model focused listening. Do all your pointing out, explaining, and question asking before the music starts. "Talking over" the example you desperately want them to listen to (as in the opening case study) makes it impossible for children to concentrate and models behavior that you don't want replicated later in the lesson.

Because young children are not yet able to comprehend abstract concepts, it is helpful to use visual representations of musical ideas when directing their music listening. Any graphic representation of the sound that might help the children focus on its musical elements is useful if it helps the children represent the sound to themselves. There are a variety of ways to show musical elements graphically which even young children can easily comprehend. Representational examples include icons (graphic representations that look the way the musical element sounds) for such musical elements as melodic direction, texture, and form. In addition, some program music can be presented to children using clear pictorial referents that relate to the music. Many of the series texts contain appealing guides that depict successive events in program music. For example, *The Music Book*, Grade Four (Holt, Rinehart and Winston, 1981) contains a pictorial referent chart to use while listening to "The Little Train of the Caipira" by Heitor Villa-Lobos. Other representational examples include simple line drawings of musical instruments to show different timbres.

Listening Maps

When a series of graphic representations for musical elements are put together to spatially represent the passage of those elements through time, the result is known as a listening map. Listening maps are constructed to guide children through a musical excerpt in much the same way road maps guide adults from point to point. They let the young listener know what to expect along the way (a sharp turn, a long stretch with plenty of curves) and provide landmarks that let them know when they've heard outstanding musical moments in the piece.

Initially, constructing a listening map for young children is often hard for music students because they want to put something in the map for every musical idea that exists in the piece. The difficult part of map construction is selecting the important musical highlights you want the primary child to hear and representing only those highlights. Fortunately, with these types of visual aids, there is no right or wrong way to represent a musical idea. You do not have to be an artist to construct perfectly adequate listening maps. You do need to own a ruler, some colored magic markers, and oaktag or poster board.

The best listening maps are those children create themselves. One approach has been described by Mary Helen Richards in her book *Aesthetic Foundations for Thinking*.[2] She suggests that each child create a map by first moving a finger in the air to capture the gestural aspects of the music and then putting this representation to paper. Each child will have a different way of mapping a given musical selection, and Richards notes that children can learn a valuable lesson about the variety of ways people respond to music when they exchange maps and try to follow each other's gestural icons. Even primary children are capable of making their own graphic representations of

---

[2]Mary Helen Richards (1980). *Aesthetic Foundations for Thinking. Part 3: The ETM Process.* Portola Valley, CA: Richards Institute.

music, and young children will have a much richer experience with the music when they are allowed to create their own listening maps.

At the end of this chapter, Script 2 uses a short excerpt from the second movement of Haydn's Symphony No. 94. Two maps that were generated by first graders in response to this music are illustrated in Figure 5.2.

Whatever type of mapping exercise you use to get children involved in a musical excerpt, you need to remember that the mapping is just a means to an end, not the end itself. The desired "end" in this case is a deeper understanding of the piece of music under consideration and a better grasp of how it does what it does. If the mapping exercise is not followed with a synthesizing activity that focuses on the musical context, the children will leave your room with a vague sense of having accomplished something rather like a social studies or art exercise. Your listening lesson, therefore, was really incomplete. You must plan your listening segments so that they culminate in an activity that lets the children experience the music unaided by any of the analysis-stage devices.

FIGURE 5.2. Two maps by primary children for excerpt from Haydn's Symphony No. 94

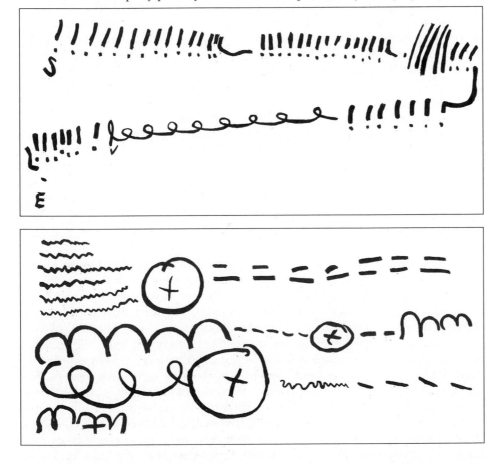

The final listening can be directed in a variety of ways. For culminating activities you might ask children to show the answer to a question about the music by using hand signs, such as thumbs up or down, or to close their eyes and respond to a question about melodic direction by showing the shape of the melody with an arm or by holding up a laminated picture of an instrument when it is heard. Sometimes, you may want to have the children learn to enjoy listening for its own sake. Directions such as "See what else you can hear in the music as we listen" or "Now that we know a lot about the melody of this music, we're going to listen one last time and see how the melody fits with all the other parts" will provide youngsters with an opportunity to truly interact with and experience the music.

Effective Affective Listening

One of the greatest challenges facing the music teacher is how to deal with the affective component of music teaching. We acknowledge that all musics have the power to move us in ways that we cannot express in language, and that much of what we hope will happen to children musically will be something that we can't expect them to be able to verbalize directly. The best way to deal with the ineffable personal musical response is to keep your lesson focused on the features of the music that seem to grab the children's attention and help them understand how and why the music has this powerful affect on human beings. Essential to this process is a classroom atmosphere in which all answers are given a receptive hearing and children are encouraged to offer divergent points of view. Due to the widespread use of music as a background in TV and films, certain styles, instruments, and genres have become stereotyped icons for a particular mood, feeling, or occasion. Although you are not charged with correcting the major musical misapprehensions of American culture, you should take care to teach your students that a particular piece of music is neither happy nor sad but that it is capable of eliciting feelings. You must emphasize that each person will experience different feelings and have different reactions to a piece of music and that each person's response is equally valid and correct.

Importance of Repetition

An exciting aspect of planning listening in the elementary school is knowing that you can revisit listening selections in successive grades. Repeated listening to the same selection enables you to further develop and deepen your students' perception and enhance their musical reaction. Producers of pop music rely on the power of repetition and know that a song becomes a "hit" only through repeated playing on many, many radio stations. Elementary music teachers need to emulate and incorporate this powerful idea when planning listening within one grade level as well as in successive grades. The music selected must, of course, contain enough depth and musical content to provide for the construction of many listening lesson segments. During the primary grades, most of the pieces selected will easily lend themselves to a second listening with focus on steady beat. You may have selected "Fanfare for the Common Man" to fit into a lesson about tone color, but you can revisit it after a few months in the same grade level and, after reviewing the timbre, listen to the piece and keep a steady pulse with fingertips. In another primary grade, you could focus on the contrasting durations in the theme. In intermediate grades, you could listen for form, changes in texture, and repeated rhythm patterns. When the students know the piece well, you can have them listen critically to two different recordings of the same piece that have obvious interpretive differences.

Repeated exposure to the same piece enables children to become knowledgeable listeners and makes it possible for them to experience music in the same way that adult connoisseurs do. Musical affect occurs only when children interact with music, and an interaction that results in an aesthetic experience is possible only when the listening child has some understanding of what is being heard. Your job, therefore, is to make it possible for children to acquire the perceptual foundation upon which a musical reaction can occur, and, most important, to provide opportunities for your students to experience a musical or aesthetic reaction.

Music teachers must not emulate the "Top 40 syndrome" too closely, however, because the Top 40 tunes do not stay static for six years—or even six weeks! A tune's position on the Top 40 list changes as listeners assimilate the musical and text content. When a song or a piece of music becomes too familiar, it no longer causes musical affect. Quite simply, it becomes boring!

What Is Good Music?

You must be very careful to select music that is rich in content so that children will not tire of it in the same manner that they tire of a tune on MTV. But prospective music teachers often are not sure that they can determine quality or "good" music. A fine article by Acton Ostling, Jr., has provided the profession with a list of ten basic criteria to use when judging the quality of music—any music![3]

According to Ostling, a quality musical composition

1. Has form and reflects a proper balance between repetition and contrast.
2. Reflects shape and design and creates the impression of conscious choice and judicious arrangement by the composer.
3. Reflects craftsmanship in orchestration with balance between transparent and tutti scoring and between solo and group colors.
4. Is sufficiently unpredictable to preclude an immediate grasp of its musical meaning.
5. Contains a route that is not completely direct or obvious.
6. Contains consistent quality throughout.
7. Is consistent in style with clearly conceived ideas and avoids trivial, futile, or unsuitable passages.
8. Reflects ingenuity in development.

---

[3]Acton Ostling, Jr. (March 1991). "Selecting Concert Band Music of Quality." *Bluegrass Music News*, 42 (3), 2. Russellville, KY: Kentucky Music Educators Association.

9. Is genuine in idiom and not pretentious.
10. Reflects a musical validity that transcends pedagogical usefulness or historical importance.

The list helps us decide whether a piece has sufficient merit to include in children's musical diets for many years. Although Ostling compiled this list in order to discuss quality band literature, it clearly applies to all music. It is particularly important to keep Ostling's guidelines in mind when considering musical selections that are written specifically for children. Prospective elementary music teachers often are attracted to the "Children's March" by Edwin Franko Goldman or the "Children Symphony" by Harl MacDonald because they contain several familiar children's nursery songs ("The Farmer in the Dell," "Jingle Bells," "Baa Baa Black Sheep," etc.) in arrangements that initially appears to be quite clever. However, after listening to these pieces repeatedly, you will find that they do not meet a number of Ostling's criteria for quality music. In addition, while young children initially can be directed to perceptive listening via familiar song recognition, intermediate children find the easily identifiable verbal referents to specific nursery rhymes "babyish" and will disengage their attention immediately upon identifying such content. These pieces may be used successfully with very young children, but their problematic nursery rhyme content prohibits their inclusion in your long-term listening plans.

Listening to Unfamiliar Styles

Can you recall how you felt when you first heard an Indian sitar, sarod, or shenai or a selection from a Chinese opera in your World Musics survey course? If you are an instrumentalist, can you recall your feelings when you initially sight-read a piece that contained nontraditional sounds and improvisation opportunities, such as "Epinicion" by John Paulson? If you are a singer, do you remember how you felt when you first sight-read a piece of music in nontraditional notation, such as R. Murray Schaefer's "Epitaph for Moonlight"? None of these experiences provided you with the context to have an initial affective musical experience because the music you were hearing or reproducing was in a completely unfamiliar style.

Those feelings of confusion are also experienced by children! You could not have an aesthetic experience with an unfamiliar style of music, and neither can a child. Fortunately, children in primary grades are receptive and open to unfamiliar styles of music. If you do your job correctly and enable them to truly experience music, all music is within their listening capability. Indeed, the primary grades are the opportune time to introduce as many styles of music as possible because these children do not yet have the strong listening preferences of older children.

Applying Learning Theory

It is important that you use your understanding of how young children learn when planning the listening portion of your lessons. As you read in Chapter 4, both Jean Piaget and Jerome Bruner (and other psychologists as well) stress that all teaching must be appropriate for the developing cognitive abilities of young children. Both theorists noted the importance of active and concrete experiences for young children. It might then seem that primary children are not capable of the abstract and passive listening act. But, of course, youngsters have been listening to music for years before they begin formal music education in the school. What you, the music teacher, need to remember is that primary children need to be *doing* something whenever possible as they listen. Incorporating the concepts of these learning theorists is not difficult if you construct directed listening instruction that requires youngsters to indicate that they hear a specific musical event.

We know from a research study in music education that young children find some musical changes easier than others.[4] Taebel found that children in Kindergarten and first and second grade were all able to discriminate changes in dynamics. The contrast that was next easiest to discriminate was tempo, followed by duration. The most difficult aspect for young children to discriminate was changes in register. It is important to know that in this research, each musical element was presented to children separately; of course, the music that you will want to use will not have one contrast but many.

How do you determine if young children will be able to hear what you want them to hear? During your initial selection process, you must be very careful to find pieces in which a single musical element predominates. It is very difficult for primary children to hear a change in tempo or dynamics if both changes occur simultaneously. It is also very difficult for them to discriminate a contrast that occurs at the same time as a new section begins. If music is not selected very carefully, young children will indicate they have heard a change—any change—rather than the specific musical change you want them to perceive. For example, when first graders are asked to listen to "Fanfare for the Common Man" and raise their hands whenever they hear the gong, even after initially listening to the first three repetitions of gong and tympani, many children will raise their hands each time they hear the tympani play alone throughout the piece. Thus, the mechanics of the listening activity can become the focus of the child's attention (raising one's hand in the right place) rather than the subtle changes in the musical example (changes in timbre of percussion instruments). Effective affective listening for young children happens only when you, the teacher, construct listening lessons that let the child perceive as easily as you do the musical element in question. Your task, of course, is to seek out those musical examples that best allow such perception to occur, and the guidelines included here will help you do this.

Materials and Sources

Choosing which music to present to students can initially appear to be an overwhelming task because the world of possible musics to use is so vast. Part of your job is to ensure that young children listen to a variety of musical styles, and an equally important part of your job is to provide youngsters with a musical education that includes their Western cultural heritage. Your task can,

[4]Donald K. Taebel (1977). "The Effect of Various Instructional Modes on Children's Performance of Music Concept Tasks." D.M.A. dissertation, University of Southern California.

however, be somewhat focused by keeping in mind the criteria for music selection discussed above: musical integrity of the piece; appropriate length; clarity of a musical element in the foreground; and of course, an obvious relationship to the rest of your lesson.

There are two important sources to consult initially. The first is your personal listening collection, and the second is the recordings that accompany the published series textbooks. Each of these two potential gold mines represents possible selections that musicians have listened to critically. Your listening collection includes music that you know well, and, as discussed earlier in this chapter, every teacher must have such knowledge before deciding *how* to teach a piece to primary listeners. The pieces used by textbook authors have already been used in other music classrooms and are selected carefully to illustrate specific musical concepts.

The easiest way to begin your search, therefore, is to consult the labels and jackets of your own records, tapes, and CDs. The next step is to examine the table of contents of available grade-appropriate series textbooks. Indexes of listening selections may be well hidden in the teacher's edition. However, careful sleuthing will inevitably lead you to a listing of the music listening examples contained in the textbook.

A third source is the music you have met in your survey, ethnomusicology, and music history courses, as well as all the music that you listen to in your own leisure time. While some of this music meets the length criteria discussed for primary children, other pieces are far too long to even consider. But you should not automatically rule out a Beethoven or Mahler symphony, a section of Handel's *Messiah,* or a piece by Claude Bolling simply because they are too long. There is nothing wrong with teaching young children to listen to an appropriate portion of a piece and gradually expanding their knowledge of the selection throughout successive grades. An appropriate portion of a piece merely means that the section sounds like it has a clear beginning and concludes with an authentic cadence. For example, you can easily hear definite sections in *The Carnival of the Animals* by Camille Saint-Saëns, the *Messiah* by George Frideric Handel, *Mass* by Leonard Bernstein, the *Hungarian Dances* by Antonín Dvořák, the instrumental concertos by Telemann, songs by the Beatles, or collections of Renaissance dances.

Summary

Two important quotations from Jerome Bruner's writings serve as a clear recapitulation for this chapter: "discovering how to make something comprehensible to the young is only a continuation of making something comprehensible to ourselves in the first place"[5] and "any subject can be taught effectively in some intellectually honest form to any child at any stage of development."[6] These two important ideas are the essence of teaching young children how to listen to music. First, the teacher must know a selection well before including it in a lesson, and second, the words "intellectually honest form" mean that

[5]Jerome Bruner (1970). *Towards a Theory of Instruction.* New York: W.W. Norton Co., Inc., p. 38.
[6]Bruner (1963). *The Process of Education.* New York: Vintage Books, p. 33.

the music selected must be short enough and clear enough to represent the musical idea you are teaching. Effective teaching of music listening depends upon these two important factors. Overriding these two ideas however, is the most important aspect of musical selection—aesthetic value. Children should never be asked to spend any of their precious time in a music class listening to music that does not meet the criteria for good music. You must never forget that perception of a musical element is not the desired end result of music listening instruction. What you want all children to learn is the value of music— that music (and all art) affects us as human beings in ways that nothing else does.

TEACHING SCRIPTS

Teaching scripts 2 and 3 not only contain the listening segment of a primary music lesson but also demonstrate how to move from a familiar song to listening. Each script uses a primary song and a musical concept first introduced in Chapter 2 and suggests a way of including a listening selection. Remember that these teaching scripts represent only a portion of a lesson. Complete lessons are given in later chapters.

Script 2

GRADE LEVEL: End of Grade One or beginning of Grade Two
MUSICAL CONCEPT: Rhythm
MUSICAL ELEMENT: Steady beat
LESSON OBJECTIVE: Students will be able to demonstrate an ability to perform a steady beat through movement and playing instruments.
MATERIALS: "One Elephant" (Figure 3.8); a recorder or another melody instrument (resonator bells, xylophone, etc.); a recording of a complete musical selection or an appropriate portion you have chosen from a non-Western musical tradition. (You may choose to use "Gambangan" played by Gamelan Anklung from Bali.) Note: If you use only a portion of the selection, dub it onto an audiotape and record it at least two times so that you waste no time trying to find the exact spot each time you play the music.

STEP ONE

If you taught Script 2 in Chapter 3 using "One Elephant" with this group of students, play the opening phrase (Figure 3.8 on p. 55) on a recorder or another melody instrument.

That was the beginning of a song that we already know. I want you to pat the steady beat on your knees while I play the entire song.

Play the song. Praise the class if students do well, but if necessary, discuss and demonstrate how to keep a steady beat without making sounds that are louder than the recorder.

I am going to sing the song one time to help you remember the words, and I want you to keep a careful steady beat while I sing.

Sing the song while the class pats the beat softly.

Now I want you to sing the song with me and show me the steady beat also.

(If you did not teach this song to this group, just play the song and have children pat the beat until they understand what you want.)

STEP TWO

Now we are going to listen to some music that you have not heard before. The reason I chose this piece was that I want you to discover whether or not this music also has a steady beat. I really like this piece because it has some wonderful instruments playing that we don't hear very much and they have such neat sounds. I think you will like it also. As you listen the first time, I want you to think about a steady beat and see if you can discover one. If you can, I want you to silently begin showing me the beat. What are some possible ways that you could show me the beat?

Elicit several alternatives and discuss the importance of children staying in their places and listening silently so they don't disturb each other. Play the musical selection.

If the class follows directions, praise them for being good listeners. If there is any noise during the music, you need to stop the music and reiterate how to listen. This step is essential. Young children can learn to focus their attention, and it is up to you to direct (or redirect) their listening to the musical selection.

We are going to listen to the music again, and I want to help some of you who did not discover the feeling of steady beat in this music. I want everyone to listen very carefully and feel the beat and quietly show the beat.

Play the music and model the beat with your fingertips in the palm of the opposite hand. If you need to play the music again or interrupt it to redirect students' attention, do so.

That was really very good listening, children.

(Use this sentence only if it fits!)

Now I want each of you to find your own space in this room. What are some other ways that we could use parts of our body to show a steady beat?

Elicit responses from the class, and discuss a variety of ways to move parts of the body silently in one space.

I want all of you to close your eyes, choose one way to show the steady feeling, and show me what you are going to do.

Watch the class respond.

I see a lot of different movements, and they are all going to work really well. We also need to remember to be completely silent when the music starts.

Play the music and monitor the class—move quietly through the class and lightly touch any child who is trying to attract the attention of his or her peers.

I like the way that everyone showed me the steady beat in their own way.

Now we are going to listen to the music one last time, and this is your time to listen for something other than the steady beat.

Describe some of the instruments in your selection, or discuss changes of dynamics or other contrasts that young children might be able to hear.

When we listen this time, let's all close our eyes so we can really concentrate on listening to other parts of this neat music.

Play the selection. Monitor the class carefully, and if children look at you, point to your eyes and model an exaggerated eye-closing motion—drawing down each eyelid with a finger.

That was really good listening, children. People who live in the country of Indonesia

(or another country whose music you selected)

listen to this music all the time, and they love the sound. We are so lucky that there are recordings/tapes/CDs

(whatever you are using)

so we, too, can enjoy this music.

Script 3

GRADE LEVEL: Kindergarten/Grade One
MUSICAL CONCEPT: Dynamic changes make the music expressive.
MUSICAL ELEMENT: Dynamics (loud/soft)
LESSON OBJECTIVE: Students will be able to identify, respond to, and discuss changes in dynamic level.
MATERIALS: "Birdie, Birdie, Where Is Your Nest?" (Figure 3.1 on p. 34); a recording of a Western classical selection (1 to 2 minutes in length) that exemplifies obvious dynamic changes, such as the third movement (Minuet, first section) of Haydn's Symphony No. 94 in G Major.

STEP ONE

How many of you remember the song we learned a few weeks ago about the bird that built a nest? Let me sing the first line for you to help you remember it.

Sing the first line after giving the starting pitch.

Who can remember it now? Good! Now I'm going to sing the whole song through, and I'd like you to join me when you remember it.

Prepare by singing "Ready, sing" on pitch and sing the whole verse, showing clear changes in dynamic level.

Raise your hand and tell me what I did with my voice to make certain parts of the song sound different from the others.

Entertain several different answers.

Yes, I changed my voice to make some parts louder and some parts softer than the others. The last time we sang this song in class, we made some

parts of it louder than others. Let's see if we can do that again as we sing it together.

Give "Ready, sing" on pitch and sing with the class.

STEP TWO

Boys and girls, you did a good job of changing from loud to soft as you sang that time. Now I'd like you to listen to a piece of music and see if you can hear any changes from loud to soft or soft to loud. The first time we listen, let's sit perfectly still with our eyes closed and just use our best listening ears. Ready?

Wait until all children have closed their eyes and are sitting still. Play the selection while watching students and model "closed eyes" for those who peek.

I saw some really careful listening going on in this room! Almost everyone had their eyes closed and their ears open, and I'll bet you heard some interesting things going on in the music. We're now going to listen to the piece again, and this time I'd like you to use your arms and hands to show me when you hear a change from soft to loud or loud to soft. Make one kind of movement with your hands and arms when you think the music sounds softer, and change to another kind of movement when the music sounds louder. Let's all close our eyes again. Are we ready?

Play the selection again, watching responses carefully to note those who consistently show changes correctly and those who are having trouble.

Girls and boys, you really did a nice job of showing the changes in the music. Musicians call changes from loud to soft or soft to loud changes in dynamic level, and you showed me that you could really hear them easily. Who would like to show us the two different kinds of movement you used to show dynamic changes?

Take volunteers to show their movements and teach them to the class.

Which of these movements do you think shows the changes most clearly?

Students respond, explaining their choices.

Let's try some and see how they feel to us.

Take three different sets of movements and have the class use them, in three listenings, to show changes, still closing their eyes as they listen.

Each movement was a bit different, and it felt a bit different when we did it. Which ones helped you feel the dynamic changes more clearly?

Let students have enough time to discuss this thoroughly; they may get to important reasons for some movements "feeling" more like the music than others.

Let's listen to the music one last time, and this time let's all see if we notice anything different in the music.

Play the piece and model attentive listening.

Thank you for such a good class, girls and boys. You did some good listening today.

Use this closing bit of praise only if appropriate. Modify it, if necessary: "Some of you did some good listening today. Maybe next time everyone will be able to listen more carefully" or "Most of you listened and moved well today. Perhaps next time we'll have everyone doing a good job." Remember that your attention tends to focus on those who are not on task, even though most of the students work well and follow directions. Don't forget to give praise where it is due!

STUDENT ASSIGNMENTS

1. Arrange to have yourself videotaped while you teach Scripts 2 or 3 to a group of primary children. After you view the videotape, write a reflection paper that includes description (what you did), information (what happened), and reconstruction (how you could do it differently.)
2. Teach Script 2 or 3 to a group of primary-age children and have a classmate use the following checklist to evaluate your teaching:
   a. The teacher motivated the class by using facial expression, voice inflection, and verbal enthusiasm. ___ yes ___ no
   b. Students understood the teacher's directions prior to each listening episode. ___ yes ___ no
   c. The teacher realized which students were not on task and adapted the lesson directions when necessary. ___ yes ___ no
   d. List the positive aspects of the teacher's presentation.
3. Have a peer use the following criteria to evaluate a listening map that you have prepared:
   a. Which musical features does the map illustrate?
   b. Are the graphics suitable for music? Why or why not?
   c. Would the map make it easier for children to understand musical relationships? Why or why not?
4. Construct a means of evaluation for script 2 or 3 in this chapter.

CHAPTER 6

Experiencing Music Through Listening:

INTERMEDIATE

Case Study

In early February, Miss Davis meets the fifth grade class at the door and says, "I hope everyone brought their best listening ears today, because we're going to listen to some music that I'm sure you've never heard before." Miss Davis hears a boy near the end of the line say (sotto voce), "Oh, brother! Not again!," but she says nothing. The students seat themselves in the two large semicircles of chairs that the teacher has set up.

Miss Davis stands in the center front of the room and says, "Today we're going to listen to a piece of music called *Holiday Symphony*. It was written by an American composer names Charles Ives. Ives lived in New England, and he wrote many pieces for orchestra. The part of the symphony we're going to hear today is called 'Washington's Birthday.' We're only going to listen to the first two minutes of this section."

Several students in the back row begin to whisper loudly to each other. Miss Davis continues, "Remember the last time we listened to a symphony orchestra?" Two students in the front row nudge each other and giggle while the whispering in the back row continues. Alicia, who is sitting on the end of the first row, raises her hand to respond to Miss Davis's question, but Miss Davis continues, "Well, in that recording we heard another piece by an American composer who used the name *Wash-*

ington in his title. Does anyone remember that piece?" Alicia raises her hand again, but this time Miss Davis is distracted by children whispering in the back row, and she decides to pick up the pace of the lesson. "All right, everybody, it's time to listen. Each of you need to find your own space in the room and find a way to move to the steady beat of this music." Students stand up and move around the room, trying to find their own space. Some children chat with friends as they move slowly to a space, but many students find their own space and wait quietly. Miss Davis stays at the center front of the room and says, "I'm still waiting for everyone to get ready. No one in this class is doing their best work today." She then stares at the clock and says, "You are all wasting your music time." Several minutes pass while Miss Davis waits until each student is in an appropriate space in the room and the entire class is quiet. Then she starts the recording.

The listening selection she has chosen ("Washington's Birthday," the first 2 minutes, 14 seconds of Ives's *Holiday Symphony*) has no discernible pulse and has very slow harmonic changes. The contrasts in timbre are also very subtle. The range of the melody is quite limited, and it moves unpredictably, with very few discernible phrase endings.

Halfway through the selection, several students begin to bump into one another, giggling as they go. When Alicia complains that she can no longer hear the selection, Miss Davis stops the recording and says, "I'm really disappointed in you. No one tried their best today. I want everyone to sit down and think about what happened here." After several minutes of uncomfortable silence, the classroom teacher returns to pick up the class. Miss Davis says, "Mr. Barnes, your class really disappointed me today." Mr. Barnes looks hurt and says to his class, "All right, folks, I warned you—no recess for the rest of the week." As they all file out, Miss Davis hears one child say, "I hate music class!"

YOUR COOPERATIVE TASK
1. Discuss Miss Davis's choice of listening example and the appropriateness of the activity she chose to get the students involved in the music.
2. List and discuss the pivotal points in the lesson when Miss Davis could have done or said something different that would have changed the outcome. Rewrite Miss Davis's commentary and directions to make this an effective listening lesson.
3. Does any other aspect of this lesson bother you? If so, how would you change it?
4. In groups of three, role-play the discussion that might ensue between Miss Davis, Alicia, and Mr. Barnes after Alicia tells Mr. Barnes that Miss Davis is not fair.
5. In pairs, discuss the positive and negative reasons for beginning a listening lesson with information about the composer or the piece.

PRACTICE TEACHING SCRIPT

The following script provides an opportunity for you to practice presenting a listening segment of an intermediate lesson to your peers or to children. The more you practice, the more confident you will become in your teaching ability. Each time you practice the script, focus on your enthusiasm for the music, and use vocal inflection and facial expression as well as the scripted text to motivate the learners.

Script 1

GRADE LEVEL: Grades Five and Six
MUSICAL CONCEPTS: Melody, dynamics, and timbre
SPECIFIC ELEMENT: Use of repetition and contrast
LESSON OBJECTIVE: Students will be able to demonstrate recognition of repetition and contrast in melody, dynamic levels, and timbre by mapping these and discussing their maps.
MATERIALS: Recordings, tapes, or CDs of Copland's "Fanfare for the Common Man," Haydn's Symphony No. 94; enough marking pens and drawing paper for entire class; and a large white plastic tablecloth upon which you have copied Figure 6.1.

STEP ONE: Song Review

I'd like to sing a song that you already know and see if you can recognize it. But I'm going to leave the words out, so you'll have to listen very carefully. When you recognize the song, give me the "thumbs up" sign.
   Sing "Emma" (Figure 4.14, p. 88) on "loo."
Great! Many of you recognized it right away. Let's all sing it together.
   Give the starting pitch on "Ready, sing" and lead the class through the entire song.

113

FIGURE 6.1. Figural map of Haydn's Symphony No. 94

Let's sing it again. This time as we sing, use the index finger of one hand and trace the contour of the melody in the palm of your other hand.

Give the starting pitch again using "Ready, sing," and monitor the children as they trace and sing.

Now I want you to use your index finger and draw the contour of each phrase in the air as we sing.

Sing the song with the class again as the children draw in the air.

STEP TWO: Listening Map

There is another way to show how music moves, and I'd like to show it to you. But first I'd like you to just listen to the next selection while sitting very still. Relax and focus your attention on the sounds.

Play the Haydn selection (1 minute, 13 seconds).

You seemed to like the surprise that Haydn put into that part of the symphony! I'd like to play it again, and this time I'm going to follow a listening map of the selection. As my finger traces the path of the map, I'd like each of you to trace it in the air with me. Are you ready? Here we go.

Trace the map while keeping one eye on the students' response.

How many of you felt that the map moved the way the music did?

Take a few responses for discussion. Emphasize that all responses are right.

I have a different piece of music for you to listen to now, and I'd like you to listen to it with your eyes closed. You may move your finger in the air if you wish.

Play the Copland selection while watching the class response. If any children have their eyes open, step toward them and motion "eyelids down."

This time while listening to the piece, each of you can create your own listening map that shows the way the music moves. Remember: Everyone will do this differently and everyone will be right, even though all our maps will look different.

Give a single piece of paper and a marking pen to each student. Play the selection, and move about the room as students work.

Let's listen to the selection again so each of you can add to your map or change it so that it more clearly shows what you hear. Before we do this, I'd like each of you to put an *S* at the starting point of your map and an *E* at the very end of your map.

When all children have an S and an E on their maps, play the selection again and circulate among the students to check progress. Be ready to offer a second sheet of paper to those who desperately want to start afresh. When they all appear happy with their maps, proceed to the next step.

A lot of musical changes occur in this piece of music. Can we make a list on the board of some of these changes? Who would like to start?

Take five or six responses, summarizing them into two- to three-word descriptors and writing them on the chalkboard. The following questions should be based on the actual responses you've listed on the board.

Did any of you show the opening percussion section the same way each time it happened? Can you show that section of your map to your neighbor now and point it out? Did anyone show the trumpet melodic line the same way each time that it came in? How many of you found a way to show the dynamic changes that occurred in this piece of music?

Let's listen once more and see if you can add to your map so that it shows changes in just one musical element. If you focus on dynamics, you might want to make the line thicker when the dynamic level is louder, or you might want to change the color. If you focus on timbre, maybe you'll want to draw the instrument that is added or change the color you use to represent the instruments. If you focus on melodic direction, you may want to use arrows to show upward and downward changes. Decide now which element you will listen for. Let's begin.

Play the selection and circulate among the students to monitor work. Expect some students to dig right in while others listen for a while and then begin to modify their maps. When the music stops, allow for questions and discussion of difficulties. Students may request an additional listening to verify or correct their additions.

Now pass your map to the person on your right; end-of-row people, take yours to the left end of your row. We're going to listen once more and see if we can follow each other's maps. Find the starting point, and let's begin.

Circulate among the students during the selection, helping those having difficulty.

Can someone tell us what it was like to follow someone else's map?

*Allow for discussion, and lead to closure with the insight that each map shows how
differently we each represent what we hear. You could extend this by splitting the
class into groups of four or five and having each group realize one of their maps in
movement.*

WHAT YOU NEED TO KNOW

Why Intermediate Children Should Listen to Music

Music is valuable to all human beings because it is one of the basic ways that
we know about ourselves and our world. Artistic expression has endured
throughout human history for this reason. Unfortunately, recent discussions of
education have focused on our nation's productivity and competitiveness in
the world marketplace; artistic knowing and intelligences have been left out of
the picture completely by those who emphasize practical skills and training
for the adult "world of work."

Even advocates of critical thinking, who emphasize the need for sorting
through knowledge to formulate good decisions in the information age, never
mention artistic thinking as an important mode of cognition. In this climate it
often seems difficult to advocate for the place and importance of music and
other arts in the curriculum. But these subjects are vital to our humanity, and
children must not be denied this important aspect of a complete education.

The ability to listen critically and carefully is the most important long-
term goal of intermediate-level music education. Because many children will
end their formal music education after they leave elementary or middle
school, it is vitally important to provide these future adults with the skills that
will enable them to participate in continued musical enjoyment. Although not
every adult will necessarily have the desire to perform music, no one in our
society can escape listening to music. But because music is ubiquitous, the
constant flow of sound can result in "audiothrombosis." This term refers to a
disease in which the primary symptom is a numbness to music. Music education that includes opportunities for focused listening will ensure that your students develop the ability to listen to the ever-present musical sounds in our
society and discriminate between those that are trivial and those of value.

Listening experiences in intermediate grades should provide both a continuation of previous instruction and an opportunity to expand children's listening skills based upon their developing cognitive abilities. As noted in
Chapter 5, if the music selected is "good" music that is rich in content, selections can be revisited in successive grades, and each listening experience can
be a very different one. After primary lessons have focused on the most accessible musical elements in a piece, such as contrasts in dynamics, tempo, and
timbre, later classes can stress the more difficult perceptions, such as changes
in melodic direction, register, or phrase length. During the primary and intermediate school years, children move from Piaget's preoperational stage to the
concrete operational stage (see Chapter 4, p. 83). This important transition in

thinking ability must be acknowledged and accommodated in the musical content and teaching strategies used in the intermediate grades.

John Dewey described the importance of the ability to reflect on art in order to experience aesthetic pleasure.[1] In order to become reflective listeners, children must be able to move beyond the perception of immediate qualities to an understanding of the relationships that these individual qualities produce in a piece of music. Reflection while listening is an ability that must be nurtured in intermediate grades, and you must not lose sight of what is really important in music instruction. Identifying, naming, or recognizing a change in dynamics or instrumentation is helpful, but understanding and feeling the effect of these changes is much more important. Instruction in listening to music needs to be organized in a structured and sequential manner so that intermediate children will be able to move from the perceptual to the reflective level of musical experience.

Approaches to Focusing Listening

Music Selection

The choice of which music to use for intermediate grades should be based initially on the music that was used in primary grades. When you begin your teaching career, however, you may discover that the children you are teaching have not had *any* listening experiences. The carefully built foundation that should have been established in primary grades may not exist. A new teacher or a teacher in a new setting can deal with this problem most effectively by introducing music listening with very short selections (as described in Chapter 5) and gradually expanding the length of the listening pieces.

Intermediate-age children are members of the "three-minute listeners' club": the commercial music selections they hear outside school never exceed this length. Advertisers know they must not overwhelm young listeners with long and complex pieces, so they rely on short, repetitive selections that produce immediate recall as well as short-term musical gratification. Teachers need to use this powerful marketing strategy as well! Even though intermediate children are older and have more sophisticated cognitive abilities, their listening attention span still needs to be accommodated with fairly short selections. However, part of your job is also to carefully prepare intermediate children to listen to music for longer periods of time.

One effective way to provide children with the tools and skills needed for sustained listening is to begin with a short excerpt of a piece and gradually add successive sections. For example, on a CD by the Kronos Quartet, *Pieces of Africa*, the final selection, "Kutambarara," lasts seven minutes. The piece consists of continually repeated phrases varied by vocal and instrumental timbre. Within the first minute and a half, there is enough musical content for an initial intermediate lesson. Children can indicate phrase length through arm movements and can determine how the composer provided contrast. Successive lessons can include more and more of the music as students continue to

[1]John Dewey (1934). *Art As Experience*. New York: Putnam.

explore how the composer incorporated repetition and contrast. The same approach can be taken with the introduction to the fourth movement of Beethoven's Ninth Symphony. Although it would seem that there is no connection between Dumisani Maraire, who was born in 1943 in Zimbabwe, and Ludwig van Beethoven, who was born in 1770 in Bonn, the use of repetition and contrast is a device used by all composers. The recognition of this commonality provides an opportunity for reflection in listening.

The attraction of commercial or popular music becomes even stronger to children in intermediate grades than when they were younger, and students may well perceive a distinction between "school" music and "real" music. For this reason, it is imperative that your choice of listening selections be eclectic. Using the criteria listed on pp. 103–104, you can select music from every genre, not just Western art music. Your selection of music must demonstrate to these impressionable learners that quality music has no boundaries.

A number of research studies in music education have shown that in the intermediate grades, peer approval and media examples have a much stronger influence than during the primary years. Of particular interest is a finding by Finnas that seventh graders expressed more preference for classical and folk music privately than in public with their peers.[2] It is important to remember that loud groans or negative comments will influence other students, particularly if this negative affect is expressed by a popular student or one who is a class leader. Preplanning is the key to preventing such possibilities. Knowing exactly what you are going to say that will intrigue or challenge intermediate students, in addition to not allowing such interference, will enable you to overcome this obstacle.

You need to consider several important factors when selecting a repertoire of appropriate listening selections for intermediate grades. As in earlier grades, it is important to select music that provides a clear illustration of the musical concept you are teaching, but now your task is to enable children to perceive much more musical content. Therefore, not one but several musical elements in a single piece must be obvious and vivid.

In addition, you must balance accessibility with complexity. Musical selections in which all of the content can easily be perceived should be a very small part of children's musical diet. You don't want to announce a listening selection and have children groan at the thought of listening to the piece again! Most of the music you select should be of moderate complexity and should provide some challenge. It is also good to choose a few pieces that represent a more substantial listening challenge. These selections will provide students with the opportunity to refine their listening skills.

Although it is always important to consider the length of a selection, intermediate students often are able to listen to more than one selection in a lesson if both are short and illustrative of a particular contrast. Within the same lesson, for example, students could reflect on similarities and differences in "Mai Nozipo" (2 minutes, 45 seconds) from the Kronos Quartet CD *Pieces of Africa* (see Script 2 on p. 127) and "Take the A Train" performed by Duke Ellington,

[2]Leif Finnas (1989). "How Can Musical Preferences Be Modified? A Research Review." *Bulletin of the Council for Research in Music Education, 102,* 1–59.

both of which are ternary form. Another approach is to use different versions of the same selection in the same lesson. You can initially use vivid contrast and later be much more subtle. Many of the recordings of the Canadian Brass, Swingle Singers, and other chamber ensembles are an excellent source because these groups have recorded many arrangements originally composed for larger and more varied ensembles. Subtle contrasts can be illustrated with two or more recordings of pieces that are already familiar to your students. You can present a real listening challenge when you use two recordings of a familiar piece and ask students to compare what they hear. Many older recordings are being remastered and released in the CD format, and they are a wonderful source of contrasts for students.

Directed Music Listening

Every time intermediate students listen to music, they must get clear directions that focus their attention so as to require active participation. An active listener is one who is involved as the music moves through time. Active participation does not, however, necessarily have to be movement-oriented. Indeed, teachers must be sensitive when they plan movement activities for intermediate students (see Chapter 7) because children at this age become much more self-conscious about everything, but especially about moving. If you are fortunate enough to teach in a setting where the physical education program encompasses a strong emphasis in movement education, you will be able to incorporate this form of expression more easily with your older students. Otherwise, students will spend their energy compensating for their self-consciousness; this will block their ability to listen to music and can derail your carefully planned listening activity.

Teachers can direct careful and attentive listening with simple verbal directions as well as with more elaborate visual assistance. Students who are directed to put their thumbs up when they hear a new section or instrument or a change in melodic direction cannot help but be active listeners. They have to be attentive if they are to move a hand or arm in a arc to indicate phrase structure or count the number of repetitions of a musical element. Active listening can also be fostered with the use of teacher-made listening maps and call charts as well as student-made maps. Teacher-made listening maps for intermediate students should be quite different from those used in primary grades, since more musical content needs to be made accessible to listeners. A listening map for "Fanfare for the Common Man" by Aaron Copland for intermediate grades should show the changes in timbre, melodic direction, rhythm patterns, and articulation (Figure 6.2; see the map for primary grades in Figure 5.1).

Call charts can be used in two ways. The teacher can call out a number that directs listeners' attention to specific sections, but this interrupts the music. The second method eliminates the verbal direction through the use of an overhead projector. The teacher uncovers the relevant section of the call chart as the music is played and simply points to the relevant section. A listening map can become a call chart with the simple addition of numbers in each section. Individual call charts can also be constructed to direct listening either with quite simple vocabulary or with much more musical vocabulary (see Table 6.1). Still other call charts can be used to evaluate listening ability (see Table 6.2).

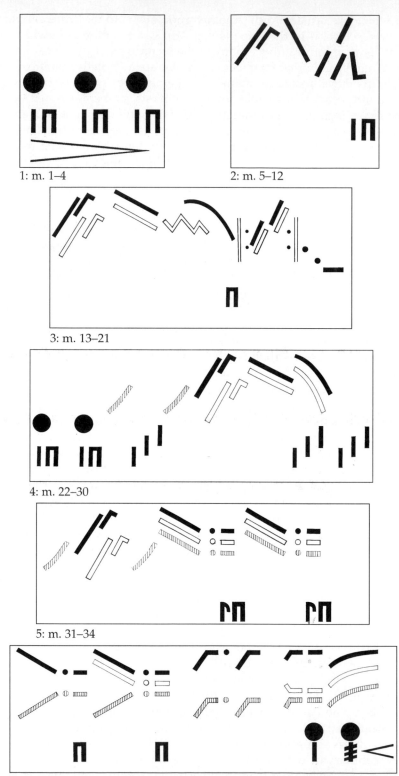

1: m. 1–4

2: m. 5–12

3: m. 13–21

4: m. 22–30

5: m. 31–34

6: m. 35–end

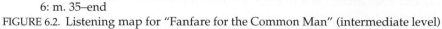

FIGURE 6.2. Listening map for "Fanfare for the Common Man" (intermediate level)

TABLE 6.1. Contrasting Directive Call Charts
("Fanfare for the Common Man")

Simple Tone Color	More Musical Vocabulary
1. Tympani Gong	1. Repeated rhythm pattern. Decrescendo.
2. Trumpet Tympani	2. Melody added.
3. Trumpet Horns Tympani	3. Parallel melodic movement. Tympani plays different rhythm.
4. Tympani Gong	4. Mostly upward direction. Tympani plays upward direction.
5. Trombones Trumpets Horns Tympani	5. Thicker texture. Accents. Contrasting melodic direction.
6. Trombones Trumpets Horns Tympani	6. Increased dynamic level. Different rhythm in tympani.
7. Brass instruments Tympani Gong	7. Parallel melodic movement. Accents. Tympani roll. Crescendo.

TABLE 6.2. Evaluative Call Chart
("Fanfare for the Common Man")

Circle the correct answer as each number is called.

1. Music gets louder. Few instruments.	Music gets softer. Many instruments.
2. Single instrument plays melody. Saxophone.	Many instruments play melody. Trumpet.
3. More instruments. String family.	Fewer instruments. Brass family.
4. Tympani plays repeated sounds.	Tympani plays upward sounds.
5. Thinner texture. Louder.	Thicker texture. Softer.
6. Accents. Thicker texture.	No accents. Thinner texture.
7. Crescendo. Accents.	Decrescendo. No accents.

The musical vocabulary used in Tables 6.1 and 6.2 is an important aspect of intermediate music instruction. By differentiating your vocabulary and your instruction for these children, you send signals that you recognize their advancing cognitive abilities. Once children begin to become abstract thinkers, they are delighted to learn and use correct musical terminology. This doesn't necessarily mean they'll use it correctly, however. A research study by Harriet Hair reported the contrast between second, third, and fourth graders' use of terminology to describe musical change (dynamics, tempo, pitch, timbre, mode, rhythm).[3] When the children did not know the correct term for a musical change, they tended to use a word, any word, that they had learned in music class. Clearly, not every child will be able to remember a myriad of musical terms from week to week. But if you provide a musical vocabulary source (a wall chart or bulletin board) and if you model the use of musical vocabulary, they will learn to speak as musicians.

Mainstreamed Students

One current trend in education is to include exceptional learners in regular classrooms. Such a "regular education initiative" or "total inclusion" policy means that all teachers, including music teachers, must be prepared to educate a wide range of learners within one class. Music and other "special" classes (art and gym) have long been settings where exceptional children were mainstreamed, mainly for social reasons, but during part or all of the remainder of the day, these students received special education services. In an effort to provide the least restrictive environment for exceptional students, special education teachers are becoming true resource teachers who assist these children in the regular classroom rather than working with them in separate self-contained classrooms. In addition, special education labels are being avoided as much as possible. Some former resource room teachers are now called "helping teachers"; their function is to provide short-term or long-term assistance to any student who needs extra educational support.

The trend toward mainstreaming all children into music means that you must plan ways of accommodating children with a vast range of learning and motor abilities within one single class. For this reason, you may need to supplement or replace listening responses that rely on children's understanding and/or writing of language. (See the discussion of evaluation in Chapter 2.) If you decide to use an evaluation call chart similar to the one in Table 6.2, you may need to prepare another version that uses icons and pictures.

Responses that require students to write answers should be used sparingly in music class. The act of writing requires the student to remember the motor patterns involved in forming each letter, correct spelling and syntax, and musical vocabulary and meaning. Even for normal achievers, the time lapse between music classes is a considerable barrier to remembering musical vocabulary. Effective individual evaluation should supply the learner with a choice of words or symbols to circle or check. In this way, you will really evaluate musical learning rather than writing or spelling ability.

[3]Harriet I. Hair (1981). "Verbal Identification of Music Concepts." *Journal of Research in Music Education, 29,* 11–21.

Materials and Sources

Listening lessons with intermediate-age children can be made more imaginative and exciting through the use of a wide variety of materials. Because they can listen for longer periods of time and can focus on increasingly more complex and subtle musical ideas, you need to be continually on the lookout for ways to expand your musical offerings for these students. In addition to comparing recordings of different groups and different artists, as discussed earlier, you can show more subtle musical contrasts by comparing an audio recording and a videotape of the same performer in the same work. Many excellent classical music videotapes are available today, and it is important to use their powerful visual influence to engage children in musical learning. It may seem that adding the visual element will distract students from the music, but the focus of your lesson will determine where their attention is directed. It is up to you to plan your questions carefully so that the comparisons made are essentially musical ones.

There are many ways to expand listening opportunities for students through live musical encounters, and part of your job is to expose students to as many live performances as you possibly can. Recorded music will always be the basic medium of musical listening in schools, but you must never forget that no matter how fine your CD player or tape deck is, recorded music is only a reproduction. Real instruments and singers sound very different from the reproductions, and students need opportunities to experience the richer and fuller sounds of live performance.

One important source of listening experiences is the community in which you live and teach. No matter where you are, there will always be many musically talented adults who could enrich your music curriculum. The best way to find this wonderful resource is to ask your students if they have any musical parents or friends, and then follow up on their suggestions. In communities with different ethnic groups, you may uncover parent performers who can bring a taste of world music to your classroom. In addition, be alert to concert announcements in local papers and on bulletin boards in malls and grocery stores. Some performing groups that do not include parents of your students may be willing to share their talents with your classes. Live performance is a powerful means of expanding the musical world for your students and is well worth your extra effort and planning.

Artists in the Schools

One way to find enrichment opportunities for your students is to investigate what is available through your local or state arts commission. Many states, counties, and even individual communities have arts councils that are partially funded by the National Endowment for the Arts. These organizations provide matching funds for artistic endeavors, which can include bringing professional musicians into school settings. The matching funds are supplied either by the school district or, in some places, the Parent-Teacher Association (PTA). A state or region may even publish a catalog that lists and describes approved artists and musical ensembles.

Before experiencing a live performance, your students must be prepared for the actual concert setting. Few students have parental guidance in how to act as audience members, so simple audience etiquette must be taught prior to a performance. In addition, the more musical preparation students have, the more they will be able to really participate in the concert as active listeners. You must not forget that the reason our major symphony orchestras perform so much familiar music is that their audiences want to listen to what they know. Similarly, your students should not be expected to sit through a performance of unfamiliar music. You must prepare your students so that a live performance provides for a musical interaction between listeners and musical performers. A live performance must not simply be a musical exposure.

Youth Concerts

All symphony orchestras, opera companies, and concert associations now recognize the necessity of educating the audiences of tomorrow. Indeed, these organizations know that their audiences are aging and that few younger listeners are attracted to their offerings. Performing organizations approach the task of education quite differently and with varying degrees of effectiveness. Some groups provide "bring your class to the symphony" experiences for young listeners; others provide "pop" offerings or other attempts at lighter entertainment. Many groups have education directors or committees who prepare and distribute helpful written materials and tapes for music teachers to use in preparing students for concert attendance.

Taking students to a performance outside of school is a complicated but rewarding experience. After you obtain approval from your principal, you may be responsible for collecting money for tickets, making reservations, arranging for school buses, and ensuring that enough chaperones (teachers and parents) will also attend. And, of course, your students must be musically prepared in class as well. Daunting as they may seem, all these efforts are worthwhile when you remember that many adults never enter a concert hall because they perceive it as a foreign place and one where they are unsure of correct behavior. A very real part of a music teacher's job is to introduce students to the social processes involved in attending live performances in addition to the real aesthetic pleasure that awaits them there.

Teacher Questioning for Student Thinking

Listening lessons are an important part of the general music curriculum because they enable students to listen to and think about musical sounds in a guided fashion. Class discussion after listening serves two purposes: it helps students make sense of what they have experienced, and it helps you find out what they have learned. It is crucial, then, that you plan each listening lesson so that the students will be required to think both during and after the listening experience. The kinds of questions you ask will guide your students' attention during listening and will give focus to their discussion.

Bloom's Taxonomy

One way to organize your own thinking about questioning is to use the taxonomy of educational objectives in the cognitive domain developed by

Benjamin Bloom and others.[4] The following six levels of Bloom's taxonomy
illustrate a progression from simple to complex and can be used both as a way
to structure your goals and objectives and as a framework for structuring
questions within a lesson. The levels in this taxonomy clearly differentiate
how prior cognitive knowledge can be used in increasingly complex ways to
gain a deeper understanding of a discipline.

1.00 KNOWLEDGE

 1.10 Knowledge of specifics

 1.11 Knowledge of terminology

 1.12 Knowledge of specific facts

2.00 COMPREHENSION

 2.10 Translation

 2.20 Interpretation

 2.30 Extrapolation

3.00 APPLICATION

4.00 ANALYSIS

 4.10 Analysis of elements

 4.20 Analysis of relationships

5.00 SYNTHESIS

 5.10 Production of a unique communication

 5.20 Production of a plan or proposed set of operations

 5.30 Derivation of a set of abstract relations

6.00 EVALUATION

 6.10 Judgments in terms of internal evidence

 6.20 Judgments in terms of external criteria

Elaboration and Sample Listening Questions

Each level of the cognitive hierarchy exemplifies a valuable progression in
teaching and learning, going from the simplest to the most complex and from
the more concrete to the abstract. The following list explains each step in the
hierarchy and gives a few examples of the types of questions you can use in a
listening segment to lead students to these different levels of cognitive understanding. Refer to this list as you construct your own lesson plans, and check
to be sure that you include questions from levels 4 through 6 in each lesson.

1.00 KNOWLEDGE. Knowledge is the simple recall of terms, facts, or ideas.

What is the name of the instrument that played alone?

[4]Benjamin Bloom (Ed.) (1956). *Taxonomy of Educational Objectives: The Classification of Educational
Goals, Handbook I: Cognitive Domain.* New York: McKay, pp. 201–207.

What three families of instruments played in this selection?

How does a double-reed instrument produce a sound?

2.00 COMPREHENSION. Comprehension is the ability to understand the meaning of material either by translating it from one form to another, interpreting it through explanation or summary, or making predictions about it.

Can you show the steady beat of this piece as you listen?

Can you put these phrase cards into the correct order, as they occur in the piece?

How did the composer provide repetition in this music?

3.00 APPLICATION. Application is the ability to use what has been learned, such as rules, principles, and concepts.

You are to create a 15-second piece with steady beat and no beat.

Your ostinato needs to have two equal four-measure phrases.

When you compose your second phrase, repeat part of a musical idea from your first phrase.

4.00 ANALYSIS. Analysis is the ability to break an idea into its component parts so that it can be understood. Included here are identification of parts, analysis of relationships between parts, and recognizing organizational principles.

How many phrases are in this section?

How would you describe the form of this piece?

How does the first selection differ from the one we just heard?

5.00 SYNTHESIS. Synthesis is the ability to create a new whole from component parts. Because of its creative nature, synthesis requires the student to use all previously learned concepts in a unique way.

Create a piece that has the same form as the one we just heard, using only metal instruments and body percussion.

Compose a movement piece that illustrates the dynamic changes in the last listening selection.

6.00 EVALUATION. Evaluation means making judgments about the material under discussion. There are two kinds of criteria for such judgments: internal criteria (how well the material is organized) and external criteria (how relevant the material is). The criteria may be student- or teacher-generated.

Let's discuss how well our metal/body percussion piece was constructed. Did it fulfill the assignment?

Which of the group movement pieces best illustrated the dynamic changes in the music?

It is important to keep Bloom's taxonomy in mind when you plan music lessons for children, so you can lead them to greater musical understanding and clearer conceptions of how music is constructed. The taxonomy is a useful structure that will enable you to check whether your questions truly challenge children to think musically, no matter what grade you are teaching. As a general music teacher, you will rarely be observed by an administrator who has any knowledge of music. However, all administrators understand Bloom's taxonomy and the importance of goals, objectives, and questions based on these important principles.

TEACHING SCRIPTS

Scripts 2 and 3 incorporate more than one musical behavior. You can begin practicing more than one aspect of a lesson and learn how to move from a known, previously taught song to a listening lesson segment designed to teach either the same musical concept or a different one. In order to teach Script 2, you will need to listen to "Under African Skies" from Paul Simon's *Graceland*. Notate the first four measures of each theme in solfège syllables and label them A, B, and C. This transcription may require several listenings to complete. Only when you have finished this task should you practice teaching this script. Your preparation for Script 3 includes listening to two tracks on the Kronos Quartet CD *Pieces of Africa*.

Script 2

GRADE LEVEL: Grades Five and Six

MUSICAL CONCEPT: Form

MUSICAL ELEMENTS: Repetition and contrast; coda; interlude

LESSON OBJECTIVE: Students will be able to demonstrate an understanding of musical form through singing and moving.

MATERIALS: "The Monster Song" (see Figure 4.15 on p. 90); a recording of "Under African Skies" from Paul Simon's *Graceland*; a chalk board with a solfège scale drawn vertically and three themes from "Under African Skies" notated in solfège.

STEP ONE

I'm going to play the opening of a song you already know, and I'd like to see you put one finger in the air when you recognize it.

Play the opening of "The Monster Song" and watch for response. Stop playing when most of the class responds.

What is it?

Take one response from one student.

Let's sing the first verse without the piano to see if you can remember all the pitches.

Give the starting pitch on "Ready, sing" and sing the whole song for review.

The last time we worked on this song we discussed its form—how it was put together. Can anyone tell me what we decided about the form of this piece?

Elicit answers and write them on chalkboard.

Today I have a different piece for you, and to begin, I'd like you to review our solfège syllables with me. Remember how these sound? Let's try it.

Point to the bottom D of the vertically drawn letters DRMFSLTD; give the pitch for do by singing "Ready, sing" and point to each ascending pitch. Then mix them up, beginning with DMS—use the accompanying hand signs if the class is familiar with them.

That was good singing. You really remember your syllables!

Now let's see if you can follow my finger and sing these three themes on the board.

Point to the themes on the board labeled A, B, and C, without imposing any specific rhythm on the singing. If necessary, return to the vertical solfège row to reinforce the sound of difficult intervals; then return to the themes and try again.

You watched and listened well, class. Now let's see if you can hear these three themes when they appear in this piece of music. When you hear them, try to sing along softly with the recording as I point to the solfège on the board.

Play the recording through the third theme.

Was there anything tricky about that?

Some students may find it difficult to sing the lower of the two parts in the harmony while listening to the recording.

I've got something else for you to do this time. Instead of singing with the recording, I want each of you to try this set of movements. Here's the "hand jive" for theme A.

Demonstrate the following hand jive: Pat thighs twice; pat shoulders twice; snap right twice; snap left twice; clap center six times, moving up higher with each clap; then hold arms up above head in a V for two counts.

Here's the hand jive for theme B—it's just the A hand jive backwards. Try it with me.

Begin with your arms above your head in a V shape for two counts; clap six times, starting above your head and moving down to waist level; snap left twice; snap right twice; pat your shoulders twice; then pat your thighs twice.

Here's what you need to do for theme C.

Demonstrate the foot jive with your back to the class so the children don't have to mirror your movements and so you can easily say and model the directions (see Figure 6.3). Start with the left foot: touch your heel in front (two counts for each move); touch your toe in back; heel; toe; feet together, lift toes to the right; lift heels to the right; lift toes to the right; lift heels to the right. Then do same with the right foot: heel touch in front; toe touch in back; heel; toe; feet together; lift toes to the left; lift heels to the left; lift toes to the left; lift heels to the left.

Now let's see if we can remember what to do when we hear the themes: hand jive for theme A, hand jive backwards for theme B, and foot jive for theme C. There's something that happens at the beginning of this piece, and between themes, that we haven't planned for, so we need to decide what we can do during those parts. What will we call these parts of the music?

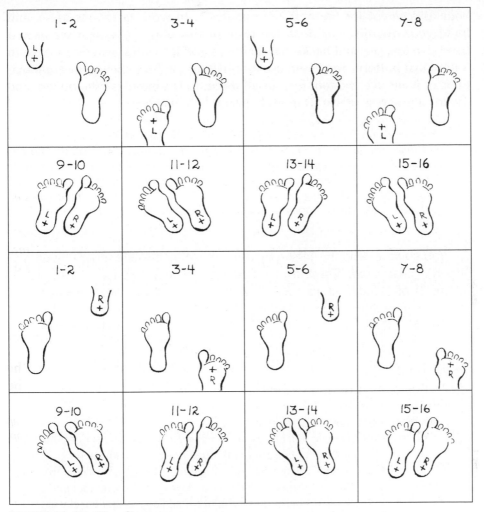

FIGURE 6.3. Foot jive diagram

*(Introduction and interlude.) Decide how to move during these sections. Then listen
and move to the music through the first appearance of theme C.*

**Could someone come to the board and keep track of the themes for us so
we can figure out the form of this piece? Each time we do the hand jive for
theme A, write a lowercase *a* on the board. Do the same for themes B and
C. When we're at the place the music stops, we should be able to look at
the board and see the form of the piece.**

*Play the entire piece, modeling appropriate movements for each theme. It will be
helpful if you call out directions for the foot jive as you do it.*

Let's look at the board now and figure out the form of this piece.

*Let the students do the talking, discussing how the various themes fit together to
make a larger whole. Allow time for students to put forward and argue various opinions. When closure has been achieved, proceed to the next step if time permits.*

Your assignment for the next ten minutes is to work in groups of six and build your own jives to show the form of this piece. Although we used a hand jive forward and backward for the A and B themes, you don't have to follow that pattern. You could use foot jive for all three themes or combinations of hand jive and foot jive for all three. In ten minutes I'll stop you and ask for a progress report from each group. You may begin.

Circulate among the groups to facilitate the process. If you allow students to form their own groups, you may not need to participate. If you form the groups, some students may not get along very well or may have difficulty staying on task. You can help these difficult groups to stay on task by offering suggestions and then leaving them to work; they may either incorporate your ideas or throw them out and find better ones. After checking progress, allow each group to complete their task and teach their movement composition to the whole class. This may take the next class period.

You could extend this lesson by using the videocassette recording of Paul Simon's *Graceland: The African Concert* (Warner Reprise Video, 1987, 38136-3) of "Under African Skies" and comparing the two performances. They are quite different, with Miriam Makeba singing the part Linda Ronstadt sang on the album in a distinctly different style and with different words.

Script 3

GRADE LEVEL: Grades Five and Six
MUSICAL CONCEPTS: Rhythm and melody
SPECIFIC ELEMENT: Use of repetition and contrast
LESSON OBJECTIVE: Students will be able to demonstrate recognition of repeated and contrasting phrases through movement and mapping.
MATERIALS: "Emma" (Figure 4.14, p. 88); guiro, maracas, and claves; the Kronos Quartet's CD *Pieces of Africa*; a CD player (or tape the selections three times); paper and markers for the class.

STEP ONE

Warm up singing voices, ending with echo patterns that contain syncopated do-mi patterns.

STEP TWO

If students already know "Emma," review the song and find repeated melodic phrases and the one contrasting phrase. If students do not know the song, teach it using the whole song method described in Chapter 4 (p. 89).

STEP THREE

Today we are going to listen to two pieces of music written by the same composer. When we listen to the first piece, I want you to listen carefully. As soon as you think you can show me where each phrase ends, I want you to put your thumb up. Who can tell me why I don't want you to raise your hands?

Discuss individual listening and response and the importance of focusing on music, not on another person's answer. Play the first ten phrases (1 minute) of "Kutambarara." Monitor students closely, modeling attentive listening. Praise the class for good listening if appropriate.

As we listen the second time, I want you to listen carefully and decide which phrases are the same and when the composer provides contrast. How could you show me which phrases are repeated and which are contrasting?

Discuss a small hand or finger movement to use—perhaps switching to the other hand for contrast.

That was good listening, class. Now we are going to listen to another piece of music written by the same composer. As we listen the first time, I want you to try to decide how the two pieces differ.

Play "Mai Nozipo" (2 minutes, 45 seconds). Solicit answers from the class. Students will identify the contrast between the opening repeated section, the middle drumming section, and the gradual reentry of opening thematic material accompanied by a shaking sound.

When we listen the second time, I want you to figure out the form of this music. When you think a new section begins, raise your thumb.

After listening, ask the class to define the form (ABA). Pass out paper to each student.

As we listen this last time, I want you to find a way to draw a map of what is happening in the music to show both the phrases and the ABA form. You will want to refer to your map in the next class meeting, so be as precise as you can.

STUDENT ASSIGNMENTS

1. Teach Scripts 2 or 3 to a group of intermediate children, and have a peer or the classroom teacher videotape your lesson. Before you view the videotape, write a paragraph of reflection about the experience. After you view the videotape, write a reflection paper that includes description (what you did), information (what happened), and reconstruction (how you could do it again differently).

2. Teach Script 2 or 3 to a group of intermediate-age children, and have a classmate use the following checklist to evaluate your teaching:
   1. The teacher motivated the class by using facial expression,
      voice inflection, and verbal enthusiasm.   ___ yes ___ no
   2. Students understood the teacher's directions prior to each
      listening episode.   ___ yes ___ no
   3. The teacher realized which students were not on task and
      adapted the lesson directions when necessary.   ___ yes ___ no
   4. List the positive aspects of the teacher's presentation.

3. Have a peer listen to one of your music selections and use the following criteria to evaluate a listening map that you have prepared for intermediate students:
   a. Which musical features does the map illustrate?
   b. Are the graphics suitable for music? Why or why not?
   c. Would the map make it easier for children to understand musical relationships? Why or why not?

4. Have a peer listen to one of your music selections and use the following criteria to evaluate a call chart that you have prepared:
   a. Does the chart indicate important musical characteristics? Which ones? If not, which ones need to be included?
   b. Is the chart clutter-free? If not, suggest ways to improve it.
   c. Is the vocabulary simple? If not, suggest ways to improve it.
   d. List positive features of the chart.
   e. Do you have any other suggestions?
5. With a partner, design a pencil-and-paper activity that can be used to evaluate intermediate students' listening skills. Present and discuss your product with the rest of the class.

Experiencing Music Through Moving:

PRIMARY AND INTERMEDIATE

Case Study

Miss Davis welcomes the fourth grade class to the music room: "Good morning, fourth graders. I'd like all of you to sit down for a moment so we can hear the directions for today's lesson." When all are seated and quiet, she continues. "Today we're going to do some movement activities, so let's review the classroom rules about moving." After stating that all should move in ways that do not touch anybody or anything, Miss Davis gives the following directions: "Boys and girls, please move to groups of five students for this activity."

Complete chaos ensues, with a variety of results. Some girls move quickly to form groups of four or six, while a few boys try to convince each other to form all-boy groups. The most popular boys hang back and try to avoid being recruited for any existing groups. Miss Davis intervenes by approaching each ungrouped boy, putting her hands on his shoulders and moving him to a particular group. Eventually, the class settles into five groups of various sizes. Several groups have mostly girls and one has three boys.

Miss Davis says, "Today I have some interesting music for you to listen to. As you listen, I'd like you to imagine a story that would go with this music. I'd like each of you to become a character in this story and act it out as the music plays.

Remember our listening rules: no talking while the music plays. Let's begin!"

Miss Davis then plays the selection (1 minute, 13 seconds of the second movement of Haydn's Symphony No. 94). The students seem completely confused about the assignment and stare at each other, hoping to find some clues as to the correct response. The all-boy group begins to mimic one boy's percussive, angular motions and act as if they are all robots, waving their arms and high-stepping. The other students notice and begin to giggle.

Miss Davis stops the music and says, "Some of you need to refocus your attention on your own group assignment. You now have fifteen minutes to work as a group to decide on your story, your characters, and your movements. You may begin." After the fifteen minutes have passed with intense discussion in the groups, Miss Davis starts the music. The children in the all-boy group begin their robot movements in earnest, this time adding grunting noises with each step. Miss Davis says, "The rule for listening is to be silent. You're making it hard for the rest of the groups to hear the music." The boys continue their moving and grunting and begin to stamp their feet as they move. Miss Davis approaches them and says, "All right, if this group can't cooperate, we'll stop practicing and start the grading. This group will be the first to be graded. Everyone else may return to their seats." Students in the other groups moan and beg to have more time to work, but Miss Davis holds firm.

She calls the three boys to the front, and when they are ready, she starts the music. Their performance sends the rest of the class into paroxysms of laughter. Miss Davis stops the music after thirty seconds and says, "I'm so disappointed in you, fourth graders. You were such good workers during our last listening lesson, but today you acted as if you'd never heard the rules about cooperation at school. I just don't know what to do with you. I'm sure your classroom teacher will be disappointed, too." Miss Davis has the class sit in silence for the remaining nine minutes of the class period, and the students shift uneasily in their seats, eyes glued to the clock. When their classroom teacher appears, Miss Davis says, "Ricardo, tell Mrs. Lucas what happened today." Ricardo, one of the members of the all-boy group, looks at the floor and says nothing. Miss Davis calls on the other two members of the all-boy group, and they respond as Ricardo did. Mrs. Lucas says, "Who would like to tell me what went on here today?" When no other students volunteer, Miss Davis says, "Your students just didn't cooperate today, Mrs. Lucas. First they didn't follow directions for moving into groups, and then they didn't follow the rules about listening, and they laughed at other students who were not cooperating." Mrs. Lucas says, "I'm sorry, Miss Davis. I hope we'll get a better report on Thursday." As they leave the room, Ricardo gives Miss Davis a mean look and says, "You're not fair. I wasn't the only one that didn't do it right."

YOUR COOPERATIVE TASK

1. In pairs, formulate a list of principles of classroom management that Miss Davis could have followed in planning this movement lesson. Discuss them with another pair of classmates and rewrite your two lists into one. Then put your combined list on the chalkboard and rank each item on the composite list from the entire class according to importance.

2. In small groups, discuss Miss Davis's choice of movement activity, focusing on ways in which she could have better directed the students' attention to the qualities of the music.

3. In pairs, discuss the gender issues raised in this case study.

4. Was there anything that made you uncomfortable with this scenario? Discuss it with a partner. Be prepared to report your reaction to the rest of the class.

5. In small groups, brainstorm a list of words you could use to describe the character of the Haydn excerpt used by Miss Davis in this case study. Formulate a question you would ask this group of fourth graders that would lead them to generate *their own* descriptions of the piece.

6. Discuss with a partner the most recent situation in which you felt that you were treated unfairly. Try to articulate your response to the situation: what you did, whom you told, any action you took to remedy the situation. Explain your current feelings about the person who treated you unfairly, and characterize the level of intensity of your feelings about this experience.

PRACTICE TEACHING SCRIPTS

Scripts 1 and 2 illustrate music teaching that incorporates movement. These scripts incorporate musical behaviors previously discussed in this text. Practice Scripts 1 and 2 with your peers and with groups of children. Repeated practice with different groups will enable you to focus less on your presentation and more on the students. Only then will you be able to begin to observe the teaching-learning process.

Script 1 (Primary)

135

CHAPTER 7
*Experiencing Music
Through Moving:
Primary and
Intermediate*

GRADE LEVEL: Grade Three

MUSICAL CONCEPT: Form

SPECIFIC ELEMENT: Music contains repeated and contrasting phrases.

LESSON OBJECTIVE: Students will be able to indicate an understanding of phrase form through singing and movement.

MATERIALS: "The Hanukkah Song" (Figure 7.1); a piano; a large space for circle movement.

STEP ONE

Warm up singing voices using a series of patterns, each repeated twice.

Try combining pulse in feet, melodic rhythm in hands

FIGURE 7.1. *From* The Gateway to Jewish Song, *published by Behrman House, edited by Judith Eisenstein. Reprinted by permission of the editor.*

STEP TWO

We're going to discuss an important idea in music today, and we're even going to dance an important idea in music—and I know that everyone in the class will have a lot of fun. I want you to listen to a paragraph, and I want you to tell me what is wrong with what I'm doing.

Read the following paragraph to the class with no voice inflection and no recognition of periods, commas, and so on:

Hanukkah, the festival of lights, is a celebration that exists to mark a miracle to the Israelites. There was a terrible battle between the Israelites and the Maccobees. The place of worship, the Temple, had to be left unprotected during the battle. Before the Israelites left the Temple, there was only a little oil left in the lamp—not even enough for one day. But after the battle was over and the people returned to thank God for their victory, the lamp was still burning.

Who can tell me what my reading needed?

Solicit answers, leading the children to understand that punctuation helps listeners distinguish parts of the paragraph. Ask children if they know what a paragraph contains; discuss the idea that there are several sentences or parts.

Now I am going to sing a song, and I want to see if you can figure out where the parts of the song are.

Sing "The Hanukkah Song" song expressively, with appropriate phrase endings every two measures.

poor response better - how many parts (phrases) are there

Raise your hand if you were able to hear the parts of the song. You were all really good listeners. Are there any words in this song that you do not know?

Solicit answers and explain the meaning of the words menorah *(a candle holder—one candle is lit each day of Hanukkah),* horah *(the name of the dance),* s'vivonim *(clay dreidels or tops), and* levivot *(potato pancakes).*

I am going to sing the song again, and each time I sing a phrase, I want you to show me the shape of the phrase with your arm.

(Show arc movement.)

Now I want you all to be super sleuths. I want you to listen as I play each phrase of this song on the piano, and you decide which phrases are the same and which are not. To be a really good music detective, close your eyes so that you will use only your ears.

Play the first two phrases, then discuss whether they are the same or different. Continue through the song, assigning one child to draw phrases on the board showing repeats, and label phrases a a b b c d d.

After we sing the song together, we're going to learn the dance.

Pass out copies of the song or put it on the overhead. Sing with accompaniment.

STEP THREE

Everyone put your hands up with your palms facing out in front of you.

Show your hands at a 90-degree angle to your arms.

We're going to learn how to do the dance with our hands first, and then we'll do it with our feet. To do the horah, we only need to learn steps for

one phrase. Then we repeat the same steps for every phrase. Watch my hands do the dance.

Right, left behind, right, hop, step, step, step (in place), lift.

Now I want you to practice the dance.

Either reverse your hands or stand with your back to the class so the children follow right and left correctly. Have the children do the dance only with hand movements until they all understand what to do on each set of four beats. You can say the words right, behind, *and so on as cues.*

Now to practice our dance, we'll all begin in a long line.

Move the class into position. If space is limited, use two or three single lines and stagger children so they can see your hands and feet. Practice the dance steps several times while you say "Right, left behind, right, hop, step, step, step (in place), lift." Then have the children watch you do the dance step while they sing the song. Then have the class try the dance together very slowly, doing only movement, no singing. Give word cues, if needed. If the children are successful, you sing the song while they move. Then have them add singing to their movements. Finally, try it in a circle, with hands on each others' shoulders while singing. The dance begins slowly; with successive repetitions, it gets faster and faster.

137

CHAPTER 7
*Experiencing Music
Through Moving:
Primary and
Intermediate*

Script 2 (Intermediate)

GRADE LEVEL: Grade Six

MUSICAL CONCEPT: Form and musical character/expressiveness

MUSICAL ELEMENT: Repetition and contrast; melody; timbre; texture

LESSON OBJECTIVE: Students will be able to respond to the music's expressive character through movement; they will plan and perform movement patterns that illustrate both the character and the form of the piece.

MATERIALS: "Daa, Daa Kente" (Figure 3.9 on p. 57), a Ghanaian folk song from the Twi people; a recording of "Turtle Shoes" from Bobby McFerrin's CD *Spontaneous Inventions* (Blue Note, CDP-546298); poster-size copies of gestural/elemental listening maps for bass, voice, and piano sections of the piece (Figure 7.2); a chalkboard for writing form symbols; sheets of paper labeled 1 through 4, taped up in the corners of the room.

STEP ONE

I have a new song for you today. I want you to listen to it carefully as I sing it, since it's in a language that I'm sure you've never heard before.

Sing the entire song. Then teach it line by line using the rote method, without saying any words but pointing to yourself and the class and using repetition for correction and refinement.

That was fine singing, sixth graders! You've just learned a song from the Twi people of Ghana, a country in West Africa. It's a song about the beautiful cloth called *kente*, from which very fine hats and scarves are made. The words tell that an upright, respectable person always wears kente. Can someone tell me about the ways in which this song illustrates the words?

FIGURE 7.2. Gestural map for "Turtle Shoes"
Bobby McFerrin from Spontaneous Inventions CD *CDP-546298, Blue Note*

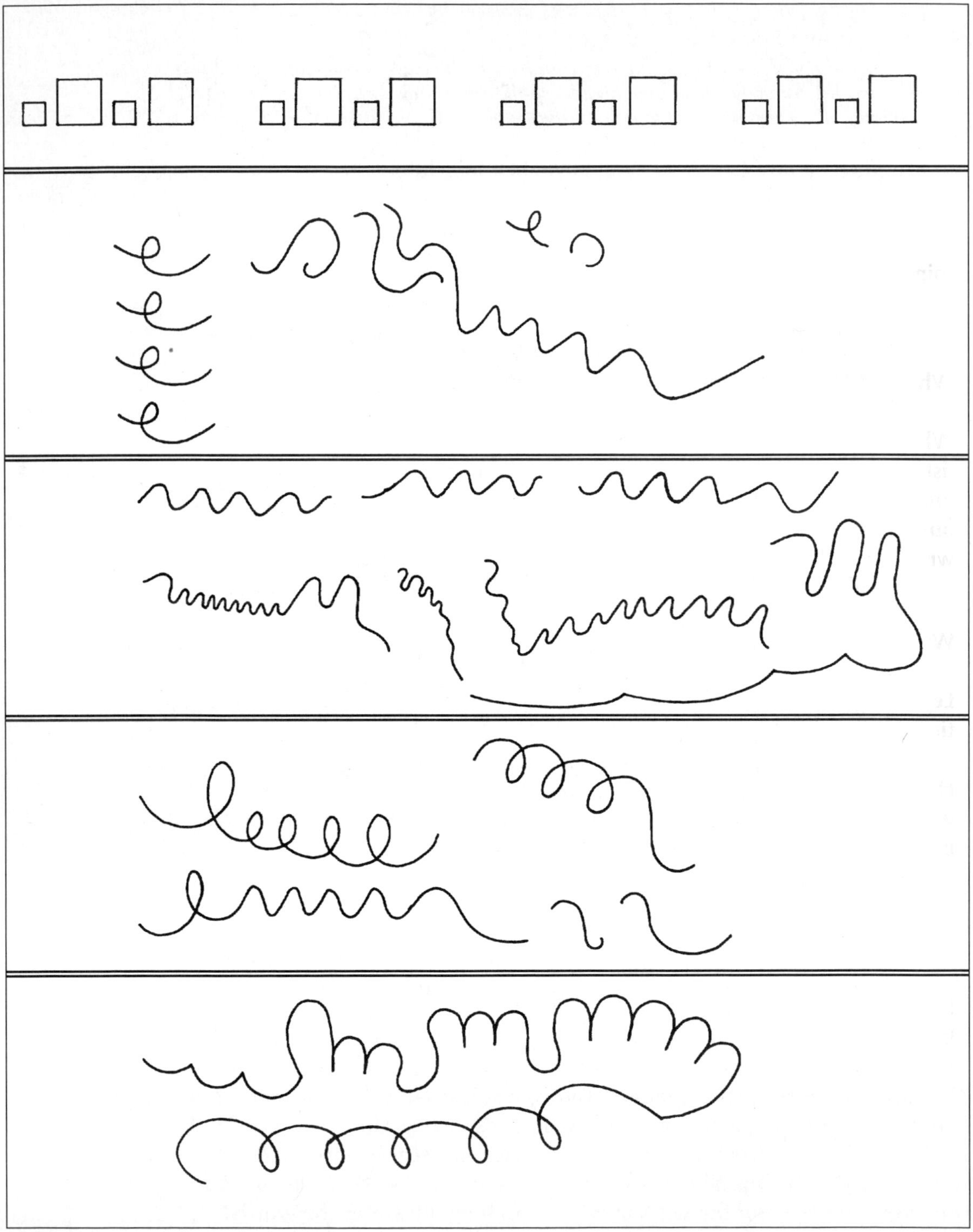

Focus the discussion on the musical elements that form the song: melodic direction, tonality, rhythm, and form.

What about the way in which we used our voices to sing it? For example, did we use any changes in dynamic level?

Discuss how different dynamic levels affect the song's musical effect: try performing it once rather softly and legato, then forte and marcato. Discuss the effects of each.

STEP TWO

The next piece you'll hear today is quite different from "Daa, Daa Kente," but I chose it because it has an interesting way of using the human voice, as well as a very different musical effect. I'd like you to close your eyes and listen to the music. When it's finished, I'm going to ask you to tell me anything you can about what you heard.

Play "Turtle Shoes." List on the board everything the class can tell you about what they heard. Put listening maps for the bass line, voice part 1, voice part 2, and the piano part on the board.

Which of these maps looks like it doesn't belong with the rest?

Elicit responses, leading the class to discover that the bass map has a different look.

Which part of the music do you think this different-looking one maps? Let's listen to the piece again, and I'll help you follow the maps. Trace along with me, in the air, as I trace the map on the board, and let's see if we can figure out the form of this piece. Would someone like to come to the board and write down the form as it happens? What will you write for us?

Have the class determine what to use for forms: shapes, letters, or symbols. Play the piece, tracing maps while students trace in the air.

What is the form of this piece?

(Introduction, A, A, B, C, A, coda.)

Let's focus for a moment on the character of each of these different sections of the piece.

Move to the bass line map.

How would you describe the way this part of the music moves? If you wanted to add movement to it, what kinds of movement would show it best?

Pursue this line of questioning for all the sections, emphasizing that the quality of the movement needs to match the musical quality of the section. As suggestions are given, have the entire class try them while listening to the appropriate section of the music. If children cannot remember each section, listen to a section and then discuss it with them.

I'm going to go down the rows now and give each of you a number between 1 and 4. When I'm finished, I want each of you to move to the corner of the room that has your number on the wall.

Point out the numbers 1 through 4. Take the maps off the chalkboard and hang one in each corner.

You have fifteen minutes to come up with a set of movements that illustrate the particular section of the music you've been assigned. If your group is working on the bass line, your movements should look different from those of the A section, and so forth. You need to discuss the character of your

assigned section and decide on the kinds of movements that would be appropriate. Then try them out with the music and see how well they fit. Any questions?

Allow students three to five minutes to discuss and/or demonstrate different types of movements. Then play the selection once, monitoring group progress and children's levels of involvement within each group. Circulate among groups, pausing at each and watching their interactions. Offer advice and praise as needed. When twelve minutes have elapsed, ask:

Who is almost ready to perform their movement with the music?

Offer two more minutes to polish and ready the performance. When three minutes have elapsed, call all to attention and start the recording.

Are there any places in the music where we have forgotten to add movement? Where are they, and what should we do about them?

Entertain suggestions, and abide by the class decision to do nothing or a lot during the transitions and coda.

I think we could make our combinations of movements more interesting to look at if we could figure out a way to use the space in the room differently. What would happen if the bass group formed a core in the center of a series of circles, and the rest of us formed concentric circles around them? Let's try it that way and see how it looks.

Is there another way to shape ourselves in the room so that we are more clearly illustrating how this piece of music moves?

Try suggestions. Then lead the students in a discussion of what they have just experienced, using the following questions:

Which group's way of moving really seemed to show the character of the music clearly? Which set of movements was the most fun to do? Which group had the most difficult assignment? Did the movement collage help you to understand what was going on in the music? Did moving while you were listening change the way you listened to your section of the piece?

Thank you for a really exciting movement lesson, sixth graders. It seemed like you really understood this assignment, since your movement compositions clearly showed how the music moved. See you next week!

WHAT YOU NEED TO KNOW

Why Include Movement in Music?

Movement, like music, is a basic form of human expression. Movement experiences provide children with another form of creative and original expression and are an important aspect of experiencing music at all ages. The partnership of music and movement is a logical one because each of these art forms moves through time. We are unable to stand and ponder a dance or a piece of music in the same way that we can look at a painting or a piece of sculpture. Indeed, most music provokes a movement impulse. Consider the difficulty that you have controlling a tapping foot or finger while listening to any piece of music. This natural human impulse is a valid one, and in music class it should be nurtured and accepted as an important aspect of musical participation.

The wonder of all art is that often we are touched in ways that cannot be explained in words. Very young children think nothing of whirling and jumping with delight when they hear familiar or exciting music. They have found a way of translating their aesthetic pleasure and experience into movement. Fostering and providing opportunities for the extension of these initial reactions is an important part of primary music instruction. Joyous movement expressions are a valid part of music class.

141

CHAPTER 7
*Experiencing Music
Through Moving:
Primary and
Intermediate*

Movement is a wonderful way to monitor how the child is responding to the music. The typical day in the elementary school focuses the child's attention on cerebral activities such as reading, listening to directions, and writing. Children come to music class ready to be stimulated in nonverbal ways through the musical experience, and they are particularly ready to engage their entire bodies in the process. Movement seems to be one of the most delightful activities any human can engage in, and children seem to lose themselves while moving to music. The simple act of moving while listening to music and essentially "becoming the music" through movement brings great satisfaction to both young children and adults, no matter how clumsy or untrained or "macho" they regard themselves. It may be that moving to music reveals to us the great wealth of feeling within us that usually is not called on in our daily lives.

Unfortunately, most young children now begin their school career not with a background of hundreds or thousands of hours of spontaneous and exploratory play but rather with a background of thousands of hours of passive television viewing. Primary children are often uncomfortable and tense with their bodies when they are directed to move in original ways. For this reason, it is more important than ever that movement be an integral part of children's music experience.

The current emphasis on accountability and evaluating learning through paper-and-pencil tests ignores simple facts about how young children really learn and can express what they have assimilated (see Chapter 4). Piaget's description of the preoperational stage suggests that primary youngsters need to be engaged in concrete experiences with each musical element before they can begin to consider abstract terminology and an unfamiliar symbol system. Bruner's terminology is different, but his description of the enactive stage supports the notion that in all classrooms, including music classrooms, children learn best when they are actively engaged. Young children best demonstrate what they have learned by physically expressing their learning in some manner.

To be an effective teacher, you must determine whether actual musical learning is occurring in your classroom. The art of teaching music to children includes using movement to evaluate whether learning is really taking place. We know that the most important initial musical concept for youngsters is the ability to feel and express a steady pulse. No matter which musical behaviors (singing, listening, moving, creating, playing) you include in your lesson, you can evaluate the ability to feel a steady pulse only when children move in some manner. You will be able to see whether each child in each class is developing an understanding of this important musical concept.

Continual evaluation (also called *formative evaluation*) is vitally important in general music class because you are able to teach music for only a brief time each week. Including movement in each lesson allows you to immediately check each student's understanding of the lesson's concept. Movement can easily be incorporated into every lesson, and you do not have to spend time passing out materials for paper-and-pencil tasks. Most important, however, is the fact that unlike pencil-and-paper tests, movement activities allow children to demonstrate their musical understanding in a way that is musically expressive while at the same time synthesizing prior learnings.

Types of Movement

Fundamental Movements

The basic ways in which human beings move include walking, jumping, skipping, and so on. In music class, usually all the children will be doing the same motor activity while singing or listening to music. Moving in any of these fundamental ways while producing or listening to music indicates the ability to feel the steady pulse. Some children may need more than one year of primary music instruction to develop this skill.

The order in which these fundamental movements should be introduced and included in music instruction is based on the difficulty of coordinating them to music. The easiest fundamental movement is walking, followed by jumping, running, skipping, galloping, and hopping. There are many ways to develop the feeling of pulse necessary for these movements, beginning with echoing simple patting movements on the body while saying a verbal cue ("Head, head, shoulders, shoulders, knees, knees," and so on) and then progressing to putting that feeling in the feet and stepping in place. Children need to succeed with simple movements and simple verbal cues before they are asked to use the movements to respond to music.

Three of these fundamental movements are particularly difficult for many mainstreamed children. When you want youngsters to skip or gallop to a song in 6/8 meter, be prepared to suggest a simpler alternative such as walking or running for children who are not at the same motor level as their age-mates. Similarly, many developmentally delayed youngsters have a very difficult time hopping on one foot, so you can tell the class that jumping is another way to move to the music.

Every primary music lesson should include some type of movement, and in Kindergarten and first grade, the fundamental movements should be stressed. Many movement specialists believe that children should initially explore their own personal tempo before they are asked to move to an established pulse. You can include beginning movement experiences in Kindergarten instruction by giving each child an opportunity to walk her or his own beat. As the child walks, the class can begin to softly pat the child's beat on their knees. You can also translate the child's pulse onto a tub or hand drum.

Another way to incorporate these basic movements is to include walking or hopping or jumping the beat when reviewing a familiar song at the beginning of a lesson. Many songs stress these movements: "If You're Happy and You Know It" tells children to clap their hands, jump up and down, step in place, and so on. "Greeting" songs, which can be used as lesson openers, require children to walk with the beat and greet a new partner (for example, "Hello, There" in Figure 7.3). You can ask children to make fundamental movements to rhythm patterns you play on a tub drum or other rhythm instruments, to simple piano pieces or improvisations, or to recordings.

143

CHAPTER 7
Experiencing Music
Through Moving:
Primary and
Intermediate

Structured Movements

Any of the fundamental movements can be incorporated into simple or intricate patterns to accompany songs or recorded music. The movements can range from walking in a circle and changing direction to intricate folk dances in intermediate grades. All these movements are teacher-directed, and every child is doing the same movement.

Organized patterns of movement reinforce many musical concepts, including with steady pulse and simple rhythm patterns as well as melodic register and direction. Young children need an opportunity to move to the beat in some manner with every song they have learned. Begin with patting or clapping. When children are relatively successful, the pulse can be "put" into their feet in different fundamental movements, such as stepping or marching. Combined movements, such as stepping the steady beat and clapping the melodic rhythm, come last.

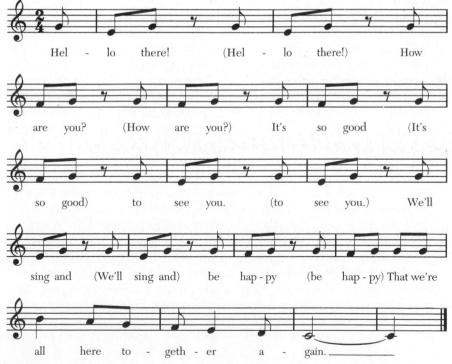

FIGURE 7.3.

If you have a clear purpose for using a particular song in your lesson, you can easily find a way to reinforce the musical idea through movement. If a particular pattern, such as quarter and two eighths, is the focus, the children can walk the pulse in a circle and put the pattern in their feet or hands when it occurs. If part of the song has an ascending or descending melodic phrase, the class can join hands and step a circle on the beat, moving their hands upward or downward when the song ascends or descends. If your focus is phrases, the children can use fundamental movements and change their movement at the beginning of each phrase. Many children, even in intermediate grades, need multiple concrete experiences in "doing" a form before they truly develop an understanding of phrase, binary, ternary, or rondo construction.

Intermediate children are capable of more elaborate combinations of movements. They enjoy learning and creating both hand and foot jives (formalized combinations of movements for hands, arms, fingers, and feet, as well as whole body movements such as jumps and turns). For an easy intermediate activity, you can have students create a hand jive with two distinct parts to show the two contrasting phrases of a song. A more advanced assignment would be to create a hand and foot jive that illustrates the changing character of a piece in rondo form. These activities require the students to synthesize many types of musical learnings and create a unique product. They also exemplify cooperative learning in that students must share and refine their understandings of the concepts involved to complete the task.

An effective way to engage students in creative movement activities is to assign them to groups. Group work allows for an exciting interchange of ideas and gives students the opportunity to explain their musical understandings to each other in ways that a teacher-led class discussion could not. Although the task may be to create a hand jive, the students will engage in actual musical decisions to fulfill the assignment. They will have to decide how many beats each section has, where the character of the sections changes, and how to explain this to each other. Creating dancelike movement patterns holds value for intermediate students; it allows them to draw on their many hours spent watching MTV, and it is a small way of bringing the world of "real" music into the classroom.

You will find numerous suggestions for structured movements in music series textbooks, but don't limit your use of movement to those suggestions. Each time you teach a lesson, think of ways to reinforce the musical learning with movement. For example, in a follow-up listening lesson using "Kutambarara" from the Kronos Quartet's CD *Pieces of Africa* (see p. 130), which consists of numerous repetitions of the same theme, you can direct children to choose two fundamental movements to use with the steady pulse, changing the movement on each repetition. Another listening might focus on the melodic rhythm, using the same type of movement reinforcement. You should also investigate the many excellent suggestions found in *Rhythm and Movement* by Elsa Findlay.[1] The book is organized by musical elements, and it includes extensive lists of movement activities which range from very simple to very

[1]Elsa Findlay (1971). *Rhythm and Movement*: Applications of Dalcroze Eurythmics. Evanston, IL: Summy-Birchard.

complex. Other sources for more structured folk dances, Phyllis Weikart's *Rhythmically Moving* recordings, are available from High/Scope Press in Ypsilanti, Michigan.

Structured folk dances are an excellent means of exploring and experiencing the nature of different cultures, and children love to learn them in music class. There may be adults in your community who are willing to share their knowledge of traditional dance with you and your students. Invite such individuals to meet with you before they come to your class so that you can help them to tailor their teaching to your students' ability level. If this initial experience with the adult dance expert proves to be exciting, you may want to explore the possibility of involving this adult in an entire day or week of folk dance so that all your students can benefit. You may even want to team up with the physical education teacher and offer combined music and gym classes for a day or a week, providing each class with a double period of folk dance where they would ordinarily have separate gym and music classes. Integrating the content of music and physical education classes is a small step toward helping children see the connections between the ideas they've mastered in seemingly disparate subject areas.

Creative Movement

Children can invent movements to express their understanding of what they hear. When children are asked to originate movements to songs or music, they often appear confused or indecisive. You may be disappointed when you ask children to create their own movements, only to see some class members imitate a child who is using a fundamental movement while others stand still and appear uninvolved. This reaction is due to a lack of prior movement opportunities and indicates that you need to provide your students with a basic movement repertoire.

Creative movement should be organized around a planned sequence of instruction with the four movement qualities of weight, space, time, and flow. When students have been introduced to each of these qualities, they can gradually begin to combine them and devise original movements that express what they hear and feel. Each movement quality can be introduced effectively with examples of opposites (light/heavy, narrow/wide, slow/fast, sustained/stop), initially without sound, then accompanied by unpitched instruments, and finally with music.

The quality of weight is expressed through light and heavy or strong and weak movements. First ask primary children to imagine an object or animal that moves lightly and to imitate the movement. Then explore the opposite quality in a similar manner. An important aspect of this initial activity is establishing the acceptance of all possibilities—there is no "right" way to move lightly or heavily. After children have explored many possibilities using fingertips, arms, legs, feet, and the entire body, you should add light and heavy sounds on a single instrument. Then you can use two contrasting instrument sounds, such as a tub drum and finger cymbals, and have the class indicate which they hear through movement. Or you can ask the children to listen to music with dynamic contrasts which you improvise on the piano, initially listening and deciding and then moving.

The quality of space can be experienced through the contrasts of up/down, narrow/wide, or in/out. Young children respond best initially to imitating the movement of an animal or object, but intermediate children should consider the ways to use this space while learning movement vocabulary. In addition, they can be challenged to incorporate ways of moving in space using more abstract vocabulary, such as *growing, spreading, exploding,* and so on. This sequence—movement exploration without sound, the addition of simple sounds, and then using the movements to demonstrate musical changes in qualities such as register or dynamics—can be used in both primary and intermediate classes, depending upon the children's background in movement.

The movement qualities of time and flow are very helpful in reinforcing musical learning. You can easily introduce time (slow/fast) in music lessons that focus on tempo. Ask young children to imitate the falling of autumn leaves at different tempi and then use the same movements or new ones when you play a maraca or a triangle, as if they are responding to the changes in the wind. You can then ask children to create movements to represent changes in tempi when you play improvisations on the piano or a xylophone. Intermediate children can demonstrate contrasts in tempo in an activity where they choose three words from a list (*drip, slither, bounce, float, glide, scamper,* and so on), decide on an order, practice in groups, and then share their movement compositions with their classmates. Their compositions can accompany teacher-selected sounds or sounds they choose themselves.

Flow (sustained/stop) is an expressive movement quality that relates to musical duration as well as to different articulations. Primary children can easily imitate moving through honey or glue; then, as they listen to a flowing piece such as "Aquarium" from *Carnival of the Animals* by Saint-Saëns, they can think about how they will move. With adequate preparation, children can create their own movements. Older children often find sustained flow more difficult, especially if they have not had numerous movement experiences in the primary years. One way to overcome their self-consciousness is to give them an object such as a 3-foot piece of crepe paper to move in a flowing fashion and then have them translate that movement into their bodies.

Children who have had continual experience in movement can often skip one or more of the steps in the movement sequence. Part of your job as a teacher is to monitor your classes carefully and decide when you think children have had enough preparatory experiences with the movement qualities so that they are comfortable with their own bodies and the space around them. Then they will be able to create original movements as a response to music. If you treat this aspect of music class as a natural and important means of expression, the children you teach will be empowered to move in creative ways to what they hear. We know that becoming a competent improviser in the jazz idiom requires a facility with a specific set of scales and patterns; similarly, becoming creative in movement requires experiences in a comfortable repertoire of motions and gestures.

Movement as Affective Response

In order for a musical movement activity to be more than just a rote exercise, students need opportunities to respond to the expressive nature of a piece rather than its component musical elements. An understanding of the musical elements is important, but it is not the end of music instruction; rather, it is a means to comprehending the musical import of any music. For movement to become an affective response, one in which the student is engaged intellectually, emotionally, and physically, you must focus the student's attention on the expressive nature of the music. Simply stated, you must lead each child to those qualities in each musical example that make it what it is.

147

CHAPTER 7
Experiencing Music
Through Moving:
Primary and
Intermediate

For example, after having the class listen for and move to a particular musical element within a piece, engage the children further in the same piece by asking them to match the quality of their movements to a quality or characteristic of the piece. Instead of leaving "Fanfare for the Common Man" after working on movements that illustrate changes in timbre, do the movements in a way that embraces the overall character of the piece: majestically, forcefully, expectantly, and with strength. If you have had children listen to different sections of *Carnival of the Animals* and develop movements that illustrate the melodic direction in "Kangaroos" or "Aquarium," be sure that you also allow time to explore the expressive ways that the melodic direction is unique in each section. The quick, jumpy nature of the ascending and descending melody of the "Kangaroo" section needs to be illustrated with very different movements than the smooth, flowing descending melodic lines heard in "Aquarium."

Movement and Classroom Management

Effective teachers give precise directions, provide children with a sense of security, and impart a sense of purpose. These competencies are essential when incorporating movement in a music period. Precise directions should begin when a class appears at your music room door. The children should be told how to enter the room and where you want them to sit. Wait until every child is in the room before you move so that you can watch the entire class and will not have your back to children for any length of time. You should begin speaking when you follow the class so not a single second is lost during the music period.

All children (and adults) feel most secure when they know exactly what is expected. You establish a sense of security through the use of clearly worded directions and consistent expectations. Carefully plan the transitions before and after movement activities so that valuable teaching time is not wasted. As you plan your lesson, decide exactly what you will say in order to organize the children moving about the room. Word your directions so that every child understands exactly what to do. If you want them not to talk when they move, tell them this. If you want each child in their own space, define what this means. You may want to limit the amount of time that children have to find a space or join hands in a circle—for example, count out loud to five. Specific and clear directions restrict the time spent in preparation and maximize the time for movement and music.

Music lessons can include movement activities even if there is not a separate music space and classes are held in the regular classroom. You can move a few desks and chairs or use an open space in the room so that a few children can move at the same time. It is important that the remainder of the class simultaneously participate in music making so that they are not merely spectators waiting their turn. Children who are not moving can accompany with song or instruments, or they can watch and decide when a contrast occurs, showing you with a "thumbs up" hand movement. Plan for ways to actively engage every child during every minute of the entire period, whether you have a separate music room or not.

It is also important that students know why their movement is a part of the lesson. What may seem very clear to you as you plan may not necessarily be clear to your students. Instead of directing children to change the direction they walk on the refrain, point out that the song changes and that is why the class is going to walk (or skip or hop) in a different direction now. In order to avoid the self-consciousness that older children often exhibit in movement activities, you must tie your purpose for movement intimately to the lesson, and carefully and enthusiastically explain and direct the activity. Never forget the importance of a clear instructional purpose and high behavioral expectations—the two concepts are embedded in good teaching at all levels.

Dalcroze Approach

The work of Émile Jaques-Dalcroze has found a secure place in the pedagogical foundations of American music education. Certain features of the Dalcroze approach are commonly found in the teaching repertoire of elementary general music teachers. When Dalcroze (1865–1950) began teaching at the Geneva Conservatoire in 1892 as a professor of harmony, he realized that his students' performances were not musically expressive because their senses of pitch and rhythm were sorely lacking. Dalcroze responded by developing a methodology for teaching music to students based on the idea that musical response is essentially a physical one. He believed that a musician knows and feels music internally and through the body:

> The important thing, as one cannot repeat too often, is that the child should learn to feel music, to absorb it, to give his [sic] body and soul to it; to listen to it not merely with his ear but with his whole being.[2]

His three-part method of musical training included solfège, improvisation, and rhythmic movement or *eurhythmics*, the best-known feature of his work. Eurhythmics relies on the body to interpret and express rhythms musically and correctly. The following list of some titles from Dalcroze's 22 movement exercises is included here to give readers a sense of the wide variety of activities Dalcroze proposed as essential to train "body, ear, and mind."[3]

1. Exercises in muscular relaxation and breathing
2. Metrical division and accentuation
3. Metrical memorization

---

[2]Émile Jaques-Dalcroze (1921). *Rhythm, Music and Education.* Translated from the French by H. F. Rubenstein. New York: Putnam, p. 98.
[3]Dalcroze, pp. 121–130.

149

CHAPTER 7
Experiencing Music
Through Moving:
Primary and
Intermediate

4. Rapid conception of bar-time by the eye and ear
5. Conception of rhythms by muscular sense
6. Exercises in concentration. Creation of mental hearing and rhythms
7. Exercises in corporal balance and to produce continuity of movement
8. Realization of musical note-values
9. Division of beats
10. Immediate realization by the body of musical rhythm
11. Double and triple speed and slowness of movements
12. Exercises in notation of rhythms
13. Exercises in improvisation (cultivation of imaginative faculties)
14. Conducting rhythms
15. Execution of rhythms by several groups of pupils (initiation into musical phrasing)

Two important resources provide useful materials for implementing Dalcroze eurhythmics in the general music classroom. The first is the Elsa Findlay book cited earlier in this chapter, *Rhythm and Movement: Application of Dalcroze Eurhythmics.* Findlay presents extensive suggestions for classroom activities designed to take children through a wide variety of movement concepts in order to teach them musical elements. The second resource is a set of two audiotapes and a booklet by Robert M. Abramson, *Rhythm Games for Perception and Cognition.* Abramson has organized an extensive collection of rhythm games to teach the musical concepts of tempo, dynamics, accent, and rests: they allow the student to progress "from moving in place to moving in space, and from movement involving isolated body parts to movement involving their entire body."[4] The games are intended to be used with musical accompaniment, which Abramson provides through the companion audiotapes, although they can be done with simple percussion accompaniment as well. Abramson also has available a useful videotape (GIA Publications, 7404 South Mason Ave., Chicago, Illinois, 60638) that introduces the concept of Dalcroze eurhythmics as he teaches it at the Manhattan School of Music. These resources will help you integrate movement comfortably into your students' experience and will provide an important way for them to respond to music.

TEACHING SCRIPTS

The following teaching scripts illustrate ways to incorporate both movement and musical behaviors and material from previous lessons. Practice Scripts 3 and 4 with several different groups of children so that you can improve your classroom management skills and focus on the important interactions between teacher and learners.

[4]Robert M. Abramson (1978). *Rhythm Games for Perception and Cognition.* Volkwein, p. 2.

Script 3 (Primary)

GRADE LEVEL: Kindergarten/Grade One
MUSICAL CONCEPT: Rhythm
MUSICAL ELEMENT: Steady beat
LESSON OBJECTIVE: Students will be able to pass a ball and move to demonstrate
an understanding of steady beat at two different tempi.
MATERIALS: "Bird Songs" (Figure 7.4); hand drum and mallet.

STEP ONE

**I'd like you to listen to a song I just learned and see if you can tell me what
it's about when I've finished singing.**

Sing the song expressively, using dynamic shaping of phrases and exemplary articulation.

Who can tell me what the song was about?

Take answers.

How many different birds were there in my song?

*If no one can tell, sing it again and have the children count birds on their fingers as
you sing each verse.*

This time as I sing it, I'd like you all to join in when I point to you. Ready?

*Teach the song by rote, pointing to yourself when you sing and to them when they
are to sing.*

Bird Songs

Traditional

FIGURE 7.4.
Reprinted by permission of D. C. Heath and Company

I'm now going to hit the hand drum five times, and on the fifth hit, I'd like each of you to be seated in a big circle on the floor. Ready? Here we go. One, two, three, four, five!

(Beat the drum as you count.) If some students aren't in place and seated by the fifth hit, have the whole class try it again, explaining that it is important to listen carefully and move with the drum.

Let's try to sing the first verse of the song, and this time we'll pat our legs to show the steady beat of the song.

Begin with "Ready, sing" and sing only the first verse.

We showed the steady beat with our patting this time. Can we stand up and show it in our feet this time? Let's walk around the circle and step the steady beat this time as we sing the first verse. Everyone put your right hand in the air.

Model which hand is the right by putting your right hand in the air.

Let's all turn to the right and be ready to step the steady beat as we sing.

When all have turned to the right and are facing the same direction, give the pitch on "Ready, sing" and begin the first verse.

Let's try it again, only this time I'd like everyone to stop moving each time we get to the part where the robin sings, and then move again until the robin sings the second time. Here we go.

Model the correct way to move and stop while carefully monitoring the class. Some students will not stop moving, even though they see others standing still while the robin sings. You may need to have these students stand still during the entire verse and watch those who are doing it correctly. Then have those who were having trouble join hands with a "correct" partner and try the verse again. This technique is called peer teaching, but young children regard it as simply helping each other.

What other movements could we do during the moving part that would show the steady beat?

Try several.

Which of these movements seemed most like a robin? Let's think up some ways to show the steady beat that we could use for the other verses, one way each for the cuckoo and the great owl.

Try several and evaluate them.

I'd like each of you to find your own space now by the time I've hit the hand drum three times. Remember: Your own space is a spot in the room where, if you turn around with your arms out at your sides, you won't touch anybody or anything. Ready? One, two, three.

Monitor "own space" and motion children who are crowded to a better space.

Now that we're all in our own spaces, can someone show me one way to move in place? I'll count to three, and while I'm counting, move in place just one way, using your arms. One, two, three.

Monitor moving in place, noticing differences in types of movement.

Now, try to move another part of your body this time, and make it move in the space above you. Ready? One, two, three.

*Monitor movements and draw attention to particularly creative ones by inviting chil-
dren to show the entire class their movement.*

**I'll bet you can find another way to move in place, this time using more
than one part of your body and moving in the space around you. Ready?
One, two, three.**

**I'm now going to play some music at the piano, and I want you to listen
to it carefully and move any way you like to show me that you hear the
steady beat. Sometimes the speed of the steady beat will change, but I want
you to still move in ways that show it to me. When the music stops, I want
you to freeze in your position.**

*Improvise a variety of tempi, interspersing lento and presto between mainly andante
sections. Use the entire range of the keyboard. Vary the tonality from major to minor,
and vary dynamic levels as well.*

**What can you tell me about how the music moved? I saw a lot of different
kinds of movements. You showed me that you can follow the steady beat in
music even when the tempo changes or when the dynamic level changes.**

Script 4 (Intermediate)

GRADE LEVEL: Grade Five/Six

MUSICAL CONCEPT: Form

SPECIFIC ELEMENT: Phrases contain different textures.

LESSON OBJECTIVE: Students will be able to demonstrate a recognition of thin and
thick texture through mapping and movement.

MATERIALS: The Kronos Quartet's CD *Pieces of Africa*; a CD player (or
tape the selection three times); blank paper; markers.

STEP ONE

(Use this lesson after teaching Script 3 from Chapter 5, p. 130). Pass out one
piece of paper and one marker per student and assign students to groups
of four.

**Who can remember the differences between the two pieces of African
music we heard last time?**

*Solicit answers leading to the idea that the first piece was very short and the second
piece was longer and had three sections.*

**Today we're going to make a map of the first short piece, and then we are
going to translate our map. Does anyone know what that means—to translate something?**

*If there is no response, say a short phrase in another language—such as "Bonjour,
mes petites"—to illustrate the idea of translating from one language to another.*

**What we are going to do, then, is to make such a careful map of this short
piece that we can use it as a guide to make movements that show us what
is happening in the music. As we listen this first time, think about the music
and decide how to make a map that shows what you hear.**

Play the music.

Now put a small *s* on your paper to show the start, and draw a map as we listen again.

153

CHAPTER 7
Experiencing Music
Through Moving:
Primary and
Intermediate

> *After listening one time, ask if the students need to hear the music again to add more to their maps; if so, replay the music.*

Now, in your group, put the four maps side by side and decide in one minute which map will be best to use to translate into movements.

> *You may need to show several maps that are very simplistic, such as one with dozens of arcs versus one with different shapes, lines, and so on. Ask the children which map would be more interesting to translate and which one shows more about the sounds in the music.*

Now, while we listen, look at the map your group chose. The person who made the map needs to show the group how the map fits the music.

> *Play the music.*

The next step is to decide which movements you will use to show what is happening in the music.

> *If the class has never done movement, let them remain seated for this activity. Let the class have about five minutes to practice.*

Now each group is going to share their movements, and the entire class is going to decide which one of the four maps the group made is the map that is being translated.

> *This focus takes some of the attention away from the movement aspect if the children are very self-conscious about moving. If they are not, just tell the groups to share their movements and display the map that is being interpreted. Play the music for each demonstration.*

Now I want us to look at the maps our first three groups used today. What did they show about the music? Can you tell where the music had only a few sounds and where there were many more sounds?

> *Elicit comments from the class based on these maps—add more if needed.*

When we hear music like the beginning of this song, we say that the music has "thin texture." At the end of the song, the texture is "thick." Which of these maps shows this idea best?

> *Lead the discussion, relating the maps to how groups moved—with one or two or many movements.*

STUDENT ASSIGNMENTS

1. Use the following format to evaluate the in-class peer teaching you do for this chapter. Checklists in previous chapters contained simple yes/no choices: this one includes space for you to make more extensive comments about each aspect of the teaching you watched. Remember to be as specific as you can about ways to address areas that need improvement. Phrase your comments in a positive, collegial way that would make *you* want to try the suggestions offered.

   I. Classroom Management:

  II. Eye Contact:

 III. Clarity of Directions:

 IV. Levels of Questions Asked:

V. Teacher's Comfort Level:

VI. Overall Impression:

2. Add a movement activity to one of the scripts in a previous chapter. The activity should be designed to evaluate musical learning.

3. In a teacher's edition of one of the music series textbooks, find a lesson that does not include movement. Describe how you could add movement to this lesson in order to evaluate musical learning.

4. Develop an observation tool you can use to categorize children's movement skills. Explain how you can modify it for use with special learners.

Experiencing Music Through Playing Instruments:

PRIMARY AND INTERMEDIATE

Case Study

The second grade class is seated on the carpeted floor in a circle. Miss Davis begins by saying, "I'd like each of you to take a pair of rhythm sticks and place them on the floor in front of you without playing them. When you've put them on the floor, fold your hands in your lap." She's holding a large can of rhythm sticks which she offers to each child as she moves around the circle. The children quickly have their hands folded in their laps and all eyes are on Miss Davis. She moves to the CD player and says, "I'd like each of you to listen to this piece of music. It has three sections, ABA. The A section is played by the piano, while the B section is sung by a single child. While you are listening, see if you can find the steady beat. If you can find the steady beat, show the steady beat by tapping two fingers of your right hand in your left palm like this." She demonstrates and the class tries it. She says, "Yes, I can see you all remember this quiet way to show the steady beat. Let's listen to the music now." As the class listens to the recording, some students begin to show the steady beat, but some watch with their hands in their laps and others begin to tap the rhythm of the melodic line. When the excerpt is finished, Miss Davis says, "I'd like each of you to pick up your rhythm sticks now, and as we listen this time, I'd like you to put

the steady beat into your rhythm sticks instead of tapping it in your palm." Some students keep the steady beat while others play the melodic rhythm. Thirty seconds into the excerpt, a boy raises his hand. Miss Davis walks up to him and he says, "This doesn't sound right. A lot of kids are playing it wrong." Miss Davis ignores him and continues to move around the circle while the music plays. As the music continues she says, "Soon the B section will begin, but when the A section returns, sing the piano part on 'loo' while you play the steady beat." As the B section begins, some children continue to play, others "shush" them loudly and try to grab their rhythm sticks, and others sing "loo." Several boys begin to use their rhythm sticks as swords, poking at each other and pretending to die on the carpet. Miss Davis stops the recording and says, "I want all the boys to put their rhythm sticks away, since you didn't follow classroom rules about use of instruments." Boys who were not involved in the swordplay protest loudly.

YOUR COOPERATIVE TASK

1. Make a list of crucial points in the lesson segment when Miss Davis could have positively influenced the direction of the class.

2. In a small group, brainstorm at least three

different ways Miss Davis could have more clearly said what she wanted the children to do each time she gave directions. Decide which your group prefers, and report your decision to the class.

3. Make a list of all the classroom management moves made by Miss Davis, and then rate them as either successful or lacking. For each "lack-ing" move, propose an alternative way to deal with the group. Present your list to the class.

4. Explain to a partner the lesson planning issues you see in this scenario. Use the following concepts as a starting point for your discussion: musical concepts, review of previously learned material, and evaluation of student learning.

5. Discuss the gender issues raised in this scenario.

PRACTICE TEACHING SCRIPTS

Practice the following script with your peers and with children. As you practice a lesson presentation, be alert to the differences in individual responses in each class. This awareness is the beginning of real teaching. After you are comfortable with *what* you are teaching, you can observe individual responses and respond to them.

Script 1 (Primary)

GRADE LEVEL: Grades One and Two
MUSICAL CONCEPT: Rhythm
SPECIFIC ELEMENT: Music contains a steady beat.
LESSON OBJECTIVE: Students will be able to sing a song and play a beat-keeping game; they will be able to use instruments to show the steady beat.
MATERIALS: "Daa, Daa Kente" (Figure 3.9, p. 57); alto xylophones and mallets; six 4-inch yarn puffs; three rhythm patterns written on the board (see Step Two).

STEP ONE

I'm going to hum a song you already know, and I want each of you to join me in humming when you recognize it.

Hum the song and note who is joining, who is not.

Who can tell me something about the song—its name, the country it's from, what it's about?

Call on children who raise their hands, and listen to responses.

STEP TWO

You remembered a lot about that song. We can add an accompaniment to that song from the Twi people of Ghana. Who remembers what an accompaniment is?

Take a few answers to see what the children remember, offering the right answer only if no one else can provide it.

Let's accompany our singing by patting our thighs like this.

Pat your thighs, alternating left and right hands and keeping the steady beat.

Join with me: One, two, ready, sing.

Sing with the class.

Now that you've done such a good job of keeping the steady beat in your patting, let's add instruments. I have three patterns on the board, and I'd like you to look at them with me.

Students look at the patterns you have listed on the boards.

1. C G C G
2. G G G G
3. G G G
   C C C *(quarter rest)*

Let's try playing each of these in the air now. Remember to start with your left hand and alternate hands as you go.

Model the correct way to play the pattern by mirroring. In other words, if the children are to use left-right-left-right for the first pattern, you face them and model right-left-right-left.

Now I need three volunteers to play these different parts for me.

Choose three students and send them to the instruments. The instruments should be set up so that the groups are next to each other in a semicircle and will be easy to cue and conduct.

Group 1 will play the C-G pattern when I point to them. Find your notes, group 1, and set your mallets up so you're ready.

Have the whole class practice in the air. Then have the players try the pattern as you cue. You may need to cue when to begin and also "play" your invisible xylophone in the air to help the students keep the steady beat and alternate playing hands. Follow the same procedure for the next two groups of players (or individuals). Then try to put the song and accompaniment together. The players should not sing; however, they should be encouraged to listen to the words and melody of the song.

Well, what happened? Can someone tell me how that sounded?

Encourage a variety of answers, and expect children to offer their reasons for their comments. You may need to ask more specific questions of the instrumentalists: "How difficult was it to follow my conducting and still look at your instruments?

Let's have three more volunteers go to the instruments and have the current player show you what to do.

Send new players to the instruments and wait a minute so the former players can explain the task to the new players. Repeat the procedure.

This time, when we sing and play "Daa, Daa Kente," I'd like the rest of you to keep the steady beat for us by playing a passing game. I'm going to beat this hand drum three times, and when the third beats stops sounding, I want each of you to be seated in a circle on the floor. Ready, set, here we go!

Play the drum and see if everyone is seated correctly after the third beat. If not, you may want to have the children return to their original positions and try it again, stressing that if they listen carefully and move quickly, all the students can find a place in the circle.

Now, in Ghana, the passing game is played with a stone or an empty soda can. We are going to use this yarn puff and pass it around the circle on the steady beat. The puff needs to stay on the floor in front of you until you pick it up and put it on the floor in front of the person on your left on the beat. Let's practice passing on the steady beat while the xylophones play their parts for us. I'll conduct the instruments while the people in the circle pass the puff to their left. One, two, ready, go!

Monitor passing, and help if children are having trouble remembering which direction is left.

Now let's put it all together. The circle people will sing and pass, and I'll help the instrumentalists play their parts. We should see the puff landing on the floor on the steady beat. I'll give you four preparatory beats this time. Any questions before we try this? OK, let's begin. One, two, ready, sing!

Repeat this after asking the children what elements they can improve with another attempt. You may want to ask for a new set of volunteers to play instruments, or you can split the class into smaller groups for the passing game so that each students gets more opportunities to pass the puff. Groups of four or five are ideal. After the second performance, ask students to explain the differences between the two performances, prompting them with questions:

How did using the puff help you understand the idea of steady beat? Can those of you who played the instruments tell us how playing the steady beat was different from passing the puff around the circle.

Allow students to ask you questions about the lesson, too.

Script 2 (Intermediate)

GRADE LEVEL: Grades Five and Six

MUSICAL CONCEPT: Rhythm

SPECIFIC ELEMENT: Syncopation

LESSON OBJECTIVE: Students will be able to demonstrate an ability to perform syncopated rhythms by playing instruments.

MATERIALS: "Emma" (Figure 4.14, p. 88); unpitched rhythm instruments (at least four of wood and four of metal and a third contrasting set, such as hand drums).

STEP ONE

Use the echo clapping warm-up described in Chapter 4 Script 1 (p. 88). Then lead the class in a rhythm canon that includes four-beat patterns that incorporate syncopation. Begin the rhythm canon process by clapping four beats and then continuing to the next four-beat pattern with no rest. Students begin after four beats, and as they clap they watch and listen to the next four beats so they can continue also. If the class has never participated in this activity, try two or three measures and then stop. If the children are familiar with the activity, include varied body sounds and hand movements in addition to clapping (patting head, patting shoulders, stamping feet, etc.).

STEP TWO

Teach "Emma" as described in Chapter 4 Script 2 (p. 88) if the students do not know the song. If they already know the song, review it once. Introduce the song review by playing it on the piano and asking students to identify the title.

We are going to focus on this word today.

Write the word syncopation *on the board.*

Can someone demonstrate what this word means with a pattern that we can all echo?

Have several children offer a short pattern for the class to echo. After each pattern,

159

CHAPTER 8
Experiencing Music
Through Playing
Instruments:
Primary and
Intermediate

discuss whether it included syncopation. If the pattern included syncopation, write the pattern on the board. Collect at least three syncopated patterns before continuing the lesson.

STEP THREE

Today we're going to write and perform a rhythm score. When conductors lead a band or orchestra or chorus, they have in front of them music that includes all the parts that everyone is playing. That music is called a score. So we are going to play several rhythm parts at the same time. Our score is going to be on the board, and we are going to use the rhythms that you just used as well as the rhythm from "Emma."

Put a four-measure rhythm on the board or overhead projector; include the pattern used in "Emma" in one measure. Make the other measures fairly simple, with eighths and quarters.

I want you to look at the first line of our score and hold up your fingers to show the number of the measure that includes the rhythm from "Emma."

If the students are not successful, have them clap all four measures as you point them out. If they are not successful, echo-clap each measure and then ask the class to show the number.

Now I am going to write another line of the score and use one of the rhythms you used earlier.

Write another four-measure rhythm directly under the first, but be sure to put the syncopated measure under a measure with no syncopation. Follow the same process, having children identify the syncopated rhythm and practice the entire line.

Before we add instruments to our score, we need to be able to perform the two lines of rhythm at the same time.

Divide the class into two parts. Have each section clap their rhythm alone and then have the class perform the two rhythms simultaneously.

Now we need to add instruments. Since we are going to add more lines, we want to have only a few instruments on these two parts.

Point to the unpitched instruments you selected for this lesson.

Which instrument should we use for the first line?

Pass out no more than three or four instruments. Have the entire class clap the rhythm while the instrument players rehearse their part.

Now think carefully about the sound of the first instrument. Which instrument should we use for the second line so we will clearly hear the two different rhythms?

Try several suggestions, and have the class decide which instruments give the best sound contrast. Divide the class in half again, and have each group accompany the instrument players with soft clapping and then perform two lines simultaneously. If the class is successful, add one or two more lines to the score, following the same process.

Have the instrument players for the first line return their instruments, then those for the second line.

That was excellent rhythm reading and playing today. Next time we have music class we will work in groups and write our own rhythm score.

Why Teach Instrument Playing?

Since the dawn of time, musical instruments have been part of human culture the world over. From simple percussive soundmakers to musical instrument digital interface (MIDI) keyboards, human beings have always found a way to create musical sounds that delight and satisfy. Even in our electrically powered technoculture, where people are often surrounded by musical sounds most of their day, individual enjoyment of music through playing instruments is still an important life experience at any age. The current sales figures of electronic keyboards and guitars stand as testimony to this fact, as do the plethora of garage rock bands. In addition, summer community bands and year-round community bands and orchestras attest to the value of musical performing for participants of all ages.

Playing musical instruments is a vital and important way to engage children in musical experiences that simultaneously increase their enjoyment of music and their musical understanding. Indeed, the verb that describes what we do with instruments, *play*, implies not only the action of producing sounds but the idea that making music is fun, not work. The addition of instruments to any song keeps children interested, extends the number of repetitions they can perform, and provides more time and opportunities for every class member to assimilate the musical idea that is being taught. The musical possibilities of classroom instruments are endless, and any musical concept can be further refined and reinforced through playing an instrument.

Children's affective knowing is enhanced by exploring a variety of instruments and hearing all the timbre contrasts possible in a single instrument. Children need to explore, assimilate, and enjoy the different sounds they can make on a xylophone when they use mallets with different heads, or the different sounds they can make on a conga drum by tapping it with fingers on the edge or striking it in the middle with the palm of the hand. These exciting contrasts are an important addition to the quality of sound produced by a group of children singing, and they help to extend and refine children's musical experience.

Playing instruments in the general music class is an important form of musical participation that allows each child to know the feeling of making musical sounds as a soloist and as part of an ensemble. And as in any ensemble, the difficulty of the parts can be set so that each class member can participate successfully. Children who are gifted and children who are developmentally delayed derive equal pleasure from playing instruments, and this musical activity can easily be adapted to accommodate the wide range of abilities found in every class. Every child, therefore, can participate in procedural, kinesthetic, and affective musical knowing when engaged as an instrumental performer.

Playing instruments is fun, after all, and play is essential to the mental health of both children and adults. A valued and sequential music curriculum lies at the heart of all general music instruction, but the affective quality of the musical encounter makes it imperative that classroom experiences be as engaging as possible. All children learn best when they are actively involved in the process, and the addition of classroom instruments to a well-planned and well-executed lesson never fails to entice children further into the musical experience.

161

CHAPTER 8
Experiencing Music
Through Playing
Instruments:
Primary and
Intermediate

Instrumental accompaniments and ensembles are popular additions to performance programs. Parents and administrators respond well to accomplished performances by children, and the instrumental playing need not be complicated to elicit this response. The sheer delight that children exhibit while performing reinforces for parents the worth of the school music program. In addition, current educational restructuring focuses on the value of "outcome-based" and "performance-based" education—just what music education has always been! Public performances can validate the music classroom experience and present what children have accomplished and learned in a delightful way.

Classroom Instruments

Children love to play instruments! When you ask for volunteers to perform any type of instrumental accompaniment, you will have a sea of hands waving at you. Indeed, a recent survey by Bowles of the music classroom activities preferred by over 2000 children found that the most preferred of 13 music classroom activities was playing instruments.[1] Because instrument playing is a favored activity, you must be very careful to provide equal playing opportunities for all children in each class. It is essential that you devise an efficient way of determining whose turn is next. One suggestion is to make a set of cards for each class, with a card for each child's name, and use two envelopes to keep track of which children have had a turn. Put the classroom teacher's name on the envelopes. You can decorate the envelopes attractively with musical symbols and staple them above the blackboard or on a bulletin board. To select who has the next turn, take a card from the top envelope, read the child's name, and put that card in the bottom envelope. When all the cards are in the bottom envelope, transfer the entire set to the top envelope. This method is much more efficient and effective than keeping class checklists, and children think it is "really fair!"

Introductory Exploration

Primary children should have ample opportunity to experiment with sounds and the way sounds are produced. Classroom instrument exploration should begin with common materials (wood, plastic, glass, metal) and ways of producing sound (scratching, hitting, shaking). One effective way to direct this type of exploration is to ask children to classify sets of sound sources that look identical but make different sounds. For example, three identical yogurt or margarine cups can contain the same material (rice, stones, sugar, or metal nuts and bolts), or two can contain the same thing and one can have different contents. You can use 35-millimeter film canisters, oatmeal boxes, ice cream

[1]Chelcy Bowles (1992). "Music Classroom Activity Preferences of Elementary School Children." Presented at the Music Educators National Conference, Research Poster Session, New Orleans.

containers, and so on. In addition, some sets should contain three containers that look different, but two should make the same the sound. What is important is the opportunity for each child to manipulate and listen to the contents of a small set in order to classify the sounds. Such an activity can be organized with pairs of children and sets of sound materials placed all around the room.

Instruments should be introduced to primary children individually and carefully. After naming the instrument, demonstrate the correct holding and playing technique. Your introduction should set a tone of respect for the care and playing of each instrument. Even the youngest child will respect classroom instruments when you present them as an authentic means of producing musical sounds.

Categories of Instruments

Unpitched Instruments

Unpitched instruments range from the ordinary, such as wood sticks, triangle, or tambourine, to the more exotic, such as the cabasa or agogo bells used in Latin American music. Each of these instruments provides a variety of sounds children should explore so they will become more and more sensitive to contrasts and gradations of timbre. Of course, the inclusion of instruments in any lesson also provides another means of reinforcing musical learning and experiencing musical expressivity.

WOOD. Wood sticks are brightly colored and are usually 14 inches long. They can be purchased in sets of smooth sticks only or in pairs with one smooth and one grooved stock, which is preferable because the players can produce another timbre. These inexpensive yet useful instruments can be used by Kindergartners to play a steady beat to a song or by sixth graders to play a rhythm score that includes complex patterns and changing meters.

A wood block is a solid rectangle about 8 inches long with a slit on the side that should be struck. The sounds produced vary depending upon the type of mallet head (wood, plastic, or rubber) that is used. They come in various sizes, and some companies sell wood blocks with attached handles.

Claves, which are shorter and thicker than wood sticks, are a Latin American accompaniment instrument. One clave should be held very lightly in a cupped hand (which acts as the sound chamber) by the fingertips. The other clave is also held lightly and should strike the held clave in the middle.

Sandpaper blocks are made with a wooden handle on one side and sandpaper on the other. One block is held still while the second block is brushed against it in rhythm.

There are also tone blocks and tick-tock blocks, in addition to wooden guiros, whips, and maracas. Wooden drums modeled on the slit log drum of Africa are also available; these come in varied sizes.

METAL. Two types of cymbals are available for classroom use, either small versions of crash cymbals or finger cymbals. When purchasing any kind of cymbal, try to buy the best, as the tone quality depends completely upon the metal alloy content. To play cymbals correctly, hold the left cymbal still and move the right cymbal up and down against it.

Triangles also come in a variety of sizes ranging from 3 to 8 inches. There are knob-type holders as well as longer handles designed for young children. The triangle should be struck either outside on the right or inside on the base of the triangle.

Tambourines can be purchased with or without heads, with single or double rows of jingles. They range from 6 1/2 to 10 inches in diameter. Be sure to buy tambourines that have skin heads, for the sake of durability as well as sound. To play the instrument correctly, hold it by the frame and tap it with your fingertips or a lightly clenched fist. Of course, you can also rotate the tambourine to produce a type of "roll" sound.

Other metal instruments include cowbells of varied sizes, jingle bells, and jingle clogs, which are metal discs mounted on a wooden handle.

MEMBRANOPHONES. Hand drums or tambours range from 10 to 16 inches in diameter. Always purchase drums that can be tuned. Cheaper drums may seem economical, but they can make a distressing "thud" after you return from summer vacation and hit one that has been sitting in a humid closet for two months. One of your first instrument investments should be a large tunable hand drum or redondo drum and a bass drum mallet; you can use these to lead movement activities exploring pulse, rhythm pattern, meter, and tempo.

Bongo drums are a pair of attached single-headed drums. You can buy sets that are not tunable, but your best investment is a set that can be tuned. Hold the bongos between your knees, with the larger of the set to the right, and play with the index and middle fingers of both hands.

The conga drum is also a single-headed drum, much larger than the bongos. It can be played between the knees or put on a stand. The authentic way to play the instrument is to sling it over your shoulder! The drum's function in Latin American music is to provide a bass-sounding steady pulse. To play the conga correctly, use the left hand to play the first and third beats lightly with the fingers; use the right hand to play the second beat at the edge of the drumhead with the fingers and the fourth beat in the middle with the palm of the hand.

Some undergraduate music education programs require general music students to take a course in percussion techniques. Such a course will be helpful for any music teacher and will give you confidence. If you understand correct playing technique, you can instill in children a respect for each instrument and a curiosity about sound production techniques and possibilities.

Pitched Instruments

METAL. Resonator bells come in sets of sized and chromatically labeled bars on either a hollow plastic or solid wooden base. Although bells with a wooden base are more durable, resonator bells with plastic resonator bases provide more access to vibration and are more useful if you teach children who are hearing-impaired. The sets come with a varied number of bells and range from a single diatonic C scale to a chromatic set of two octaves. Mallets are available with rubber or wooden heads. A most helpful device is a bell

163

CHAPTER 8
Experiencing Music
Through Playing
Instruments:
Primary and
Intermediate

stepladder (see Figure 8.1) upon which you can place bells in size and pitch order. Resonator bells are a standard classroom instrument that reinforce initial pitch concepts such as contrasts of register or direction, as well as the more advanced concepts of chord structure and scale construction.

Handbells come in chromatic sets of 25 or 37 bells, with or without carrying cases. Additional individual bells can also be purchased for other pitches. Tone chimes, a popular and more affordable adaptation of the handbell sound, are hand-held tubes with attached clappers. They come in chromatic sets,

FIGURE 8.1. Resonator bells and bell stepladder
Courtesy of Peripole-Bergerault, Inc., Salem, OR 97301

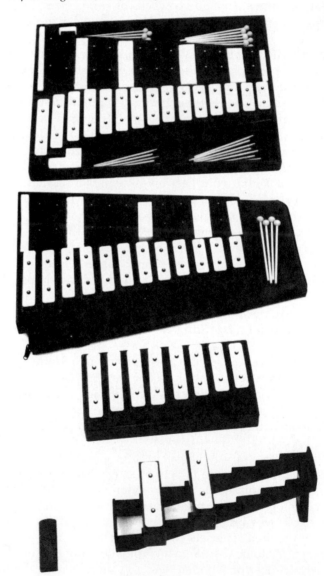

165

CHAPTER 8
*Experiencing Music
Through Playing
Instruments:
Primary and
Intermediate*

color-coded to match a piano keyboard, and each tone chime also has the note name on the bar. These bells cost approximately half as much as bronze handbells. Tone chimes should be considered an enrichment possibility for older children rather than a general classroom instrument. There are several reasons for this. It is difficult to play a single handbell note in the right place, and the sound is not as musically satisfying as a sustained tremolo block of sound. The physical skill of synchronizing rhythm and melody requires greater precision than the average general music student possesses. If you find the sound of these instruments appealing, a short course in handbell ringing will prepare you to incorporate these instruments in your music program.

Metallophones and glockenspiels are the two metal melody instruments used in an Orff instrumentarium. These instruments have detachable individual bars, which means that they can be used by your youngest students (when you remove all the bars except the few you wish them to play) as well as by your oldest students, whose motor control is more advanced. The instruments are diatonic, and separate sets of chromatic bars are available so you can convert the instrument to other keys. Glockenspiels are available in soprano and alto sizes, and the metallophones come in soprano, alto, and bass sizes. The instruments can be played when placed on the floor or on a low table, and you can buy commercial stands to position the instruments so children can play them while standing. Mallets with wooden or plastic heads are available for glockenspiels, and felt, wool-wrapped, or wood-wrapped ones with rubber heads are available for metallophones.

WOOD. Xylophones used in an Orff instrumentarium (Figure 8.2) come in three sizes—soprano, alto, and bass—and are similar in construction to the

FIGURE 8.2. Orff Instruments

Courtesy of MMB MUSIC
© 1994 Studio 49 Musikinstrumentenbau Gmblt. Used by permission. All rights reserved.

metallophones, except the bars are wooden. The sound is pleasant and light, and it quickly decays, in contrast to the long decay of the metallophone. Xylophones are played with felt, woolen, or plastic mallets. The correct mallet-holding position for all of these instruments is illustrated in Figure 8.3. The bars of all the instruments should be struck in the middle for the best sound.

Temple blocks consist of five different-sized wooden blocks mounted on a frame. They may be square or ornately carved into various rounded shapes. Temple blocks are played with either rubber, felt, or wooden mallets.

MEMBRANOPHONES. Tympani for an Orff instrumentarium are available in a variety of sizes with heads ranging from 10 to 28 inches. They can be purchased with skin or plastic heads (since the instruments are tunable, plastic heads are recommended). They are available in a cylindrical shape with adjustable legs or in a more expensive kettledrum shape.

AEROPHONES. Recorders are often used as a classroom instrument beginning in third grade. Plastic models are available at very moderate cost and are sometimes used by instrumental teachers in the grade that precedes beginning band and orchestra instrument instruction. There are only a few rules for playing a recorder:

1. Blow easily. (Breathe into the instrument!)
2. Use the left hand on the top three holes.
3. Blow softly. (Breathe into the instrument!)
4. Cover each hole completely.
5. Blow gently. (Breathe into the instrument!)
6. Release air with the tongue whispering "too."

FIGURE 8.3. Correct mallet-holding position

Rules 1, 3, and 5 are important! Children become excited when they are first learning to play this instrument, and these three rules provide a way of eliminating potential musical distress—for you and for your students. You must continually emphasize to each child the importance of producing a beautiful and musical sound with their plastic instruments. Always purchase recorders that come in at least two pieces so that you can modify the tuning, if necessary. In addition to the widely used soprano recorder, sopranino, alto, tenor, and bass recorders are available in plastic; they can be used with intermediate students in ensembles.

167

CHAPTER 8
Experiencing Music
Through Playing
Instruments:
Primary and
Intermediate

There are numerous recorder methods on the market, and some of the latest materials come with accompaniment tapes. These materials, with their synthesized and sampled sounds, may seem appealing to youngsters of the MTV generation. However, you should select beginning recorder music with the same care you take in choosing song or listening materials. The selections should be musically valid and should contain interesting melodic, rhythmic, and harmonic construction. Any recorder music you use in your classroom should provide children with an affective musical experience. You can enhance the quality of this experience by generating your own accompaniments on the piano or on different-sized recorders. It is suggested that you use a recorder book that has relatively few familiar songs so that your students will actually learn to read music as they are learning to play their instrument.

Harmony Instruments

The Autoharp and Chromaharp (both trade names) are strummed string instruments that have labeled pushbuttons for chords. Their sound is somewhat similar to that of a metal-stringed guitar. The playing technique is very simple: push a chord button with your left hand, and reach over with your right hand and strum from the lowest string (on the bottom) to the top. You can alter the strums rhythmically, and you can also produce a broken chord sound by strumming the bass notes and then the remainder of the chord. The sound of these instruments is very appealing to youngsters, and they can be played by younger children in pairs (one pressing the button and one strumming) as well as by older individual students. The drawback of these instruments is the amount of tuning time required, especially if you plan to use several in a class.

The Omnichord is an adaptation of the Autoharp which needs no tuning. This battery-operated digital device produces 84 chords, 10 different tone colors, and 10 rhythms that can be controlled for tempo. This instrument is more useful for some students with physical handicaps because they do not have to hold a pick in order to produce a sound. The advantage of this instrument over an Autoharp is that you never need to tune it, but the sound is quite different from the acoustic, metallic sound of an Autoharp.

The instrument of choice for most intermediate students is the guitar. You can buy reasonably priced student guitars. Older intermediate students with a large hand grip, firm finger pressure, and independent finger control can learn to play guitar in a class setting. Some schools own sets of soprano and/or baritone ukuleles; with their four strings and narrow necks, these are simpler to master. You should not use either of these as a classroom instrument, however, if you teach your classes only once a week. The technique needs frequent reinforcement so students will experience some musical success and satisfaction. Unlike recorder and Autoharp, which any college music major can easily master in a very short time, competent guitar playing takes considerable effort and practice, even for adults. Teach guitar to intermediate students only if you can demonstrate correct playing technique and have adequate instructional time.

The piano should not be overlooked as a classroom instrument, and the use of electronic keyboards should also be explored. Several young children can explore pitch concepts at a keyboard at one time if you give careful directions for movement and playing. You can use a similar procedure with older children when they are learning about chords or tonality.

Most elementary music classrooms already have a supply of unpitched instruments. After taking a careful inventory, look at catalogs and decide which additional instruments you wish to purchase. It's best not to buy complete sets of rhythm instruments as you have no control over the quality of the individual pieces. Make a list of what you need, and prepare a long-term acquisition plan based upon your projected annual budget.

Orff Approach

The work of Carl Orff (1895–1982) has had a great influence on music education practices worldwide. The Orff approach involves a specified sequence of musical activities designed to lead children into an understanding of musical concepts and skills. The prescribed teaching sequence begins with rhythmic speech; next is imitative singing, then instrumental accompaniment taught through imitation, and finally movement.

Orff began working with adult dancers in 1926 at the Guenther Schule, a school for gymnastics, music, and dance in Munich. Here he conceived the idea of the instrumentarium known today as Orff instruments. These barred percussion instruments, based on Javanese gamelan instruments, are both easy to play and beautiful to listen to.[2] Orff, who was fascinated by the connections between music and movement that Émile Jaques-Dalcroze was making in his work in Geneva, took his adult musician/dancers on tours and to appearances at teachers' conventions prior to World War II. The Guenther Schule and the instrumentarium were destroyed during the war. However, a prewar recording of the group led to an offer to compose music which children could play easily for the Bavarian Radio.

Orff called this music "elemental." He wrote, "What does it mean? . . . Never music alone, but music connected with movement, dance, speech—not to be listened to, meaningful only in active participation. Elemental music . . . contents itself with simple sequential structures, ostinatos, and miniature rondos. . . . It can be learned and enjoyed by anyone. It is fitting for children."[3]

The application of the principles of Orff's elemental music to American music teaching has been clarified and expanded through the work of Jane Frazee in her 1987 book *Discovering Orff.* Frazee organized the teaching princi-

---

[2]Carl Orff (1963). "The *Schulwerk*—Its Origins and Aims." *Music Educators Journal, 50* (8), 69–74.
[3]Ibid. p. 70.

ples derived from Orff's approach into a useful text that outlines musical concepts, discusses principles of scope and sequence, and clearly illustrates many ways to implement Orff's ideas in the music classroom. Script 4 in this chapter, which is based on a lesson written during an Orff certification course taken by one of the authors of this book, exemplifies Orff principles. For further information regarding this interesting approach to music teaching, as well as summer certification courses and workshops, contact the American Orff Schulwerk Association (address listed at the end of this chapter).

169

CHAPTER 8
Experiencing Music
Through Playing
Instruments:
Primary and
Intermediate

Methods of Reinforcing Musical Learning with Instruments

Of the many reasons to include instrument playing in the general music class, reinforcement of musical learning is probably the most compelling. Once you understand how to incorporate instrumental experience in your teaching, you can easily include it in all your lesson plans. The following section focuses on three of the many musical elements which you can reinforce through instrument playing: rhythm, melody, and harmony. (See Appendix A for a list of musical elements.)

Rhythm

The concept of rhythm is probably the easiest to reinforce. Children enjoy clapping and patting the rhythm of music, and you should expect to see all sorts of rhythmic or arhythmic accompaniments! They can keep time to the steady pulse, subdivisions of the pulse, and the melodic rhythm. If you are focusing on steady pulse, select those children who can consistently show the pulse to play rhythm sticks, claves, or small drums. Use these children as models for the rest of the class to follow, and continue to add instruments as more children approximate the steady feeling. You can also reinforce the concept of pulse by having half the children play the instruments while the other half engage in another musical behavior (singing, listening, or moving). Then have them switch parts, and discuss the difference between the two experiences.

The next step is to reinforce the idea that there are rhythm patterns in the melody that contrast the pattern of the steady pulse. You can have the class sing, for example, "Bird Songs" (Figure 7.4, p. 150) and clap the rhythm of the words. Then the children need to "think" the melody while clapping the rhythm of the words. Next divide the class into two groups, with one group clapping the rhythm of the words and the other group clapping the steady pulse. Then you can hand out instruments of contrasting timbres, so that the children with wood instruments (rhythm sticks, claves, maracas, temple blocks) play the rhythm of the words while those with metal instruments (triangles, finger cymbals, jingle bells) keep the steady beat. This technique is most effective when you have the groups exchange parts and play or sing the piece again; the children's musical understanding changes when they experience both steady beat and melodic rhythm and feel the difference between them. Don't pass up the opportunity to have the children discuss their reactions to this experience. It is appropriate to ask such questions as "How did it

⁴Jane Frazee (1987). *Discovering Orff*. NY-Mainz: Schott.

feel when you played the steady beat?" "What happened when I asked you to play the different part?" "Was it easier to keep the steady beat or play the rhythm of the words?" "Why do you suppose it was harder/easier?" Asking children to reflect on their experience helps them to "own" the experience and put it into the context of their musical understanding. It also gives them the opportunity to use their musical vocabulary in a musical context, and this is extremely important to their musical development.

You can reinforce a particular rhythm pattern by singing a song that contains the pattern and having the class clap the pattern whenever it occurs. You can then add instruments to reinforce the rhythm pattern, with some of the children playing the pattern while the others sing. Here is a chance to let the class make creative aesthetic judgments about which timbres best fit the song and most effectively bring out the rhythm pattern. Ask the children which instruments they think would be most effective, and then try their suggestions. Follow with questions about which ones they liked the best, which ones were most fun to play, which ones made the music sound the best, and which ones weren't as pleasing. If you always ask your students to give reasons for their answers, you'll give them practice at using their own creative imaginations and powers of thought as well as their musical vocabularies.

You can use instruments to reinforce the musical element of meter by following the same teaching sequence. For example, when students have learned "Clementine" (Figure 4.10, p. 71), they can first step the steady beat, then clap and step the strongest beat, and then play instruments of contrasting timbres (such as skin heads and metals) in place of the claps and steps. This activity would best be followed by a discussion of triple meter: Ask students to describe how triple meter feels to them, whether it reminds them of any particular type of music, or what adjectives it brings to mind. You can then further reinforce triple meter by introducing a contrasting musical example in duple meter, such as "John Henry" (Figure 4.3, p. 63), following a similar sequence of musical activity and discussing the differences between the two types of meter.

Melody

You can easily illustrate the musical concept of register by using the Orff barred percussion instruments: xylophones, metallophones, and glockenspiels. For example, you can have students demonstrate the octave skip in "One Elephant" (Figure 3.8, p. 55), by having them play the low C and the high C whenever the skip occurs in the song. You will need to cue them to play, acting as the conductor or having another student act as conductor. It is very difficult for students to successfully play a single note, on cue, in exactly the right place, even when you conduct them. It is much easier for them if you create an ostinato accompaniment using the concept reinforcer, in this case the low and high C, and have them play the ostinato in half notes throughout the song.

For the concept of melodic direction you can use barred percussion instruments or even tone bars. For example, half the class can sing "The Flea Song" (Figure 3.2, p. 41) while the others play the pitches of the ascending and descending melodic line as dotted half notes (one per measure). By isolating the feature of the known melody, bringing it to the children's attention by hav-

171

CHAPTER 8
*Experiencing Music
Through Playing
Instruments:
Primary and
Intermediate*

ing them play it, and then putting it back into the context of the song, you allow your students to become better perceivers of the inner workings of music. When you take them one step further—by asking them to tell you about what happened, whether the music sounded different after they had played and sung, whether playing helped them to notice the melodic direction—you help them to think musically, synthesizing the vocabulary of experience and their growing musical understanding.

Contour

When choosing songs to reinforce the concept of contour, be sure to use selections that have ascending and descending scalewise patterns of four or more pitches. "The Flea Song" lends itself well to contour reinforcement with children playing resonator bells or barred melody instruments. Another song that has an extended scale pattern is "Taffy" (Figure 8.4). Be sure to place the bells so that children see the size change from low to high. If you are using xylophones or metallophones with very young children, you should remove all unneeded bars, and you may wish to space out the remaining bars as well in order to facilitate a successful playing experience. You can be flexible when you choose an instrument for children to play to reinforce melodic contour. Use whatever is readily available in your own teaching setting. The important thing is that children be led to produce musical sounds that complement their singing and enhance their musical experience.

Phrases

Before having children play melodic instruments to reinforce phrase structure, you must analyze the song you are considering. If you wish to use bells

FIGURE 8.4.

or barred melody instruments with primary students, you must choose either a song where they will only play a section of a repeated melodic phrase (as in the beginning of the first and third phrases of "Birdie, Birdie, Where Is Your Nest?," Figure 3.1 on p. 34) or else a song that has very simple melodic patterns (such as the first and third phrases of "John the Rabbit," Figure 3.4 on p. 47, which are all repeated pitches). Since young children are unfamiliar with musical notation, their playing is a rote motor response, and you want to ensure that what you select has the potential for successful execution. Older students can play the same instruments as well, and the lesson will be most effective when it reinforces a repeated melodic idea. If you attempt to have older students play each phrase, you may spend far too much time on notation and end up with frustrated or disinterested students. The intermediate song "Emma" (Figure 4.14) contains a repeated melodic motif that uses only three notes (at the beginning of the first, second, and fourth phrases). Older students can play this as a way to reinforce the concept of phrase beginnings. After you teach "Erie Canal" (Figure 4.7) to intermediate students, they can play the first, second, and fourth phrases on melodic instruments, with one student playing the first half of a phrase and another concluding the phrase. In this manner, students get a feel for the question and answer musical ideas in the phrase in addition to the *aaba* phrase structure of the verse.

Harmony

MELODY AND DESCANT. The partner songs that children learn in primary grades are an excellent source of material for experiences in playing harmony with recorders. If necessary you can transpose each song to the key of C and put the notation and words on an overhead transparency. In addition, children can play on the recorder any descants that they have learned to sing. Writing simple descants for any song is not difficult; follow the harmonic structure and write melodies that have primarily contrary motion and simple rhythms. The recorder 1 part in Figure 8.5 is from the text *Music and You*, Book Five. It was written to be played as accompaniment for "Wabash Cannonball" (Figure 4.1). The recorder 2 part in Figure 8.5 is one way of adapting this recorder ostinato for individual students who have poorer visual and motor coordination, or for students without prior recorder instruction who move into your school district.

CHORDS. When you begin to teach the basic harmonic concepts to intermediate children, you must remember that you are not replicating your college theory class! Children want to play chords, not learn about voice leading. Through a simple exploration, which can be teacher-led or structured for groups, children should experiment with tone combinations until they discover which sets of three (or four) sound best together. It is very important that after this discovery, you explain the concept of how a chord is named so that children understand why the G bell or bar is used in both the C chord and the G chord.

Playing harmonic accompaniments should begin with slower songs that use only two chords, such as "All Night, All Day" (Figure 3.7a, p. 51). The slow tempo lets children prepare for the next time they hit a bell or press a bar

173

CHAPTER 8
*Experiencing Music
Through Playing
Instruments:
Primary and
Intermediate*

FIGURE 8.5. Descant for "Wabash Cannonball"
Appears in Music and You, *Book 5, Teacher's Edition, Barbara Staton and Merrill Staton,
senior authors.* ©*1988 Macmillan/McGraw-Hill School Publishing Company.*

of the Autoharp. When introducing chordal accompaniments, always allow
the entire class an opportunity to look through the song and discover where
the chord symbols are printed. In addition, if the class includes developmentally delayed students, provide hand signals for chord changes when the student playing begins. (For two chords, palms facing the class for tonic and
palms facing the floor for dominant will work well.) If you have three children
each playing a resonator bell in a chord, have them stand together so they can
coordinate their movements and produce a block chord sound rather than an
arpeggio. Or you may wish to have only one child play all three bells. You can
order sets of three mallets on a single handle from instrument catalogs. Even
more effective is to have the entire chord played by several children on a
tremolo, with each child maintaining a quick, soft repeated pattern of hits that
continues for the duration of the chord. With such simple harmonic structures
you can also add a recorder descant, such as the one in Figure 3.7b (p. 51).
Older children usually do not want to sing songs they learned in primary
grades (they are "baby" songs), but it is possible to use some of this material
when you are playing instruments if you provide a musical challenge and a
rich performance experience.

   When children are successful in accompanying songs with two chords, it
is time to include songs that contain the subdominant chord. The only initial
caveat is to ensure that chord changes last for an entire measure. Unless the
tempo is exceptionally slow, children will have great difficulty playing two
chords in a measure or a dominant chord on the final beat of a measure and
then a tonic on the next beat. "Red River Valley" (Figure 8.6) is a good example to use because the chord structure gives the accompanist enough time to
prepare for the change. It is also helpful to have the entire class sing the chord
roots while different children practice the chord changes. Use the Curwen

Red River Valley

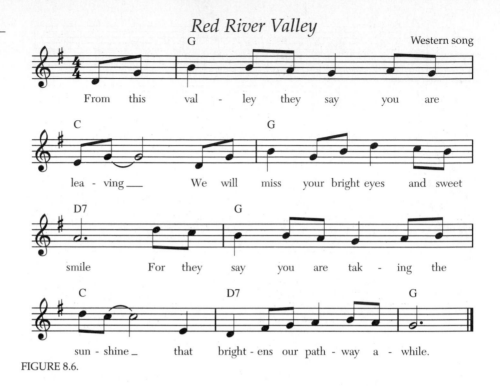

FIGURE 8.6.

hand signs for the three chord roots as a useful visual signal and reinforcement for the chord changes.

During all these playing experiences, lead your students to consider the
roles of performer, critic, and conductor. Ask them to focus on the visceral and
kinesthetic aspects of playing in order to make thoughtful decisions about
what they hear and feel: "How does the song sound different when we add
accompaniment?" "Which instruments make the song sound best?" "How can
you manipulate the instrument to make it change in sound?" Include class discussion time in your lesson plan so that students can evaluate the effect of
their instrument playing. You need to model musical judgments for students
for playing in the same way you do for singing. Instead of using a question
such as "Did you like the way that sounded?," which requires only a one-
word response, ask the class, "What did you notice about the way that
sounded?," which requires the students to draw on their tonal memory, musical terminology, and conceptual understanding. Class discussion is an important way for you to model the components of musical thinking and to emphasize the importance of reflection about all aspects of musical production. The
questions you ask to stimulate class discussion need to be thought out and
worded carefully in order to enable the children to grow as musical thinkers.

TEACHING SCRIPTS

The following scripts provide additional practice material for teaching lessons
that include instrument playing. Script 3 illustrates an approach to teaching a

rote song and reinforcing the melodic concept with pitched instruments. Script 4 illustrates a typical Orff teaching sequence, moving from expressive speech to rote singing to instrumental accompaniment taught through simultaneous imitation. It incorporates the song "One Elephant," which was introduced in Chapter 3 (Figure 3.8), and assumes that the children already know the song.

175

CHAPTER 8
Experiencing Music
Through Playing
Instruments:
Primary and
Intermediate

Script 3

GRADE LEVEL: Grades One and Two
MUSICAL CONCEPT: Melody
SPECIFIC ELEMENT: Direction
LESSON OBJECTIVE: Students will be able to demonstrate an understanding of melodic direction through movement and playing.
MATERIALS: "One Elephant" (Figure 3.8, p. 55) and "Taffy" (Figure 8.4, p. 171); a set of resonator bells or a wood or metal barred instrument.

STEP ONE

Today we're going to be using an instrument to help us learn something important about two songs. One of the songs we already know. It sounds like this.

Play "One Elephant" on a recorder.

Who can raise their hand and tell me the name of that song?

Call on a child to answer.

As we sing the song together the first time, I want you to watch what I do with my hands.

Play the initial pitch and sing the words "Ready, sing," and motion the class to join you in singing. As you sing, show the contour of the first and third phrases, using an exaggerated gesture for the octave.

Let's sing the song again and see if each of you can show me how the melody of the song goes down and then up.

Play the initial pitch and sing "Ready, sing," and motion the class to join in.

Now we are going to learn a new song that also has a part that goes down and a part that goes up.

Teach "Taffy" using the rote method described in Chapter 3 Script 1 (pp. 33–35).

Can you figure out who or what Taffy is while I sing?

(Taffy is a Welsh terrier.) After the song is learned, proceed as follows:

You are singing that song really well, class. I want you to sing it again and watch how the melody goes down and then up. Ready, sing.

As they sing, show steps progressing upward and downward with two hands and space the upward leaps.

As you sing it with me and show the way this song goes up and then down, I want to show you how we can also play this song on the bells.

Place resonator bells on a bell stepladder or on a music stand so that children can see the size change as the sound ascends and descends. Lead the children in singing the song while they move their hands and you play the bells.

Who can tell me which direction this part of the song moves?

Sing and play the first phrase.

We need one player for that section.

Select a child to play, and provide an opportunity to practice before the class sings.

How about this part of the song?

Sing the second phrase.

Who would like to play that part?

Provide a practice opportunity before adding the part to class singing. Repeat the same procedure for the third phrase.

Now let's perform the song with our instruments playing, and let's all also show with our hands that we know when the melody of the song goes up and when it goes down.

Change players and have the first players demonstrate correct procedure to the new players before the class sings again.

Script 4

Before using this script, review the Curwen solfège hand signs (Figure 3.3, p. 42). Practice the hand signs needed in this script before you attempt to teach this lesson either to a group of your peers who are not in this class or to a group of intermediate children.

GRADE LEVEL: Grades Four and Five

MUSICAL CONCEPT: Form

SPECIFIC ELEMENTS: Ternary form; tonic and dominant phrase endings

LESSON OBJECTIVE: Students will be able to demonstrate an understanding of ABA form and contrasting phrase endings through singing, playing and reading, and improvising.

MATERIALS: "The Monster Song" (Figure 4.15, p. 90); "Welcome Here" (Figure 8.7); poster-size staff paper with four 2-measure segments of the entire melody of "Welcome Here"; poster-size staff paper with instrument parts to hang on the chalkboard; finger cymbals, soprano glockenspiel, bass metallophone, mallets.

STEP ONE

Review "The Monster Song" (Figure 4.15, p. 90), having the class show the melodic direction while singing the first verse.

STEP TWO

I have a new song for you today, and it has leaps between notes and changes direction a lot like "The Monster Song." I'm going to teach it to you in a way that's different from what I usually do, so be ready for anything!

Teach the song by first reciting the words expressively, one line at a time. Indicate to students that they are to echo you by pointing to yourself when you speak and to them when they are to speak. Next, sing the whole song with words, using the Curwen solfège hand signs. Then sing two-measure sections, building two phrases, and indicate to students to echo. When students have learned the sections, say:

Welcome Here

177

CHAPTER *8*
*Experiencing Music
Through Playing
Instruments:
Primary and
Intermediate*

FIGURE 8.7.
Arranged by CPR

Now I'd like you to listen to the song in your head while showing the hand signs for the pitches. We won't sing this time, just sign and listen in our heads. Ready?

Sing the song while students made hand signs.

STEP THREE

Ask for four volunteers to come to the front of the room and hold up four poster-size sheets of staff paper (available in tablets from West Music, P.O. Box 5521, 1208 Fifth Street, Coralville, Iowa, 52241) on which two-measure segments of the melody are notated. The song should appear in scrambled order; the volunteers are to hold the sheets up for class perusal, not unscramble them themselves.

Can someone come up and unscramble this melody for us?

Take a volunteer who rearranges students into the correct order.

Let's have a show of "thumbs up" if you agree with this choice and "thumbs down" if you think there is a better way to rearrange this melody.

Let majority rule, and then have the students check their decision by clapping the rhythm of the melody as it is arranged.

STEP FOUR

Teach the bass part through simultaneous imitation: say the note while showing how to play it, alternating hands and pretending to hit the bass metallophone with your mallets. Have the students join you. When all seem competent, have one student come to the instrument and try the part. Teach the glockenspiel part in same fashion. Point to the finger cymbal part on the board and ask:

Can anyone clap this part for me?

Take volunteers, and allow the first child who claps correctly to try the part on finger cymbals after you review the most effective way to play this particular pattern on the instrument. Next combine all three instrumental parts: have the class clap the steady beat, give instrument players two measures of preparation before they begin, and cue each instrument and point to the notation on the board.

STEP FIVE

Let's see if we can play and sing it together now. Players, just play, and the class will do the singing. I'll give you two full measures before we start. One, two, ready, sing.

After the first attempt, ask students what was good about the performance and what could be improved. Ask for volunteers to have a turn at the instruments. Then repeat this step with new players.

STEP SIX

I'd like to try something new now, using this song. Remember what we did before, when we played question and answer? One person played some music that sounded like a question, and then another person played an answer. Do you remember the rules for making a musical question and answer? Who can tell me?

Solicit responses that lead to the idea that a question ends on dominant and the answer ends on a tonic.

Let's do the whole song again and build an ABA form. Let's use the song as the A section, and in the B section, let's have two people play a question-and-answer improvisation on the alto xylophones. Who would like to play the question and answer parts?

179

CHAPTER 8
*Experiencing Music
Through Playing
Instruments:
Primary and
Intermediate*

Take volunteers and let them decide who will play the question and who will play the answer.

The question needs to be eight beats long, and the answer needs to be eight beats long. Question and answer players, you can experiment with your instruments now, and we'll count eight-beat patterns for you. Ready, go.

Let them work for two sets of eight beats; then check to see if they are ready. Let them try at least two different question-and-answer series. Then put the song and the improvised segment into an ABA form, with the whole class singing.

Let's try it a different way. This time, let's use different instruments for the question and answer sections. What shall we use in place of the alto xylophones?

Take suggestions and try one. Then have the class try putting it all together, using the new B section. Discuss how this version sounded different, and ask students to support their statements with specific reasons.

SOURCES FOR CHAPTER 8

AMERICAN ORFF SCHULWERK ASSOCIATION
P.O. Box 391089
Cleveland, OH 44139-8089

Companies that sell percussion instruments:

MMB MUSIC
10370 Page Industrial Boulevard
St. Louis, MO 63132

OSCAR SCHMIDT INTERNATIONAL
230 Lexington Drive
Buffalo Grove, IL 60089

PERIPOLE-BERGERAULT, INC.
2041 State Street
Salem, OR 97301

RHYTHM BAND, INC.
P.O. Box 126
Fort Worth, TX 76101

SUZUKI MUSICAL INSTRUMENT CORPORATION
P.O. Box 261030
San Diego, CA 92126

STUDENT ASSIGNMENTS

1. Teach one of the scripts in this chapter to a group of children. Have a music teacher observe your teaching and write an observation summary using the following categories:
   a. Classroom management
   b. Eye contact
   c. Clarity of directions
   d. Levels of questions asked
   e. Teacher comfort level
   f. Overall impression
2. Rewrite one of the scripts in this chapter, using different instruments to reinforce different musical concepts.

Apples

FIGURE 8.8.
By CPR

3. Find two appropriate songs for primary level and two for intermediate level that contain a repeated rhythm pattern. Include complete citations for your song sources.

   a. For each song, describe how you would reinforce the rhythm pattern using unpitched instruments.

   b. For each song, score an accompaniment using pitched instruments.

4. Study the score in Figure 8.8 and derive a list of rules for Orff orchestration of a speech poem. Then replace the body percussion designators with unpitched instruments. Practice your score with two peers, and present it to your class.

5. In a small group, discuss unobtrusive ways to evaluate and document children's progress in playing instruments.

181

CHAPTER 8
*Experiencing Music
Through Playing
Instruments:
Primary and
Intermediate*

Experiencing Music Through Composing:

PRIMARY AND INTERMEDIATE

Case Study

Miss Davis returns from the teachers' lounge to find that her third grade class is already seated and waiting silently for her. "Well, hello!" she says. "I guess Mrs. Percell brought you early today." She continues, "Thank you all for surprising me with a roomful of silently waiting children! You were so quiet I didn't even know you were here!" As she moves to the front of the room to begin class, Miss Davis notices a new face in the class and says, "Welcome to music class. My name is Miss Davis; what's yours?" The new girl smiles shyly and the child next to her says, "Her name is Maya."

Miss Davis then begins to review a previously taught song by playing it on the recorder and asking for hands up when children recognize the tune. When most of the children have their hands up and one child has given the name of the song, Miss Davis leads the class in singing it.

She then leads the class through a review of musical questions and answers, focusing on the fact that the musical question begins on the tonic and ends on a dominant, while the musical answer begins on any note but needs to end on the tonic to feel complete. Miss Davis moves to her name envelopes and pulls out the last two names in the envelope. One of the children whose name she has pulled is absent, so Miss Davis says, "Maya, why don't you have a turn at the instruments today. Come up to the xylophone and take your turn."

Maya looks confused but moves to the xylophone with Elena, the other child whose name was chosen, and watches her intently as she picks up the mallets. Maya then picks up the mallets and watches as Elena begins to explore her musical question. As Maya continues to watch and explores, Miss Davis leads the class through the song and explains that the song will be the A section while the question-and-answer improvisation will be the B section.

Miss Davis asks the children what they would like to have happen during the C section, and they decide that they'd like to make a movement that shows the contour of the A melody while the question-and-answer playing continues. Miss Davis agrees that this is a great idea and says, "Are we ready? Xylophone players, have you figured out what you will do for question and answer?" Elena says she is ready. Maya simply smiles at Miss Davis, who then says, "Here we go! One, two, ready, sing." The A section proceeds successfully, and the question is played in the B section.

When it is her turn to play the answer, however, Maya just smiles at Miss Davis. The class breaks into loud laughter, whereupon Miss Davis says, "Would someone like to come up and help Maya with her answer?" Several boys and girls raise their hands, and Miss Davis chooses Tiffany, who comes up to the front of the room and sits down on the bench next to Maya. Maya gives her mallets to Tiffany and sadly walks back to her seat. When Miss Davis looks puzzled, Tiffany says, "She doesn't speak English, you know. She just moved here from Mexico."

YOUR COOPERATIVE TASK

1. Compose a list of cues found in the case study that, had she noticed them, would have helped Miss Davis meet Maya's needs.
2. With a partner, discuss an experience you have had that helps you understand Maya's actions and feelings.
3. Discuss some possible next steps that Miss Davis can take to salvage Maya's introduction to music class.
4. Propose a list of things Miss Davis needs to do before she meets with this class again.

PRACTICE TEACHING SCRIPTS

Script 1 (Primary)

GRADE LEVEL: Grades One and Two
MUSICAL CONCEPT: Timbre
SPECIFIC ELEMENT: Different timbres have different expressive qualities.
LESSON OBJECTIVE: Students will be able to select and perform appropriate unpitched timbres for expressive reasons.
MATERIALS: Overhead transparencies with story prompts and blanks to fill in; classroom instruments sorted into sets of woods, metals, and skin heads; a blank cassette tape and a tape recorder.

STEP ONE: Story

Use the following prompts to have the class compose a story. Be sure to use only one prompt at a time. Put each prompt on a separate overhead transparency to show only after the class has filled in the blank. Read the prompt, write in the response, and then read the next prompt. Decide ahead of time how to choose children for responses. You may want to go down rows, alternate blue-eyed and brown-eyed children, or alternate birthday months. Whatever you choose, explain your procedure to the class before you begin constructing the story.

1. *Once upon a time there was a _____.*

2. *(He/She/It) lived in a great big _____.*

3. *(He/She/It) had lots of _____ and liked to _____.*

4. *One day, as the _____ was playing in the _____ , (he/she/it) saw a _____ in the _____.*

5. *"Oh, dear!" thought the _____. "That _____ is so _____, I'm sure it will _____!"*

6. *The _____ ran as fast as (he/she/it) could to the _____.*

7. But it was too _____. (His/Her/Its) heart was pounding as (he/she/it)

_____.

8. Suddenly the sky looked _____ and (he/she/it) heard birds

_____.

9. Then a friendly old _____ came out of the _____ and said,

"_____."

10. Now the _____ felt much better, and (he/she/it) ran back to

_____ and said, "I'll never _____ again!"

11. So (he/she/it) walked along home and _____.

STEP TWO: Adding Appropriate Sounds

When the story is complete, read it through and let the children follow along on the overhead transparency.

Now let's add some sounds that help to make the story more interesting. There are many ways to do this. We could add a different sound for each line, or we could add only a few sounds. We could add certain sounds to particular words, or we could add sounds only in between words. Let's begin by trying out some different sounds with the first line. We'll have to read it once more and suggest a few sounds to try. Ready?

Using your predetermined method for choosing children to respond, take suggestions for each line or section and let the class add sounds they think will enhance the meaning of the story. Try several suggestions per line or section, and allow the group to discuss which sounds enhance the meaning of the story for them. If you guide the discussion carefully, the children's focus will remain on the quality of the sound enhancement rather than on whether they like a particular student's suggestion.

STEP THREE: Recording and Evaluating the Performance

When they have added sounds to the entire story, have the class try performing the entire set of sounds as children read the different lines. Record the performance and play it back for them immediately. Then lead a discussion based on the following questions:

1. **Which parts were particularly interesting to you? Why?**
2. **Which parts would you like to change? Suggest alternatives.**
3. **What did you notice as you listened to each of the different children's voices while they read? Is there anything you'd like to suggest that would make the reading more effective?**
4. **How did the sounds that we used change the story for you? Did the sounds make the story feel different to you? Describe how it changed.**
5. **If we were to start over again and do this completely differently, what would you do this time?**

Take suggestions and work with them, as time permits. Conclude by saying (if appropriate):

That was fine work, children! You worked well together, and you listened carefully to your own composition.

Script 2 (Intermediate)

185

CHAPTER 9
Experiencing Music
Through Composing:
Primary and
Intermediate

GRADE LEVEL: Grades Five and Six

MUSICAL CONCEPT: Form

SPECIFIC ELEMENT: Theme and variations

LESSON OBJECTIVE: Students will be able to compose a theme after hearing a teacher model of a theme and variations composition.

MATERIALS: Paper and pencils for each child; sets of instruments of your choice placed in four groups around the room; a list of members of four groups; a recording of your theme and variations piece.

STEP ONE: Creating Your Own Model for Class Use

The sound piece that the fifth grade will construct in this lesson will be based on a model that you provide, and this time you need to compose your own music for the model. Using what you already know, compose and record a 90-second piece for classroom instruments that illustrates theme and three variations.

1. *Use a clearly recognizable theme that lasts no longer than 20 seconds. The theme can be pitched or unpitched.*
2. *Compose three variations in which the theme is still obvious enough for fifth graders to recognize.*
3. *Use only those compositional devices that you can explain easily to fifth graders. Changes in timbre are more easily recognized than changes in the rhythm pattern or meter. Inversion of the melody or rhythm is harder to recognize than changing the dynamic level or articulation. When you perform your piece, emphasize each variation's characteristic by exaggerating it slightly.*

STEP TWO: Teaching Theme and Variations

I have a brand new piece of music for you to listen to today. I composed it myself! It's a theme and variations piece. Can someone tell me what that means?

Entertain suggested definitions, and lead the class to your own definition.

A theme and variations piece has a single musical idea, called a theme, that is modified each time it is played in a variation. The theme might be a series of pitches played slightly differently each time, or it might be a rhythm pattern that is changed slightly each time it is played. My theme and variations piece is played on (fill in your instrument). **It lasts only ninety seconds. Here is the theme:**

Play it on classroom instruments.

See if you can tell me how many variations there are in my piece. When you know, write the number on a piece of paper and turn it over. I'll then ask you to turn your papers over and show us your number. Here we go.

Play your composition again and then ask to see papers.

Good! Most of you heard the theme and the three variations. Now I'd like to show you how I varied the theme in each of the three variations.

Explain the technique you used by demonstrating it and asking the students to describe what they heard that constituted the variation. Then lead a discussion in which you solicit ideas for other ways you could vary your theme. Have individuals come to your instruments and demonstrate these ways of creating a variation. When you are confident that the class comprehends the many ways to create a variation, proceed to the next step.

STEP THREE

Now I'd like you to move to the sets of instruments, work in groups of six, and compose your own theme and variations pieces. First you need to move to your groups, so listen carefully as I read the list of people in each group. Group 1 meet here:

Move to the first set of instruments and read these names from the list; then tape the list to the wall in group 1's area. Do this for each group.

You have fifteen minutes to work on building a theme, and I'd like each group to have a theme ready to play for each other in five minutes. This time is for brainstorming, which means that everybody participates and everybody's musical idea is listened to. You may begin.

Move from group to group, listening, answering questions, and making suggestions as you go. Monitor the time and give a two-minute warning. Then call on each group to give a progress report by playing the theme they've chosen to work on. Allow each group to play and discuss the various choices they made in arriving at this particular theme.

STEP FOUR: Notating the Theme

Before you leave, you need to write your theme on paper so you won't forget how to play it. We're going to work on these next time, so you'll need to remember how your theme goes. Everyone in the group needs to write out the theme. It doesn't matter how you write it down, just as long as you can tell what you mean. You now have three minutes to write your themes.

Monitor the time carefully, and move around the room to offer suggestions to those who need more explanation. At the end of three minutes, say:

Group 1, please put your papers into this envelope

(hand them an envelope)

and move to line up.

Dismiss other groups in similar fashion.

Thank you for your good work today, class. We'll work on your variations next time.

WHAT YOU NEED TO KNOW

Why Include Creating?

The general music classroom is the place in which every elementary child experiences all the facets of the art of music, and one important aspect of this experience is learning to use the materials of music as a composer does.

Understanding music as a composer develops the child's musical thinking beyond the level of performer or recreator to that of musical decision maker. Just as the goal of reading instruction is to enable children to enjoy independent reading throughout their lifetimes, the goal of general music should be to empower all students to realize that they are musical beings who can express themselves with musical sounds. Including creating and composing activities in your classroom provides another way for children to become musical.

187

CHAPTER 9
Experiencing Music
Through Composing:
Primary and
Intermediate

"Messing around with music" in the composer's role is the perfect way to let each child synthesize the musical understandings gained through singing, listening, playing instruments, and moving. Because music is a nonverbal art, this important final synthesis provides the perfect opportunity for learners to combine the elements of music they have experienced in teacher-led activities and begin to use them independently. If music class does not include this important process, children leave elementary school believing that all music making must be initiated and led by another person and cannot be an individual exploration. Clearly, creating is an essential component of the general music program.

Because all children are naturally creative beings, their inclination is to play with whatever materials are available to them. Making sounds and recombining them is both stimulating and fun for children, particularly in our age of prepackaged entertainment and video-induced passive enjoyment. Manipulating sound sources for simple enjoyment enhances children's understanding of how sounds behave when combined in random or haphazard ways, and these activities are the foundation for later use of the same sounds in well-thought-through ways.

As a musician, you know that musical thinking involves a very different way of knowing. So many of our musical decisions cannot be verbalized because we intuitively "feel" that certain sounds should be manipulated in different ways. It is often impossible to describe this feeling in words. The opportunity to experience similar thinking must be included in general music classes so that youngsters realize that they too can make musical decisions independently.

Young children "make" art in visual art classes constantly. Every house with children has a refrigerator door covered with original works of art that youngsters have proudly carried home. Music classes often do not move to this final original production stage because music is more often thought of as an interpretive art. Most of us believe that composers are "special" people, but children can learn composition skills very easily. Parents do not compare their child's drawing with that of Michelangelo, and they will not compare their child's compositions with those of Bach. Children's artistic expression is a unique and valued part of their education. An important part of your job is to ensure that every child creates music, just as all students paint, draw, and make clay pots.

Musical Problem Solving

Problem solving is a currently popular educational term that describes a process in which children are presented with a situation or set of parameters as a stimulus and then set free to solve the situation or find the answer in any way they choose. This procedure, often called the discovery method, allows children to draw on prior knowledge and not only sort out the answer but discover ways to find the answer. Although currently a popular approach to teaching, problem solving and discovery learning were first espoused and explained by the progressive American educator John Dewey in his 1933 book *How We Think*.[1] Dewey emphasized that the first stage of problem solving is the point at which the student senses that there is a problem to be solved, something that needs to be figured out or discovered to resolve a situation. Dewey is very clear that unless the student is involved in the actual discovery of the problem, there is no real problem solving.[2]

When you plan to give students a musical task to complete, as in the teaching scripts at the end of this chapter, you need to remember that simply telling children that you want them to create a composition according to particular parameters does not necessarily engage them in musical problem solving. The task you set merely gives them the stimulus; the problems that arise in completing the task need to be framed and solved by them, either in groups or as individuals. The most important point is that if students do not become engaged in framing the musical problem for themselves, you have merely given them another assignment, and no particularly engrossing activity will follow.

So your task becomes one of asking the questions that will help your students to take ownership of the process and find their own paths to solving the problem. For example, you might assign groups to use their mouths and bodies to create a 15-second piece that sounds like a pond at night in spring. Ask the children what they think they need to do first, second, and third in creating the piece. Helping groups or individuals to prioritize steps in the process will guide their thinking and may provide the "hook" you seek to engage their prior musical knowledge in the present task. The questions you ask are the most important means you have to get students directly involved in the composition process, and it is critical that you continue to ask them once the work is under way. If you pursue a line of questioning that focuses on what the students think and how they might proceed, and always encourage them to follow their own inclinations, you will allow them to discover their own solutions to the problems they perceive. This is real musical problem solving that goes far beyond the level of task completion for teacher appeasement that characterizes much of what happens in school.

Changed Role of the Teacher

When you begin to engage your students in creating music and provide opportunities for them to become musical thinkers, decision makers, and composers, your classroom may not resemble any that you ever participated in as a student. However, if you look carefully at the classrooms in present-day schools, you will find that the groups of children may not be similar to the

[1]John Dewey (1933). *How We Think*. Lexington, MA: Heath.
[2]Ibid., p. 12.

groups you remember from elementary school, either. It is a reality that most
elementary teachers in our country are white, middle-class, and female. But in
many sections of our country, the student population is very diverse. In a single school twenty different languages may be spoken by children who are all
Americans. Your role as a teacher may therefore be quite different from what
you remember of your own teachers. You must be prepared not only to let go
of your concept of classroom control when students are composing but also to
let go of your own stereotypes of what a group of students should look and
sound like.

189

CHAPTER 9
Experiencing Music
Through Composing:
Primary and
Intermediate

Different Classroom Structures

As is evident from the preceding section, your role in the composition
process is one of mentor, coach, and source of suggestion rather than critic,
participant, and fount of all wisdom. While not changing your role completely,
in the spirit of the creative process you are more of a bystander than in other
musical activities. Because of this subtle shift in role, your experience while
teaching a composition lesson may feel different from what you're used to
feeling while teaching singing or playing, for example.

It may be frightening to allow students to move into groups, pick up
noisemakers, and start making all sorts of sounds over which you have no
control. You may feel that you have lost your classroom management ability.
You may also feel confused by all the scattered activity and not know where to
focus your attention, or even whom to answer when several students in different groups raise their hands and invite you to come to help their groups.

These feelings are to be expected when engaging in a more student-
focused activity, and you can feel assured that, in spite of the seeming confusion, musical learning is happening. Getting control over your feelings of dis-
comfort and inadequacy is easier when you realize that all that your students
really need from you in this activity is an enthusiastic ear and some helpful
suggestions. Children love to create their own music, and you are the lucky
one who has the privilege of watching them, listening to them, and enabling
them to do it.

Different Classroom Members

The other important aspect of the teaching role that you need to keep in
mind, whether leading a composition lesson or not, is the sensitivity, knowledge, and tact required to teach all the students you encounter. Children from
cultural backgrounds you may have never heard of, children who speak languages other than yours, and children who are at risk of failing to learn will
certainly be among your students. They may be hidden from you, as was
Maya in the case study at the beginning of this chapter, or they may come to
you in self-contained classroom groups. In order to reach these children, you
need to expand the repertoire of teaching skills on which you rely when teaching "typical students." The best way to begin is to seek help from classroom
teachers, resource teachers, and your building principal.

No one will expect you to know exactly how to communicate with the
child who does not speak English. However, you can learn a lot by asking the
classroom teacher which words of English the child does know and building

on those. You may also want to seek out the ESL (English as a Second Language) teacher in your district to learn some useful words in the child's native language. While it's helpful to know *yes*, *no*, and commands such as *come here*, *over there*, and *sit down*, words of praise are especially important and will enhance the classroom environment of children who are struggling to learn a new language.

Students are identified as "at risk" of failing for a wide variety of reasons, including emotional upset, poverty, malnutrition, and family situation. Because you, the music teacher, may see them only an hour or less each week, it is difficult for you to identify such children, and you will have to rely on faculty colleagues for help in this matter. Knowing what to expect from children in this category is difficult, as each child's case is unique. You can, however, make a habit of consulting regularly with classroom teachers to keep abreast of developments in the lives of those children with special needs, and you can learn to read the signals they send you in the classroom.

For example, in the opening case study in this chapter, Miss Davis should have noticed Maya's inability to follow directions. Maya's pattern of following another child and watching for cues as to the right thing to do indicated that she did not understand the directions. Another signal of confusion was her smile, which was her way of saying, "I don't understand this, and I'm trying my best to cope. Please help me!" Miss Davis didn't need to be able to diagnose Maya's specific difficulty to read her distress signals. She should, however, have stepped in immediately and moved next to Maya, showed her what to do, and talked with her. In doing this, she would have discovered whether Maya was hearing-impaired or simply did not speak English. The teacher's personal concern and individual contact can go a long way to bridging all sorts of learning difficulties by creating a caring, supportive atmosphere. All children respond to respectful, warm, and caring treatment; ESL and at-risk children are particularly in need of your consistent, reaffirming presence and the order of your classroom for their own stability.

Perhaps the best way to run a classroom that embraces children of all possible backgrounds, native tongues, and emotional states is to build your music curriculum in a way that resonates for these children. Your students should know that you are an accepting person and that you think each child is unique and equally capable of every task you set. Your acceptance and continuing high expectations are an important aspect of their education, and your class content should not be watered down or undemanding. You must provide engaging musical experiences for all students, using the best music possible. Just how your curriculum will look will depend on your district and the resources available to you. But even in the poorest districts in the largest cities in our country, teachers with high expectations and a burning desire to share their love of music are able to provide a rich and valid music education for their students.

Good teachers communicate their beliefs in the equal worth of each student in many ways. One way, described earlier in this text, is to ensure fairness in taking turns, instrument playing, and so on. In addition, classrooms where children work together and show respect for individuals through attentive listening contribute to children's belief in themselves as valued and equal participants in the educational setting. The recent AAUW report *How Schools Short-*

change Girls suggests that teachers need to reconsider the value of cooperation

191

CHAPTER 9
Experiencing Music
Through Composing:
Primary and
Intermediate
and listening to others:

> Across the whole spectrum of the K–12 curriculum there is currently more
> emphasis on the development of assertive than affiliative skills, more reward
> for solo behavior than collaborative behavior, more reward for speaking than
> listening. The curriculum can be strengthened by consciously focusing on the
> development of reflective, caring, collaborative skills as well as those empha-
> sizing individual performance and achievement.[3]

An excellent principle for creating an inclusive curriculum is found in the
above quotation. In classrooms where some children are struggling to understand and express themselves in English and others are trying to cope with the
daily unease of inner-city life or the limitations of poverty, music curricula are
strengthened by continual opportunities for cooperation. Although the focus
of the AAUW report was gender fairness, the idea is one that would ensure a
curriculum in which every child would feel valued. The authors of this text
have adapted a set of guidelines for an inclusive curriculum originally outlined by Gretchen Wilbur.[4] Consider the following suggestions when planning
an appropriate and inclusive music classroom. A curriculum that embraces all
children has six attributes:

1. It acknowledges and affirms variation—the similarities and differences
   among and within groups of people (and the musics of all peoples).
2. It is inclusive and allows all participants to find and identify positively
   with messages about themselves (music making provides an opportunity for success for every participant, and class content includes music
   by both male and female composers and performers).
3. It is accurate and presents information that is data-based, verifiable,
   and able to withstand critical analysis (the musical information selected
   reflects current scholarship and is not based on stereotyped, subjective
   interpretations of historical events or groups of people).
4. It is affirmative and acknowledges and values the worth of individuals
   and groups (all musical encounters depend upon the participation of
   every member).
5. It is representative in that it balances multiple perspectives (the music
   used represents the Western cultural heritage as well as the wide variety of other cultures).
6. It is integrated and weaves together the experience, needs, and interests
   of all participants (the music teacher is flexible and able to incorporate a
   variety of content and to focus on different learning styles and individual backgrounds).[5]

These six guidelines describe a decidedly different kind of music curriculum from the one you may have experienced. When you take multiple perspectives, use multicultural musics, and include music by composers of both
genders, your inclusive general music curriculum fosters a much broader

---

[3]*How Schools Shortchange Girls*, p. 67.
[4]Ibid.
[5]Gretchen Wilbur (1991). "Gender-Fair Curriculum." Research report prepared for Wellesley College Center for Research on Women, August, 1991. Quoted in *How Schools Shortchange Girls*, p. 64.

outlook on the musical world than is typical of so-called school music. And when improvising and composing in these various musics is an integral part of children's experience, you open unlimited musical horizons.

Composing and Improvising

An important consideration when planning instruction is an awareness of the difference between improvisation and composition. When children are given sounds to play with and begin working on compositions, they often move blithely from idea to idea, working on what to the observer seem to be random bits and pieces. When asked to perform their chosen melody or segment of a melody, they often return to a melody they worked on much earlier in the lesson without using any visual prompt, such as notation or a picture or diagram. Is this melody now a composed piece of music, or is it still an improvisation? This question is often asked by musicians trained in the Western classical tradition. But many musicians, in our own culture and in nonwestern cultures, have stores of compositions in their heads which they have assimilated. Their teachers may or may not have been formal instructors, but they all are steeped in a particular musical tradition.

In a similar manner, children's improvisation also depends upon a stored repertoire of sound possibilities. To expect children to improvise without a rich fund of musical knowledge is unrealistic; unreasonable expectations are often the source of less-than-successful composition lessons. Your students need time and opportunities to explore the ways they can use the many musical ideas they carry around in their heads. This exploration is as important to a child as it is to the finest jazz musician.

The idea that children need to know notation to compose music is absurd when considered in this light. Children learn to compose by playing with sound, and whether they write it down or not, they are composing. When they have worked on a piece and have found their own way to save it, to show it to others, and have others play it, they are also composing. Composition, by definition, implies a creation and sometimes a saving and a sharing process.

Approaches and Materials

Primary Grades

Composition with young children is an exciting undertaking, for their enthusiasm and uninhibited joy at making their own music create an atmosphere in which musical ideas seem to bubble up within them from a hidden source. Young children respond best to composition activities that are exploratory, with plenty of short, focused activities and a variety of stimuli. It is essential that primary-age children explore a wide variety of sound sources so that they can begin to form their own repertoire of ideas about how sounds are made and how they can be manipulated to the player's or composer's satisfaction. Focused exploration can be as simple as finding three interesting sounds that can be made on a single instrument or finding three different ways to make a sound with the body.

Adding sounds to enhance the meaning of stories or poems is another way to involve young children in sound exploration and to integrate the activities of the regular classroom into the music lesson. Stories or poems that the children are reading, writing, or acting out in language arts are a fine source for orchestrating in music class. The musical activity presented in Script 1 at the beginning of this chapter integrates reading, language, and writing instruction with sound exploration in music class.

193

CHAPTER 9
Experiencing Music
Through Composing:
Primary and
Intermediate

Children can also make up simple accompaniments for songs they already know. You must organize this exploration by setting specific parameters for the activity. If you want the children to use pitched instruments, limit their choice of pitches to the tonic and dominant of the key in which the song is written, and have them figure out which pitches sound best. If you want them to make up an unpitched percussion accompaniment, limit their choice to instruments that produce the desired timbre. No matter what the task, always allow children to work on their own for a few minutes to explore sound possibilities and to reacquaint themselves with the instrument. It is helpful to precede any playing activity with a reiteration of the correct way to play the instrument in question, as well as any special rules you may have developed for playing activities (for example, "We use our mallets only for playing music. Anyone who uses a mallet as a weapon will lose their turn").

Another way to explore sound possibilities is through building a particular form. Primary children easily grasp the concept of binary form if you explain it as "same or different." Use descriptive language for the character of the music you'd like them to create. Words such as *bumpy* and *smooth* or *swirling* and *straight* are effective stimuli for primary children's explorations. Visual reinforcement of the stimulus helps all children to remember the task and is essential for special learners of many types. Instead of simply saying the two contrasting words, write them on the board and then draw an icon for them as well. Children in primary grades are just learning to read and are greatly helped by the combination of picture and word.

A more elaborate process, taking several class periods, is involved when you help children to turn a poem into a song. The song composition process may seem cumbersome, but it is an activity primary children love and is well worth the effort. As in the activities mentioned earlier in this section, the more you are able to limit their choices of sounds, the more easily they'll be able to create. In the first class period, have the children read the poem together, and discuss various ways to make it sound different through voice inflection, articulation, and accent. When the children have decided which way they like it best, have them chant the poem several times as a class. Then try it with individual voices reading single lines but still using the agreed-upon inflection, articulation, and accents. This step could take an entire class period. In the second class, offer the class a choice of appropriate pitches to use as accompaniment, such as the roots of IV V I, or appropriate others of your choice. Have the class decide which patterns sound best. This could take the entire second class period. In the third class, play the chosen accompaniment and have the class chant the poem over your playing. Then ask the children to sing what they have been chanting, and tell them that you will expect to hear lots of different melodies when they do this. If they try the accompanied chant several times, those children with the stronger voices will prevail, and a melody or several different melodies will emerge. Record these and have the entire class listen to them. You can write these out on staff paper and create a collection from each class to publish as a school songbook. Song creation is an exciting activity in which the entire school takes great pride, and the class songs are a great source for performance program material. In addition, if you are teaching in a school that emphasizes whole language, where children's stories and books are "published," these songbooks are a way of validating your curriculum to your professional peers.

The question-and-answer technique commonly used in the Orff approach to music teaching is an effective way to involve primary children in instrumental improvisation and can lead to explorations with the voice as well as with unpitched percussion instruments. Question and answer can be explained in either melodic or rhythmic terms. As discussed in Chapter 8, the melodic version is based on the Western musical tradition that musical questions begin on the tonic and end on the dominant, whereas musical answers begin anywhere and end on the tonic. With unpitched instruments, you can drum a rhythm pattern of any length to serve as a musical question, and the appropriate answer will have parallel length and opposing or differing patterns. The teacher usually gives the class the task of working in pairs to build a question of a particular number of beats and an answer of (usually) the same number of beats. One way to use this activity as a culminating task is to go around the room and have each pair play their questions and answers in turn without missing a beat. This results in a much longer composition than primary children are used to creating. Recording this long improvisation allows these young players to step back from their own work and hear it in the context of others' improvisations.

Intermediate Grades

If sound exploration and composition are part of the primary music curriculum, intermediate students will be ready and, in fact, anxious to engage in more sophisticated composition activities. Intermediate students are capable of more subtle manipulations of sound sources, and they have a more extensive vocabulary of musical experience as well as a firmer grasp of musical terminology and genres. They are poised for a wider variety of compositional activities.

Fourth, fifth, and sixth graders often have a solid performance base in a musical instrument, which can be an important source for improvisation and composition activities in the general music class. An effective way to find out who can play an instrument is to invite everyone to bring an instrument to class on a given day, promising them all that they won't have to play a prepared piece in front of the group. Pianists can share the keyboard of the class piano, or you may want them to move to barred percussion along with any students who do not play an instrument outside of class. In some districts, recorder is introduced in third grade and many students are proficient recorder players by fifth grade. You can then lead them through a variety of group playing exercises, such as all finding the same note and playing it at a variety of dynamic levels at your direction. This activity can culminate in the question-and-answer activity described in the previous section. Once you have laid the groundwork for composing on a known instrument, you can split the class into groups of like instruments to improvise together or assign them individual or partner tasks tailored to their own playing proficiency. For example, if the pianists play only single-line melodies, have them make up melodies that they can play together. If some of your students have been studying violin since age 3, involve them in composing a countermelody to one of their repertoire songs. Some of your recorder players may be proficient enough to improvise on a harmonic background that is supplied by Autoharp or piano.

Another rich source for ideas appropriate for composing with intermediate children is the Manhattanville Music Curriculum Program (MMCP), a sponsored research project that was developed during the 1960s. This project focused on creating a composition curriculum for general music students that would allow them to understand contemporary music by composing it themselves. The book that best explains the aims and implementation of this project is *MMCP Synthesis*, a classic music education document available in most music libraries.[6] The curriculum delineated in *Synthesis* is based on the spiral curriculum proposed by Bruner, with the musical elements of pitch, rhythm, form, dynamics, and timbre revisited sixteen times throughout the school year. Each visit builds on the previous one and refines the musical element further. Although designed for secondary school, this program presents listening examples and group composition "strategies" that can be used as inspiration for composition with intermediate students. Although it is not widely used as the basis for music curriculum design today, MMCP established the basic principles of group composition, performance for peers, and critical analysis of each other's work, and this legacy makes the MMCP an essential part of your knowledge as a music teacher.

Notation

The need for notation skills begun in the primary grades continues to grow in the intermediate grades as students begin to develop better playing skills and need more efficient ways of notating both melodic and rhythmic elements. There are two distinct ways to handle this need, and both are equally valid. The first is to use invented notation, which may evolve into standard notation, and the second is to use electronic media such as MIDI technology.

Invented Notations

Students are prepared for writing their own notation through many prior musical experiences, such as experimenting with moving to sounds, tracing the contour of a melody, and doing the gestural mapping activities proposed in Chapter 6. By the time they are in intermediate grades, students are ready to invent notation for their own compositions. Such experimentation is time-intensive, but it allows children to explore music writing because they want and need to record their own work, not because they have to learn notation to

[6]Ronald B. Thomas (1970). *MMCP Synthesis*. Bardonia, NY: Media Materials.

pass a quiz or get a good grade in your class. *Children can experience music deeply and fully without knowing anything about notation.* When you allow students to develop their own notations for their compositions and let them explain their notations to each other so that they can play each other's music, you create a need and provide the motivation to learn the universal notation system.

Once they are convinced that it is necessary, intermediate students will enthusiastically develop their own notation. The development of this skill has been explicated by Rena Upitis in her 1992 book titled *Can I Play You My Song?* Upitis presents a detailed description of the sequence in which notation skills seem to develop in children and shows the parallels between the development of language-writing skills and musical notation skills. Upitis focused her investigation on children who were involved in notating their own compositions, not on children who were learning to play an instrument and needed to learn to read someone else's notation. She found that children pass through several stages:[7]

1. *Precommunicative—early communicative/iconic.* At this stage, children playfully use notes, rests, and other musical symbols to represent their music, without any understanding of what the symbols mean. They may also draw pictures, letters, and numbers, along with the musical notation.
2. *Semiphonetic—units.* At this stage, children begin to use a single symbol for a musical unit, such as a note or a phrase. The earlier stage might be written from right to left, but notation in the units stage is usually written from left to right. Children at this stage of development often attempt to represent the vertical dimension of music, usually two lines of melody or two different instruments playing together.
3. *Phonetic—contour/intervals/grouping or pulse.* Upitis found this stage most difficult to categorize as her subjects took on the task of notating more and more musical elements. Attempts at combining pitch, rhythm, dynamics, texture, and repetition often lead children to an elaborate yet difficult-to-explain notation system that even they have difficulty following.
4. *Transitional—regulated.* At this stage children may be able to notate some of the elements of music consistently, while still not being perfectly accurate. Their notation of pitch and rhythm, for example, may be relative rather than exact, and it may seem to develop in relation to the instrument on which they perform. For example, if a pianist notates the starting pitch incorrectly, it doesn't matter, since all the following pitches will be correct in relation to it.
5. *Correct—standard.* Children at this stage understand that pitches have absolute values and that rhythms occur in patterns that form meter.

Upitis stresses that unlike the stages of cognitive development proposed by Piaget and Bruner, the stages of notation development do not seem tied to particular ages but are a function of the child's composition experience. Children seem to pass through all these stages in their use of invented notation, no matter what age they begin composing. Upitis's findings are a useful guide to the music teacher embarking on the task of composing with children of all ages.

[7]Rena Upitis (1992). *Can I Play You My Song?* Portsmouth, NH: Heinemann, pp. 58–77.

Electronic Media

197

CHAPTER 9
Experiencing Music
Through Composing:
Primary and
Intermediate

Today the possibilities for composing music using electronic media are much greater than they were even ten years ago. The widespread use of computers in educational settings and the development of software specifically for composing music make it possible for general music teachers to incorporate technology in their composition lessons. A technology component may have been incorporated in your undergraduate degree program, and you may already be familiar with software for printing music or drilling music theory or aural skills. Whatever your computer background, you need to avail yourself of every opportunity to use technology in your classroom. Many school districts have invested large amounts of money in computer labs and software libraries, and you may be expected to make use of these facilities in your music curriculum. Computer literacy and software knowledge are desired skills which are appearing more often in job descriptions for general music teachers.

More important, however, is that children enjoy composing with computers because they can create music in a variety of timbres and genres and then listen to it, edit it, and notate it. The more elaborate composition programs, such as "Finale," are far beyond the abilities of children, but simplified composition programs such as Songworks (Ars Nova Software, 500 Kirkland Way Suite 140, Box 637, Kirkland, WA 98033) may enable your students to compose in this medium. Because both hardware and software change rapidly, it is imperative that you explore what is available for your school's computers.

It is your responsibility to find software that is appropriate for your students, and just as you choose song materials that meet certain criteria, your standards for composition software should be exacting. Sources for software are many and include university music computer labs, your local software dealers, and the technology column of *Music Educators Journal*. The only way to know if the program is suitable for your students is to spend time with it yourself, doing the kinds of things you would expect your students to do. Address questions of cost, time effectiveness, and hardware requirements before you make your decision. In addition, it is important to find software that enables your students to actually think as composers think and that requires them to make musical decisions. This detective work is time-consuming, but the benefits to your students are well worth the effort you make to choose the best technological tools for them.

Group Composition

An exciting and engaging task for intermediate children is to compose a class song based on their own set of lyrics and to perform it with instrumental accompaniment. Several class periods may be needed for the many steps of the process, depending on the tempo and level of consensus of each class. However, the time spent is very worthwhile as the process enhances students' capabilities for thinking and integration. In addition, the end product can be shared with other classes, parents, and teachers and is a source of pride for the student composers.

One type of song that children can compose is the blues song. Begin by playing a recording of a standard twelve-bar blues song, such as "Good

Mornin' Blues" by Lightnin' Hopkins or a selection by a performer of your own choice. Limit the number of verses students will listen to, and be sure that all the language included is age-appropriate. If you choose a recording with a straightforward guitar accompaniment, it will be easier for students to hear the chord changes and to approximate the harmonic structure. After the second hearing, ask students to tell you what the song was about, and write the words of the lyrics on the board. Discuss the character of the song, focusing on the mood expressed by the combination of lyrics and music. Ask them to tell you about how this kind of music sounds to them, and ask if they know what it means to be "blue."

Your next step is to give the children a title for their own class piece. You can use anything, including the month ("January Blues"), their classroom teacher's name ("Jones's Blues"), or simply "School Blues." Have them refer back to the lyrics they heard and decide how many lines of text they'll need for each verse. The children should then look at the rhyming scheme, if any, and decide whether their piece will fit that pattern. They may choose to do theirs differently, perhaps with no rhyme scheme or with nonsense syllables for text. You are now ready to lead students through text creation, taking suggestions, writing them on the board, and evaluating them through discussion. Complete three verses using this procedure.

Once the group achieves consensus and the verses are set, you are ready to have the class add the chordal accompaniment found in the standard twelve-bar blues progression and chant their words while they play the accompaniment (D is an easy-to-sing key). During the second playing, have the children begin to sing their chants. Expect to hear a wide variety of melodies. You can ask for volunteers to sing their versions; discuss the differences between them when you've heard all who want to perform. Record all attempts; play them back, with the children singing along if they wish to try out how each of the various melodies feels. When you achieve consensus about the "best" version, have the whole class try it, record it, and then discuss whether it sounds authentic, perhaps by comparing it to the listening selection. At this time you may want to discuss blue notes and how to add some to the song. The final step is to notate the melody, write out the words with the chord symbols, and make a copy for each student. You can package the product of several classes' work by compiling a grade-level blues songbook. Children may want to add illustrations and color. The songbooks can then be circulated among classes, shown to parents at open house nights, and even serve as the core for a performance program.

Summary

Composition is an invaluable musical experience for children and has as many manifestations as you can think of. The activities suggested in this chapter are intended to get you started on the path to including composition as a regular feature of your music teaching. Although some of these ideas are time-consuming and will not fit into a single class period, you must remember that authentic creative activity requires time. If your students are to become independent musicians, you must plan your instruction to accommodate the time required for creativity to flower.

The process of leading children through creative musical endeavors puts a different spin on your role as teacher, as you move from adult in control to facilitator. When you include composition as a regular activity, you give children an opportunity to construct their own unique meanings from what they have previously learned in your music classes. In addition, your students come to understand the purpose and value of our shared musical notation system. And finally, you have the privilege of watching children at their best, fully engaged in musical thinking and musical creation.

199

CHAPTER 9
Experiencing Music
Through Composing:
Primary and
Intermediate

TEACHING SCRIPTS

Script 3 (Primary)

GRADE LEVEL: Grade Two

MUSICAL ELEMENT: Timbre

LESSON OBJECTIVE: Students will demonstrate an ability to select appropriate sound sources for visual prompts and to organize the sounds into a meaningful whole.

MATERIALS: The set of pictures in Figure 9.1, enlarged and mounted on the chalkboard or on cardboard; four additional sets of these enlarged pictures; identical sets of classroom instruments placed in the corners of the room.

STEP ONE

Warm up singing voices by having children sit up tall and take a preparatory breath, exhaling on a hiss for five counts. Lead them through "ooo" and "aah" on D; then add the consonants m and d to each vowel. Emphasize dynamic contrast by having the children follow your conducting gestures for louder and softer. Discuss ways in which the character of the sound changes as you change dynamic levels.

STEP TWO

Have the class sing "The Flea Song" (Figure 3.2) with no dynamic changes. Then have them follow your conducting gestures to change dynamic levels. Next ask them to think of appropriate percussion sounds to add to the song. Try a few additions and discuss very briefly how these additions change the way the song sounds.

STEP THREE: Inspiration for Composition

I have a set of pictures I'd like you to look at today. I'm going to show them to you in order, and I'd like each of you to think about them as I show them to you. When I've shown you the entire set, I'll ask you to tell me about them.

Show the pictures one at a time, in order, placing them on the chalkboard (with tape or simply leaning them on the chalk tray) in order from left to right.

Who can tell me what happens in this set of pictures?

Let a few children suggest what each picture tells them.

STEP FOUR: Composing a Sound Story

Today you are going to work in groups of four and make a sound story from our set of pictures. First, let's count off one, two, three, four, and as I give

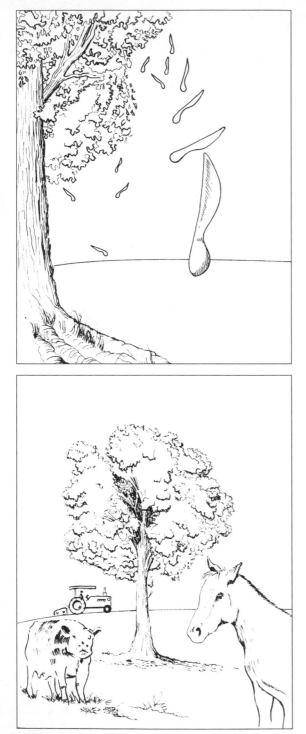

FIGURE 9.1. Sound story
Pictures by Robert Atterbury

FIGURE 9.1. *(Continued)*

you your number, hold up the number of fingers that shows your number. Now, group 1 move to this corner.

Send all groups to their corners.

I'd like you to work in your groups. Look at each picture and figure out a sound that tells what's happening in the picture. Begin with the first picture and ask, "What kind of sound would show what's happening in this picture?" Listen to each other's ideas, try them out, talk about them, and decide which ones you think are best. We'll work on this for ten minutes, and then we'll play our sound stories for each other and record them. Are there any questions?

Monitor group work, moving from group to group, watching the time carefully. Give a two-minute warning. Then record the pieces, announcing each group's number before recording. When all groups have recorded their compositions, replay each performance for the class.

These were beautiful sound stories, second graders! Next time we'll begin by listening to each one and talking about how the different groups' sound stories were similar or different.

Script 4 (Intermediate)

Plan to take two class periods to complete this lesson for building a percussion rondo.

GRADE LEVEL: Grades Five and Six

MUSICAL CONCEPTS: Rondo form, timbre, melody

MATERIALS: Recording of "Eldorado" by Ney Rosauro, performed by Evelyn Glennie (percussionist) on *Light in Darkness* CD 60557-2-RC; a variety of pitched and unpitched percussion instruments, including found sound sources (glass, metal, and wooden objects); paper and pencils for each group.

1. *Rondo form = A B A C A (three different parts).*
2. *30 seconds long.*
3. *Use at least three different types of instruments.*
4. *May include body percussion.*
5. *May include pitched as well as nonpitched percussion.*

Write on board before lesson begins.

STEP ONE

Warm up singing voices by having students stand, roll their shoulders up and back, and take a cold air sip. Have students sing solfège syllables on the correct pitches as you give the Curwen hand signs. Make up your own patterns for them to follow; then ask for volunteers to take your place in leading the singing and signing.

STEP TWO

Ask three volunteers to come forward and lead three different groups in signing and singing the solfège syllables reviewed in Step One. Split the class into three groups, and have the leaders practice signing and singing with their groups. When the students have practiced for a few minutes, tell them that they now need to create a rondo form, and write A B A C A on the board. Assign each leader to a part of the form (A, B, or C), and have the leaders decide as a group which musical controls they will be able to show in their signing. For example, A might be piano *at the beginning and build to* forte, *while B may be* pianissimo *and C may begin* mezzo forte *and finish at* piano. *Have the class try to follow both the solfège and the dynamic levels of the leaders as they build the ABC form.*

203

CHAPTER 9
*Experiencing Music
Through Composing:
Primary and
Intermediate*

STEP THREE: Listening for Inspiration

I have a really exciting recording for you to listen to today, class, and I'd like each of you to close your eyes as we listen. I'll play the CD when each of you shows me that you're ready.

Monitor the class and make sure all eyes are closed; then start the music. This piece is nearly four minutes long, but is full of interesting changes in timbre, texture, dynamics, rhythm, and meter, so it will easily keep the attention of your listeners.

Open your eyes. Who can raise their hand and tell me something about this piece?

Take a few responses.

Let's close our eyes again and listen once more. This time see if each of you can tell me how many sections are in this piece.

Move around the room, monitoring listening and checking that eyes stay closed. When the piece ends, ask for volunteers to report the number of sections. Discuss various responses and take a preliminary vote. Then ask the class to listen once again to check their response.

This time, instead of just listening, let's move some part of our bodies as we listen, and every time the music changes, find another way to move. Here we go.

After the music ends, discuss the number of different movements that were required. Ask the class to diagram the form in some way on the board. Any method will do (graphics, words, letters, symbols, etc.). Review the rondo form and discuss ways in which this piece differs from the usual rondo form.

STEP FOUR: Composing

Our next task is to compose our own percussion rondo using the same form as the composer of "Eldorado," the piece you just heard. We're going to do this in small groups, and each of you will have a part to play in the process.

The first thing we need to do is form groups of six. I'll count to twenty, and when I reach twenty, I'd like everyone to have found a group in which you'd like work. Groups that are ready will be sitting on the floor in a circle. Here we go. One, two, three. . .

When you reach twenty, there may be some children who are still wandering around or sitting at the periphery of a circle, wanting to join. You can let these children join groups already formed or include all of them in their own group. Try to keep each group's membership to six; larger groups allow children to hide and not participate as fully.

Our next task is for each group to build a rondo percussion piece and then play it for the class. I have some directions I'd like you to follow in composing your piece, and they're written on the board. Let's look at them now.

Move to the board, where you have written the following:

1. *Rondo form = A B A C A (three different parts).*
2. *30 seconds long.*
3. *Use at least three different types of instruments.*
4. *May include body percussion.*
5. *May include pitched as well as nonpitched percussion.*

Explain the parameters and take questions. Then say:

You now have ten minutes to work in your groups, and during these ten minutes I'd like you to work out some ideas for the A section. I'll circulate among the groups and help you if you have questions. You may begin.

Move around the room, pausing at each group and listening to the proceedings. Interject ideas where you perceive they are needed. In some groups where no one has taken a leadership role, you may need to ask for a volunteer to be in charge of the A section. Children will attach their own meaning to this, but you can facilitate the composition process by having one student committed to being leader for at least one section. You may have to explain that the leader just does what you, the teacher, do: ask questions and get everyone to try out musical ideas, make things up, and play around with the sounds. Give a one-minute warning and prepare the class for the next task by saying:

We will play our A sections for each other in one minute, and then we'll work on the rest of the piece.

After one minute, have each group give a progress report by playing their preliminary ideas for the A section.

Now we'll return to our group work and begin working on our B sections. Remember all the different ways you can change the music for the B section: think about instrumentation, rhythm, texture, dynamics, pitches. It may help to think about how the composer of our listening selection made the B section different in that piece. You have ten minutes to work on the B section now.

Move around the room, monitoring progress, and allow groups to move at their own pace. Some may speed through and want to work on the C section, while others will take the entire ten minutes to decide on what should happen in the B section and will then need a lot more time to work on it. Still others may have trouble deciding whose ideas should be used in the final product and may need your intervention in the decision process. As the class period draws to a close, give a three-minute warning.

We need to come to closure on today's work. Each group needs to play their piece once more, and then we'll complete them next time. Use the next three minutes to make notes for yourselves that will help you to remember your piece so that you can work on it again next time. You may want to notate the rhythm patterns or write down the letter names of the notes you used, or you may just want to draw symbols for each section and write the names of the instruments you used. I'd like each group to turn in a completed sheet that includes two things: the name of each member of the group and the directions for your composition. Hand this to me as you line up. You now have three minutes to complete this task.

Collect all "scores" before dismissing each group, making sure that the list from each group includes each child's name.

205

CHAPTER 9
*Experiencing Music
Through Composing:
Primary and
Intermediate*

STUDENT ASSIGNMENTS

1. Using what you have learned in previous chapters, develop an evaluation form which you would like a music teacher to use to comment on your teaching. Then arrange to have the music teacher observe and fill out the form as you teach Script 3 or Script 4 to a group of either primary or intermediate children. After debriefing the teacher, write a reflection paper on the experience that covers these two points: the effectiveness of your evaluation form, and your perceptions of the effectiveness of your teaching.
2. Rewrite one of the scripts in an earlier chapter to include a synthesizing composition activity.
3. Develop a form for evaluating a small group composition assignment. Explain how each child will receive a grade for the assignment, what role participation will play, and what role self-evaluation will play in assigning the grade.
4. *Cooperative or partner assignment*: Find five sound sources and bring them to class, along with directions for three different ways to play each of them to achieve three different timbres. Be prepared to lead the class in an improvisation exercise using your sound sources and to lead a discussion of the experience.

Experiencing Music Through Reading:

PRIMARY AND INTERMEDIATE

Case Study

It is April and Miss Davis is preparing for her first sixth grade class of the week. This month she went to her first MENC In Service Conference and found materials she could use with the oldest students in her school. At the MENC conference she found a book for sale, *Personalizing Music Education, A Plan for Implementation*, which described almost a hundred games for teaching notation.[1] She bought the book and spent all of her spring vacation preparing games for the sixth graders to play.

Miss Davis greets the class at the door. "Good morning, girls and boys. I hope you had a wonderful spring vacation. I have a different kind of lesson planned for today. I want you to quietly come into the music room, find your seats, and see if you can figure out what we are going to do."

The children file into the room, go to their assigned seats, and look around curiously. They see signs around the room that say "Station 1," "Station 2," and so on through "Station 8." Under each sign they see either a shoe box or a large laminated chart or stack of cards.

"Does anyone have any idea what is going to happen today?" Miss Davis asks. The children are silent. "Well, at each of the stations posted around

the room, there is a game. The directions to each game are on a card for you to follow. The music games all require you to use what you know about how we write music. For example, the game at Station 1 is called Sad Sam. The directions tell you to deal all the cards to your group and then see how many pairs or matches you can put down. A match is when you have a card with a note such as a whole note and another card that has the words 'Four beats.' Then you continue to play the game by drawing a card from the person on your right, just like Old Maid, only the final card is Sad Sam. I am going to divide you into groups, and each group will have seven minutes to play the first game before you move to another station. When I pull up the overhead screen, you will see a list on the board of the members of each group and the station number that tells you where to start. If you start at Station 2, when the lights flick off and on you will move to Station 3. If you start at Station 8, you will move to Station 1. Does anyone have any questions?"

The children look at Miss Davis. Finally Amanda raises her hand. "Do we get to sing today?" Miss Davis replies, "No, we are going to

---

[1] J. A. Fyfe (1978). *Personalizing Music Education, A Plan for Implementation.* Sherman Oaks, CA: Alfred Publishing Co.

follow this different plan. Are there any other questions?" Jeremy raises his hand. "What about the composition project we were working on before spring vacation? My group worked on it at my house, and we're ready today. We all brought our instruments so we could perform what we wrote."

Miss Davis says, "Well, it will have to wait until next week. Today is game day." She pulls up the screen and says, "Now move to your correct places, please."

The children get up, read their names off the board, and start to move to different parts of the room. Each group sits on the floor and begins to figure out how to play their assigned game. The period proceeds fairly smoothly, and Miss Davis is feeling quite pleased with her lesson. As the groups get to Station 6, however, they all seem to have a lot of trouble. The game directions tell the children to take a card and play the printed melody on a glockenspiel, then turn the card upside down and play the melody again. The player gets one point for each correct pitch and one extra point for playing the correct rhythm. When the card is upside down, the score is doubled. After the first child plays, each group spends the remainder of the time arguing whether or not the rhythm was played correctly.

At the end of the period, Miss Davis turns off the lights and says to the class, "Please return to your seats, class. It is almost the end of music time." The children talk among themselves as they move to where the chairs are set up, and Miss Davis waits for them to come to order. She asks a question to conclude the lesson: "What was our music class about today, boys and girls?" The children all sit and look at her, and no one volunteers an answer. Finally, Amanda raises her hand and says, "Miss Davis, can we sing next week?" Miss Davis replies, "Yes, of course. It is time to line up, sixth graders. Will the people who have birthdays in January and February please walk to the door."

YOUR COOPERATIVE TASK
1. Discuss the purpose of the lesson as seen by the teacher and the children in the above scenario. Create the lesson plan that Miss Davis should use next week.
2. Did the children in this sixth grade class have a musical experience in their music class? Brainstorm a list of ways that the period could have been a musical one and still use the games that were prepared by Miss Davis.
3. Discuss the class control directions and techniques that Miss Davis used. How do they differ from the ones used in earlier scenarios?
4. Reread the model of motivation described on page 61 in Chapter 3. Apply that model to the children's reactions in this lesson.
5. Does anything in this script bother you? Discuss your reactions with your peers.
6. Discuss the levels and types of questions used in this lesson.

PRACTICE TEACHING SCRIPTS

The following two scripts differ from the introductory scripts in prior chapters because they illustrate complete lessons and are constructed to be used not with your peers or friends but with actual groups of children. The scripts, however, are not necessarily appropriate for the class you will teach. You will need to talk with the regular music teacher about which grades or classes are suitable for practice with the script. Teaching music notation is a carefully planned and sequenced part of music instruction in elementary grades, and different teachers stress different aspects of notation at different grade levels. In order for you to succeed with either of the following lessons, students will need to have a background you cannot possibly supply in one music lesson.

Script 1 (Primary)

GRADE LEVEL: Grades One and Two
MUSICAL CONCEPT: Melody
SPECIFIC ELEMENT: Melodic direction can be symbolized.
LESSON OBJECTIVE: Students will be able to demonstrate an understanding of melodic direction and the way that it is notated.
MATERIALS: An overhead of "Taffy" (Figure 8.4); a painter's drop cloth or white disposable tablecloth with a five-line staff drawn on it with marking pen; ten 6-inch white paper plates; Telemann's Suite in A Minor for Flute and String Orchestra, Menuetto, No. 2 (tape the first minute and 10 seconds three times; you can find this in Record 2 from *Music*, grade 2, published by Silver Burdett); a flute or a picture of one.

STEP ONE

Warm up singing voices, emphasizing correct posture: begin with a cold air sip and a hiss on four eighth notes and two quarters (the rhythm pattern in "Taffy"), and end with singing the scale while using clearly spaced Curwen hand signs.

STEP TWO

Review a familiar song that illustrates scalewise melodic direction with at least a five-note pattern. Use "The Flea Song" (Figure 3.2, p. 41) if the class knows it, or ask the children's regular music teacher for a suggestion. In your review, include simple hand movements that show the ascending or descending steps. Then sing the song on "loo," using the proper solfège names on the scalewise pattern with accompanying Curwen hand signals.

STEP THREE

Teach the new song "Taffy" using the rote song procedure outlined in Chapter 3. You may wish to put the song on an overhead; most second graders will be able to read the words. Begin with a sentence or two of motivation:

I have a really neat song for you to learn today that uses all the hand signs we know.

Use the following questions prior to each listening:

1. **Can you figure out who or what Taffy is while I sing the song?**
2. **Watch my hand draw the melody as I sing the song again, and see if you can tell me how the song moves.**
3. **As I sing the song a third time, I want you to move your hand and show how the melody goes up and down.**

Now I want you to look at what I have on the floor. These lines are what we use to write music on. We use every line and the spaces between lines for the circles or notes that tell us if the sounds in a song go up or down or stay the same. Today we are going to have two kinds of notes. You are going to be notes, and these paper plates are going to be notes.

Have the entire class move and arrange themselves so they can see your floor staff.

Have one row of children sit cross-legged, one row kneel behind them, and one row stand. Then put four plates on the staff on the same line or space. Demonstrate by singing the first four sounds of the song that the sounds would be the same. Then use five plates and demonstrate ascending sounds and five more to demonstrate descending sounds.

209

CHAPTER 10
*Experiencing Music
Through Reading:
Primary and
Intermediate*

If our first sound in "Taffy" stands here

(puts one child on D below the staff)

and we sing "Taffy was a," who can figure out where to stand for "Welshman"?

Sing that much of the song, and have the two children standing on D and E do the Curwen hand signs for do and re. Continue with this process until you have eight children standing on the staff. Have those children sit and ask the class:

Can anyone figure out where we would put people for "I went to Taffy's home, Taffy was in bed"?

If a child volunteers, select four other children and have the volunteer place them on the staff.

How many of you know how to stand on the staff for the last phrase of the song?

Sing the last phrase. If enough children raise their hands, select eight and have them arrange themselves, and then ask the class if they are correct. If there are not enough volunteers, do the descending line one sound at a time until the children figure out the pattern. If your staff is long enough, you can have children represent the notes while you sing the song with hand signs. After the students finish representing and singing the song, evaluate their understanding of the process.

This song had three parts. The first part went up. Sing that with me.

Provide the beginning pitch and sing the first phrase.

The second part went up and down.

Provide the beginning pitch and sing the second phrase.

And the third part went down.

Provide the beginning pitch and sing the phrase.

Now I am going to put paper plates on the staff for either part 1 or part 2 or part 3, and you must decide which part it is. After you decide, you must close your eyes, and then I will ask you to raise one finger or two fingers or three fingers. Be sure not to raise your hand until I tell you to, and be sure to close your eyes.

Mix up the phrases and repeat some also so children will actually determine direction, not eliminate possibilities or guess.

STEP FOUR

Now we are going to listen to some music that has upward and downward sounds. The first time we listen, I only want you to decide which instrument is the most important. Then, after that, we will find the upward and downward sounds.

Play a recording or tape of the Telemann piece.

Who can tell me the name of the instrument that was most important?

If no child identifies the flute, shows a flute (or a picture of one) and identify it.

While we listen the second time, I want you to close your eyes and figure out where the music goes up and down. If you can tell, move your hand and show me.

Play the music again and monitor the class. If children do not identify scalewise ascending and descending passages, repeat this step, having them keep their eyes open while you demonstrate where these passages are.

For today, we can listen to this music only one more time. As you listen, I want you to see what other sounds and musical ideas you can hear. We will discuss what you heard after the music is over.

After listening, ask children to describe what else they heard in the music.

STEP FIVE

We are going to end our lesson today by singing the new song we learned, "Taffy." I have an overhead of how this song looks in a music book, and as we sing, I am going to show you how the notes, which are black circles, are placed going up and down just as you placed yourselves on our floor staff.

Sing the song and point out the notation on the overhead.

You remembered that song well, girls and boys. Thank you for a very fine music class.

Script 2 (Intermediate)

GRADE LEVEL: Grade Five

MUSICAL CONCEPT: Melody and rhythm

SPECIFIC ELEMENTS: Major and minor mode; rhythm pattern

LESSON OBJECTIVE: Students will be able to demonstrate an understanding of how rhythm and mode contribute to musical expressivity through singing, listening, and playing.

MATERIALS: An overhead of "Erie Canal" (Figure 4.7, p. 68); two sets of resonator bells; a chart with an A group with ten children's names, a B group with seven names, and equal C and D groups with the remaining names; copy of work song; chalkboard with two sets of bar lines for group work.

STEP ONE

Warm up singing voices with a cold air sip and hiss on the rhythm pattern of the first full measure of "Erie Canal." Then have the class echo short arpeggiated patterns based on scale degrees one, three and five in major and minor.

STEP TWO

Your singing voices sound just great today, class. I want to begin today with a work song that you already know, and then I want to teach you a new work song. Who can raise their hand and tell me what you remember about work songs?

Solicit as much information as possible from the class, and then add whatever is needed to emphasize the ideas that singing made work easier and that in times before radio and TV, singing was a very useful form of personal entertainment. Sing a familiar work song with the class. (Ask their teacher to tell you which ones they know; be sure to prepare so you can sing it without looking at the music.)

We are going to learn another work song now. It was made up by people who worked on the Erie Canal.

> *Show the children where New York State and the Erie Canal are on a map. (The Erie Canal went from Albany, to Buffalo, from the Hudson River into Lake Erie.) Solicit from the class their understanding of a canal and its purpose; fill in any gaps in their information.*

I am going to sing the song to you, and as I sing, I want you to follow the words carefully. The song tells you quite a bit about what it was like to work on the canal.

> *Sing the first and second verses. Then ask the children what they can tell you about canal life and work. Be sure they understand that the boats were pulled by mules, that the canal was shallow, and that the bridges over the canal were low. If necessary, explain the purpose of a lock on a canal.*

I want to sing the song to you again, and this time, I want you to track the chord symbols over the song. We are going to play the chords today.

> *Sing only the first verse.*

Now I want you to sing the song with me, and then we will work out playing the chords.

> *Sing the entire song with the class.*

This song has two parts. How does the printed music clearly show you where those parts are?

> *(The printed copy includes the words* verse *and* refrain *and has a double bar at the end of the A section.)*

There is another way that the two parts of the song are different. Are the chords the same throughout the song?

> *Solicit answers.*

All but two of the chords in the verse are from the D minor scale, which sounds like this.

> *Play the scale and then play three chords.*

The chords in the refrain come from the F major scale.

> *Play the F major scale and the F and C7 chords.*

If I play the first three notes of each scale, can you figure out which of the three tones is changed?

> *If the class cannot tell with D minor and F major, use D minor and D major.*

The third step or tone in a minor scale is lower, and that one difference makes the scale and the chords sound very different. The people who made up "Erie Canal" used major and minor chords to make the parts of the song sound and feel different. Read the words of the verse to yourself, and then read the words of the refrain. What is there about the meaning of the words that would make the composer use such a contrast in the music?

> *Solicit answers, and lead to the idea that the refrain describes coming to a town and that this part of a trip would be more enjoyable.*

I have placed the bells for the chords in the A section on this side of the room and the bells for the B section on the other side of the room. Each set of bells is labeled so that you know which chord you are playing. One

group is going to practice the bell part for the A section, and a second group is going to practice the bell part for the B section. We are also going to have two other groups who will be today's composers. They are going to write out a rhythm pattern for the bells to play in each measure in the A and B section. You will have ten minutes to work on your assignment, and then we will listen to how you sound. But first, let's look carefully at the rhythm of this song. When we add accompaniment, we want a contrast. Let's all clap the rhythm of the first measure.

Clap the rhythm.

Now listen again while I clap it, and think of a rhythm pattern that would be a contrast.

Solicit several responses and try them together, with you clapping the song rhythm and the class clapping the contrast. Follow the same procedure with the first measure of the refrain. Have the two rhythm groups work at separate chalkboards on which you have set up the correct number of bar lines for each section. Move from group to group; encourage cooperation and help children remain on task. You may wish to appoint a conductor for each bell group. After ten minutes, listen to the A and B groups play the bells, and have the rhythm groups clap their rhythms. If groups need more time, let them resume work. If not, have the bell players for the A section play the rhythm on the board while the A composer group softly claps it. Follow the same procedure for the B section. After practice, have a final performance with singing and playing. After the complete performance, lead a discussion, asking the following questions:

1. **How did the rhythm patterns work in each section?**
2. **Could we change them in any way to provide more contrast?**
3. **How does it feel to sing the song with this type of accompaniment?**
4. **Are there other ways we could make the song sound better?**

You did a nice job today, class (*if this praise is warranted*). **Next week we are going to sing some other work songs and also listen to some music that uses major and minor scales. Thank you for your hard work in music.**

If time permits, include a listening selection with major and minor sections, such as "Possum Rag" by Geraldine Dobyns on the recording titled Pickles, Peppers and Other Rags by Women, *Northeastern Records 225.*

WHAT YOU NEED TO KNOW

Why Teach Music Reading?

It is an unfortunate fact that music education ends for the majority of American children when they finish elementary school. It is therefore imperative that students going on to secondary school possess not only the desire to continue participating in musical experiences but also the means by which to do so. Children should not leave fifth or sixth grade musically illiterate! Your students should not be restricted for the rest of their lives to learning any music they want to sing or play via the rote approach. They should possess an important skill that helps them become independent adult musicians: the ability to decipher and interpret musical notation.

213

CHAPTER 10
Experiencing Music
Through Reading:
Primary and
Intermediate

As an elementary music teacher, you will see the same students for a number of years, and your long-term planning must incorporate both readiness for, and the actual process of, performing music while reading musical notation. Because of the short amount of time that is normally allotted for music instruction, you will need a very clear long-range focus for teaching literacy. A comprehensive music education includes experiences in singing, listening, playing, moving, and creating. Each of these musical behaviors is a way to involve children in the expressivity of music. But in addition, each of these behaviors also provides a means by which you can introduce and teach children the language that Western musicians use to preserve what they have created.

You must always remember that notation is not music! As you know from your music history courses, the way we notate music evolved from the way musical sound is produced by performers. The circles and lines we use are actually just another symbol system, as are the words we speak and the numbers we use. Music symbols (or signs) represent or stand for something else. But a naming knowledge of the signs or symbols is nearly useless to children or adults because identification does not necessarily imply the ability to understand and use the symbols in a meaningful way.

You know that music instruction must take children's developmental stages and cognitive abilities into account. Children in primary grades learn most effectively when the experience of music precedes the representation of music. And as children mature, they are better able, in Piagetian terms, to assimilate and accommodate the concepts that constitute the structure of music. When you demonstrate a graphic representation of musical ideas, you provide the necessary connection between the enactive or action stage and the symbolic stage of representation described by Bruner. As the concepts (rhythm, melody, timbre, harmony, and so on) gradually coalesce in children's minds, they also then can be represented in a musianly way.

Fortunately, in addition to maturation and changes in thinking from concrete to the more abstract, another facet of childhood assists you in teaching children to read notation. Children delight in deciphering codes, and a code is just what musical notation is! Whether you are showing melodic direction with icons or with notes, children who can decode your representation and discover that you have drawn or written a song they already know will become intrigued and involved in learning how the new system works.

Another reality of elementary general music teaching is that unless you are the only music teacher in a K–12 district (and there are still many such jobs in our country), you will be one of many music specialists. Since you will be teaching the youngest children in a community or school district, your music teaching peers at other levels (the band, orchestra, or choral director or even the fifth grade instrumental instructors) will expect that when they teach these students, the children will be able to read musical notation. All of your peers expect and assume that teaching the notational system is part of your job. And it is!

Music Reading in Primary Grades

All of the systems of representation that human beings learn are best assimilated if students are allowed to experience the content before being presented with the symbol for the experience. Years of using spoken language as toddlers and preschoolers prepare Kindergartners and first graders for learning to read what they speak. Similarly, counting and numbering experiences are the prelude to learning addition and subtraction. In teaching both of these subjects, professionals understand that children must be ready to learn symbolization and that prior experience produces that readiness.

Teaching music reading in primary grades must follow a similar path. Readiness experiences must be provided prior to beginning instruction in musical notation. These experiences include all of the singing, moving, listening, playing, and creating found in each of your lessons. But in addition, you must carefully plan your curriculum from Kindergarten through second grade to enable children to move quite readily to simple and then progressively more complex reading experiences.

To begin this process, you must clearly understand music as a discipline with its own conceptual structure (as outlined on p. 40 and provided in Appendix A). Your conceptual outlines of the discipline of music are the framework for your short-term and long-term planning. Your personal musicianship and your understanding of the structure of music will enable you to carefully sequence introductory experiences with rhythm and pitch notation in the primary grades.

Rhythm

Readiness for reading rhythm begins with a multitude of steady pulse experiences. Some children begin Kindergarten possessing the ability to clap or pat a steady pulse, but most do not. It may take all of the first and even some of the second year of music instruction before the groups you teach can express a steady pulse to music with unanimity.

Once children can feel and show pulse, you can begin to teach rhythm patterns. Begin with a simple pattern, such as quarter, quarter, two eighths, quarter, and teach the children to clap echoes that alternate between four steady beats and the simple pattern. Once your students can successfully clap this pattern, move the eighth notes to the second beat and alternate with straight quarters as well as with the initial pattern. The next step should be to use a pattern with quarters and a rest on the fourth beat. Then you can combine patterns with quarters, rests, and eighths in your rhythm echoes.

When you introduce echoes, include songs in your lessons that have contrasting meters as well as repeated rhythm patterns. After children feel and demonstrate the pulse, you can have them clap, pat, or step the repeated pattern (see Script 1 or 3 in Chapter 3) and reinforce the pattern with unpitched instruments (see Chapter 8).

Another important distinction children need to experience before they are presented with notation is the contrast between pulse and melodic rhythm. It is best to wait until second grade to introduce this important distinction, as it is easier for older primary children to understand the difference between these two concepts. When the children you teach can pat and clap a steady pulse to known music, echo-clap simple rhythm patterns, and switch from pulse to melodic rhythm, then they are ready to encounter simplified ways to represent what they are doing.

215

CHAPTER 10
Experiencing Music
Through Reading:
Primary and
Intermediate

The simple way to introduce rhythmic notation is to use *stick notation*, or the stems of quarter, eighth, and sixteenth notes and triplets. For four pulses, draw four straight lines. Indicate eighth notes by drawing and connecting two lines. Form half notes and whole notes as in regular notation. With adequate preparatory experience, children at the end of first grade and in second grade will easily be able to read and clap simple patterns using this notational system.

In addition, we know from research in music education that it is helpful to young children to include a verbal mnemonic with these introductory patterns. Calling a quarter note "ta" or "du" or *something* is important. Some teachers use word cues for notes—such as *Ford, Honda, Oldsmobile, Masarati,* and *Pontiac*—while others use nonsense syllables. Different systems exist (see Table 10.1) and all are equally valid. What matters most is that you combine a verbal system when reading rhythm patterns and that you use the verbal cues constantly and consistently.

As you introduce simplified rhythm notation, you need to evaluate whether every student understands the relationship between sound and symbol. One effective approach is to use flip charts like those by Mary Helen Richards in *Threshold to Music*.[2] One chart in this series, titled "What One Do You Hear?," contains simple numbered patterns. The teacher performs a pattern and the students hold up the appropriate number of fingers to indicate the pattern they hear. You will want to sequence your evaluation from easier (with verbal syllables) to more difficult (only clapped, or played on an unpitched instrument). Another form of evaluation is to have children construct the pattern you perform using cut in half popsicle sticks, which can be purchased very cheaply at crafts stores.

Pitch

Pitch readiness evolves throughout Kindergarten and first grade as you teach lessons that provide experiences with register, direction, and contour. These three musical concepts are very difficult for children to verbalize

TABLE 10.1. Verbal Rhythm Mnemonic Systems

Note	Mary Helen Richards	Edwin Gordon	Zoltán Kodály
Quarter	ta	du	ta
Eighth	ti-ti	du-de	ti-ti
Half	ta-a	du-u	ta-a
Whole	ta-a-a-a	du-u-u-u	ta-a-a-a
Sixteenth	ti-di-ti-di	du-ta-de-ta	ti-ri-ti-ri
Triplet	tri-ple-ti	du-da-di	tri-o-la

[2]Mary Helen Richards (1967). *Threshold to Music*. Palo Alto: Fearon.

because musicians use the words *up* and *down* to indicate pitch direction and children (and their parents) use these words to indicate volume ("Turn the TV down"). Therefore, introductory experiences must be multisensory in order to overcome children's prior associations. Children must sing, play, and move to songs that have high and low contrasts (such as "One Elephant," Figure 3.8 on p. 55, or "Taffy," Figure 8.4 on p. 171) as you introduce the labels *high* and *low*. ① Children are able to accept these terms as "words we use in music" when they are stretching high and then crouching close to the floor or moving their hands or arms up and down as they sing and play.

*register
direction
contour*

While you are teaching lessons that focus on these three pitch concepts, you can also begin slowly and carefully to introduce the Curwen hand signs ③ (Figure 3.3, p. 42). As discussed earlier in this text, these hand signs provide a clear spatial cue for young children. Introduce them in the echo format following the sequence described on page 46. This process should not begin until after most of the children in a class have found their singing voices, probably ② sometime in first grade.

Iconic representations of pitch direction and contour also prepare young children to read pitch direction on the staff. For example, after teaching "The Flea Song" (Figure 3.2, p. 41) to first or second graders, sing the song again ④ and simultaneously draw the contour on the board. Then have the class sing the song, follow the contour, move the way the contour is drawn, and then decide where the drawing shows "my hair grows." Whenever you teach primary children a song that contains a clear pattern of melodic direction or register contrast, include a similar iconic activity.

Toward the end of first grade and in second grade, begin to move from reinforcing melodic patterns in songs to the recognition of similarly con- ⑤ structed patterns on other pitched instruments. When your students can listen to patterns you play on the piano and move their hands in the appropriate direction, identify intervals with the correct hand signs, sing what you sign, and correctly select which of three patterns descend or ascend by raising their hands or thumbs, you are ready to move to representation.

Pitch representation needs to begin on large surfaces! Some authorities ⑥ believe that the introduction to the staff should begin with two lines instead of five. Whichever way you proceed will be effective if you make the staff large enough. You must not skip this important step—do not begin directly on the chalkboard. Children need to stand on a floor staff (made of masking tape or on a drop cloth with marker lines). They can manipulate paper plates or beanbags on this staff in first and second grade. This process gives children experiences that prepare them for reading pitch notation. By the end of second grade, students should be able to read note heads that represent scalewise patterns, repeated tones, and the arpeggiated patterns they have learned with the ⑦ Curwen hand signs (sol-mi, sol-mi-do, and so on).

It is very important that you identify which line or space represents do as you begin the transfer of Curwen hand signs to the floor staff. In the Kodály approach, a note at the beginning of the line represents do. In the Richards materials, a key sign, which represents the bottom of a skeleton key, is used (see Figure 10.1). Again, your choice of system is not important. What is important is that you move do around the staff so that children become

217

CHAPTER *10*
Experiencing Music
Through Reading:
Primary and
Intermediate

FIGURE 10.1. Key sign
From Threshold to Music *charts by Mary Helen Richards, published by Fearon Publishers (1967), Palo Alto, CA.*

familiar with the patterns on lines and spaces and that you be consistent in visually illustrating which line or space is do.

Intermediate Grades

Teaching music reading to older students begins with two important transitions. The first is changing from reading stick notation to reading rhythms on note heads, and the second is moving from the large floor staff to reading the staff in an actual music book. This transition must be very careful and gradual so that every child will succeed in the reading process. After third graders become adept at reading combined simple tonal and rhythm patterns on the floor staff (make stems out of construction paper), the transition to the chalkboard is a simple one. If children are aware that they are learning to read music in the same way as "real" musicians, they eagerly look forward to deciphering notation and demonstrating their ability to sing and/or play what is written.

Throughout the intermediate years, you must continue to foster the reading process in every lesson. Music classes that meet once or twice a week do not provide the important reinforcement that children receive in their daily language and mathematics instruction—but remember, you teach each child for six or seven years. Multiply the number of minutes over that span; you will find that it is a substantial amount of time. Using a few minutes each period to teach reading really does produce students who are musically literate.

Rhythm

As you teach rhythm reading in intermediate grades, continue to use stick notation until you have made the transition to using the staff. Stick notation is an effective way to introduce more challenging rhythm patterns, and the clarity of this approach should not be eliminated too soon. As children gradually make the transition to reading what is on the staff, they are often confused by all the symbols and are unable to visually differentiate only the rhythm. Practicing the new rhythm pattern (without note heads) on the board or from an overhead is an important preparatory activity in intermediate grades.

In addition, the stick notation approach will enable many of the main-streamed children in your classes to participate successfully. These learners are often incredibly confused by the visual clutter found in music notation. Separating the pattern in this way is particularly helpful for developmentally delayed youngsters. Some mainstreamed students may require other adaptations; you may need to add color to your charts, point to the beginning of each line on an overhead, use a larger staff or page size, or partially cover the material to eliminate distractions.[3]

As early as the 1960s, music education researchers found that meter is the most difficult rhythmic concept for children. Like any other musical idea, meter is actually a feeling, an impression of how pulses are grouped. Meter is not simply what the top and bottom number of a time signature represent. The ability to feel metrical groupings is based, of course, on all the musical experiences children have had with different meters in the primary grades. As you gradually introduce actual staff notation, you can also explain why we group pulses in the notation, but be sure that each explanation is reinforced with actual experience with the meter.

Each intermediate lesson should include at least one activity that requires students to improve their auditory memory. One approach is to write out the "mystery tune of the week" on the board before each class. Songs that children have learned in primary grades serve as a rich resource for this activity. Another way to challenge older students is to clap the rhythm of known songs and have them determine which song it is. Both of these "challenge" activities can begin with songs the students have just learned and can be extended to songs or music they learned in earlier grades or to music they hear on the radio.

As described in Chapter 9, one important goal of your teaching is to give children the ability to use symbols and musical learnings in a creative manner. Children can use the particular rhythm patterns or contrasting meters you are emphasizing as the content of rhythm compositions they devise in groups or with partners. They can follow single-line compositions with two-line scores or even more complicated rhythm compositions as they mature in their rhythmic ability. Your oldest students might be challenged to write a rap composition: the group can write a simple four-line poem, determine the beat, translate the text to rhythm, and perform for the class. The sound sources for all of these rhythm activities can range from body and mouth and found sounds to any of the unpitched instruments described in Chapter 8.

Pitch

The transition from the floor staff to a smaller staff is easily accomplished in third grade. The basic principle to remember and follow is to move from the known to the unknown. Students can easily be introduced to pitch notation based on their prior knowledge of "The Flea Song" and other songs with ascending and descending scale patterns of at least a fifth. Put the iconic repre-

---

[3]See Betty Atterbury, *Mainstreaming Exceptional Learners in Music*, Englewood Cliffs, NJ: Prentice-Hall, 1990.

219

CHAPTER 10
Experiencing Music
Through Reading:
Primary and
Intermediate

sentation of the song on the board and sing it with syllables, but first challenge the class to identify the song, which they already know. After the children read the iconic representations and sing the scale syllables, simply draw note heads on a staff while again singing the syllables. Next, write out the rhythm of the song in stick notation and have the class perform the rhythm. Then simply transfer the rhythm to the note heads, and your students will be excited to find they can read "real music." The same process can then be followed with songs that have shorter scalewise patterns and songs that have octaves or other large intervallic skips.

Once your students become competent at recognizing songs they already know in staff notation, you should immediately begin to build an understanding of movable do. Children in third and fourth grade need to become familiar with the patterns commonly found in music (scales and arpeggios) in many different placements on the staff. Each time a song or pattern is sung from notation, it should be notated both on lines and then on spaces (for example, in the keys of F and E flat). In this way, children become familiar with this concept. When you eventually introduce the reason we have key signatures, your students will have the experience necessary to understand the formal system.

It is particularly important to teach that key signatures are derived from scales. By fourth grade, your students will have been singing the major scale with Curwen hand signs for four years. They know the sound of a major scale! You can clearly demonstrate with a set of resonator bells on a bell stepladder or music stand that when a scale begins on C, there are no accidentals, but when the same scale begins on any other diatonic pitch, accidentals are required. The transfer to a key signature can then be clearly demonstrated. Of course, you must use children's language, not musicians' terminology, and the discussion should build on many previous experiences with different scales.

Because they are moving from Piaget's concrete operational stage to the formal operations stage (or from Bruner's iconic stage to his symbolic stage), upper intermediate students are better able to decipher more of the notation and markings found in the musical score. And because their voices are capable of more musical singing, they can actually follow and execute more of the dynamic, expressive, and articulation markings found in the music. As you gradually replace the iconic notation of rhythm and pitch with formal notation, you can introduce all the other symbols we use in music. Crescendo and diminuendo symbols, staccato and legato markings, and phrase markings that offer visual reinforcement of the composer's musical intent should be introduced individually and performed in a meaningful musical encounter.

If you carefully plan your teaching of musical notation, you will, after five years, be teaching fifth and sixth graders who truly are able to read music. Because you meet your students only once or twice a week, you may still have to interpret the key signature or indicate where do is for some children. But if you focus on the importance of this skill as a lifelong asset and make it one of your goals for music instruction, you will have fifth or sixth graders who can decipher their chorus music. They will not have to learn by rote in your chorus or in any other musical group they belong to in the future. Your students will be musically literate.

The Approach of Edwin Gordon

Edwin Gordon is a music psychologist and music education theorist whose interests are far-ranging and whose ideas regarding the learning of music reading are particularly pertinent. His interest in music aptitude has led to the development of a number of standardized tests of music aptitude as well as textbooks on music psychology and music learning theory.[4] Gordon believes that the foundation of music literacy is "audiation," which he defines as the ability to hear music silently through recall. Gordon has postulated that there are seven types of audiation, which occur when we are

1. Listening to music.
2. Reading familiar or unfamiliar music in performance or silently.
3. Writing familiar or unfamiliar music from dictation.
4. Recalling familiar music in performance or silently.
5. Writing familiar music from recall.
6. Creating or improvising unfamiliar music in performance or silently.
7. Creating or improvising unfamiliar music in writing.

Gordon believes that these types of audiation are necessary to understand music.[5]

Edwin Gordon believes that learning music depends not upon merely knowing notational terminology but on prior experiences with tonal and rhythm patterns. The sequence in which these patterns should be presented is detailed in his text *Learning Sequences in Music*. Here the reader will find a taxonomy or classification of tonal and rhythm patterns and the suggested order in which these should be introduced. For example, the tonal patterns begin with 21 two-note patterns based on the tonic and dominant triads and then progress to 59 three-note patterns based on the same two tonal functions. This systematic and sequential approach and the accompanying instructional adaptations can be learned in detail in summer workshops, which are offered at various universities.

Planning Complete Lessons

The last two scripts in this textbook provide an opportunity for you to practice your planning skills as well as your teaching skills. The scripts each demonstrate how to introduce a lesson and begin teaching notation. You will create the remainder of each lesson. All of your previous experiences with this text have prepared you for this step, and the following guidelines will help you to refine even further your concept of lesson planning.

Lesson Plan Format

The lesson plan format included here (Table 10.2) is just one of many ways to organize your planning. This format lays out clearly the essential elements

---

[4]*Musical Aptitude Profile* (1965); *Primary Measures of Music Audiation* (1979); *Intermediate Measures of Music Audiation* (1982); *Instrument Timbre Test* (1986).
[5]Edwin Gordon (1984). *Learning Sequences in Music: Skill, Content, and Patterns.* Chicago: G.I.A. Publications, p. 19.

TABLE 10.2. General Music Lesson Plan

221

CHAPTER 10
Experiencing Music
Through Reading:
Primary and
Intermediate

Grade Level:

   I. Musical Concept:

  II. Learning Outcome or Objective

       Entry ability: Students can . . .

       Exit ability: Students will be able to . . .

 III. Lesson Evaluation Procedures:

 IV. Materials and Board/Space Preparation:

  V. Teaching Procedures:

     A. Setting the Stage:

     B. Developing the Lesson:

         Step 1:

           Transition question:

         Step 2:

           Transition question:

         Step 3:

           Transition question:

         Step 4:

           Transition question:

     C. Concluding the Lesson:

 VI. Self-evaluation:

of lesson planning that you need to know and understand so you can complete the teaching scripts in this chapter.

Elements of Lesson Planning

Begin formulating a lesson plan for the musical concept you wish to teach by thinking about what your students already know and what they are capable of doing. Your learning outcome or objective should lead your students beyond what they presently know or can do, and it should be stated in such a way that you can either observe success directly or infer students' understanding from their discussion. A synthesizing activity, such as composing a movement piece that exemplifies the concept of binary form, might also serve as an evaluation.

Since you may not have the foggiest notion as to how many second graders can demonstrate the concept of steady beat, observe the class for whom you will be planning a lesson, and take the time to consult with their music teacher. You will remember from Chapter 2 that the most useful verbs for learning outcomes or objectives relate directly to musical behaviors: *sing, listen, move, play, create,* and so on. These verbs are avenues to real musical learning and are readily observable bases for evaluating whether your students learn what you want them to learn.

It is important to carefully list all the materials you need, from instruments to props to recordings. Including such items as composer, title, and recording label and number will save you from last-minute panic when you realize that your CD case is empty and you'll need to dash to your school's learning materials center (LMC) to find a replacement. Similarly, listing the Orff instruments you need, as well as the configuration of pitches you want to use, will save you precious class time since you will be able to arrange the instruments in advance.

The heart of the lesson plan is the procedures section. It is here that you carefully set out exactly what you want to do and the order in which you will do it. The beginning of each lesson needs to grab students' attention and get them completely involved in what you are doing. You may wish to show a poster or picture as a stimulus to discussion, or you might use a prop such as a hand puppet to focus their attention. You could also use a question from previous lesson content (based on your consultation with their music teacher) to draw students into your lesson. Whatever you use to set the stage needs to be age-appropriate and interesting to your audience, but it is only a means of leading them to the real meat of your lesson, the teaching procedures.

The steps you decide to follow in teaching your lesson should proceed logically and leave your students with some sort of changed musical understanding. In order to formulate these steps, you must give a lot of thought to what will happen first, second, third, and so on. The most crucial part of leading children through a lesson is the transition question you pose to take them from one step to the next. Write out your transition questions in your lesson plan, and *highlight* them in neon yellow or orange. That way you can easily refer to your prepared questions and refocus the direction of the lesson if you begin to digress while teaching.

Your conclusion should summarize and synthesize for your students what happened during the lesson, putting it into the larger context of prior musical learning and, perhaps, foreshadowing what will happen during the next music class. One of the most effective ways to conclude a lesson is to ask a volunteer to make a one-sentence statement about what she or he learned during that class period and then let others add to or modify that statement.

223

CHAPTER 10
Experiencing Music
Through Reading:
Primary and
Intermediate

The self-evaluation section of the lesson plan format is a place where you can record your immediate reactions to your teaching. Here you may want to note where the lesson went awry, or where you ran out of time. You may want to make notes about what you wished you had said or how you will rephrase something when you teach the lesson again.

TEACHING SCRIPTS

An important rule to remember in planning a lesson is that the length of an activity should be equal to the children's age. So, if you teach 7-year-olds and you have a 30-minute period, the lesson should contain at least four different activities. If any singing, listening, playing, moving, or creating activity lasts longer than seven minutes, you may find that you have lost the attention of many class members. Until you know the abilities of the children you teach and are familiar with their prior musical experiences, you can rely on this rule in your lesson planning. As with the introductory scripts in this chapter, you must investigate the background the children have in notational readiness and/or their actual experience with notation before teaching either of these scripts.

The new song outlined below is one of these four lesson segments. You must decide which other musical behaviors to incorporate in this lesson (listening, moving, creating, playing) to reinforce or complement children's experience with sol and mi.

Script 3 (Primary)

GRADE LEVEL: Grades One and Two

MUSICAL CONCEPT: Melody

SPECIFIC ELEMENT: Melodic intervals

LESSON OBJECTIVE: Students will be able to demonstrate an understanding how one interval, sol-mi, is represented on a floor staff by placing note heads on a floor staff and singing.

MATERIALS: "Hello There" (Figure 7.3, p. 143); a large floor staff (use masking tape on the floor, or use a white drop cloth or disposable paper tablecloth and draw a large staff); a pitched instrument (either barred or resonator bells).

STEP ONE

Warm up singing voices: begin with an emphasis on correct posture for singing, then focus on abdominal breathing. Show the children how to put their hands below their rib cages, inhale, and bark like dogs. You can have children volunteer the names of different breeds to extend the exercise. Then have the class echo different melodic patterns using the Curwen hand signs, ending with several that use sol and mi in different rhythm patterns.

STEP TWO

The first song we are going to sing today is one that you already know. Raise your hand when you know which song I am playing.

Introduce a familiar song that contains a descending minor third, such as "This Old Man," by playing it on a recorder or another pitched instrument. (Check with their regular music teacher.)

As we sing this song together, watch my hands. I want to show you where sol and mi are in the song.

Give class the starting pitch by singing "Ready, sing" on the pitch and motioning them to begin singing with you. Use the Curwen signs for sol and mi at the appropriate places in the song.

We're going to play those sounds on these bells, but first let's sing the song and practice where sol and mi go by taking out the regular words and putting in sol and mi.

Sing "This Old Man" with the class, providing the starting pitch on the words "This is sol, ready sing" (replace "This old man, he played one" with sol and mi). As the children practice in the air, demonstrate how they are to play the pattern on the pitched instrument that you have prepared. If you are using a barred instrument, remove the surrounding and intervening bars. If you are using resonator bells and have a bell stepladder, leave an empty stair between bells to reinforce the interval. Select one child to play each measure, and sing the song again, replacing the first two measures with the syllables.

STEP THREE

Now I am going to teach you a new song. It also has sol and mi in it. Will you be able to tell where they are?

Sing "Hello There."

As I sing the song again, if you think you know where sol and mi are, show me with your hands.

Sing the song and monitor the class.

I want to be sure that everyone knows where these two sounds are in this song, so as I sing this time, watch my hand and move your hand where sol and mi belong.

Sing the song and model movements.

Let's sing this song the way we did "This Old Man" so that we are really sure where to put sol and mi and where to play them on the bells.

Sing the song, replacing the pattern in the first, third, ninth, and tenth measures with syllables. Then as above, model playing movements while leading the singing again and adding instrument players.

STEP FOUR

We have a way in music of showing where these sounds are, and we don't have to use any words. It is a really neat thing to know because when we write out our songs, people far away can look at what we wrote down and know exactly how our music should sound. We're going to start learning about where to put just sol and mi today, and then we'll add other sounds during other music classes.

225

CHAPTER 10
Experiencing Music
Through Reading:
Primary and
Intermediate

Spread out the floor staff.

These lines and the spaces between the lines are where we will put sol and mi. If sol goes around a line, the mi will always go around the line below. And if sol is in between two lines, then mi will be in between two lines right below it. I want one of you to come and stand on a line (choose a volunteer) and be sol. Then we will see if someone else knows where to stand to be mi.

Continue with this activity until all children are able to participate. Have three children figure out where to stand for the beginning of the song, and sing the song once more with bells and hand signs.

Note: *You now need to create the next two steps of this lesson.*

STEP FIVE

STEP SIX

Script 4 (Intermediate)

GRADE LEVEL: Grades Five and Six
MUSICAL CONCEPT: Texture and expressive symbols
SPECIFIC ELEMENT: Layering texture, accents, dynamics, phrasing, and staccato
LESSON OBJECTIVE: Students will be able to play a rhythm score and interpret the notation and expressive symbols.
MATERIALS: Rhythm score on an overhead transparency; piano part on transparency from *Let's Have a Musical Rhythm Band*, Figure 10.2 (Phoebe Diller, Alfred Music, 1976); bells and triangles; tambourines; wooden instruments; drums and cymbals; piano; Bach's Minuet.
Before you teach this lesson, practice the piano part so you can play it without looking at the music. You will need to be able to monitor the class and even use your head and eyebrows to cue students.

STEP ONE

Good morning, sixth graders. As you can see by what I have out today, we are going to play a lot of instruments, but we are going to do so in a very different way. First I want you to follow my rhythm patterns after one measure, and we'll see how long we can make our canon.

Begin the class with a rhythm canon as explained on page 158. Begin with a one-measure canon using the rhythms in the score, and alternate between clapping and body percussion. Then expand to a two-measure canon, where the second measure is a dotted half note or a quarter and two rests.

STEP TWO

Now we're going to read those same rhythms on this overhead. But first let's look at each part and see what else we have to do besides reading quarter notes, eighth notes, and rests. Look at the bell and triangle part. Are there any other symbols in that part?

Minuet

J.S. Bach

FIGURE 10.2. **Minuet by J. S. Bach**
Let's Have a Rhythm Band, page 3, by Phoebe Diller. Published by Alfred Music, (1976), Van Nuys, CA. Used with permission of the publisher.

227

CHAPTER *10*
*Experiencing Music
Through Reading:
Primary and
Intermediate*

FIGURE 10.2. *(Continued)*
Let's Have a Rhythm Band, *page 3, by Phoebe Diller. Published by Alfred Music, (1976), Van
Nuys, CA. Used with permission of the publisher.*

Jazz Version

FIGURE 10.2. *(Continued)*
Let's Have a Rhythm Band, *page 3, by Phoebe Diller. Published by Alfred Music, (1976), Van Nuys, CA. Used with permission of the publisher.*

Solicit answers and discuss dynamic markings.

Let's all clap this part together and see if we can change our dynamics when the score tells us to.

Clap the bell and triangle part.

Now let's look at the next part. Do the tambourines have other markings?

229

CHAPTER 10
Experiencing Music
Through Reading:
Primary and
Intermediate

Solicit answers; discuss and model accents, having the class echo-clap several patterns with and without accents.

Let's clap the tambourine part together and follow the score markings.

Continue in this manner through the other two parts. Then divide the class in half and clap the first two parts simultaneously. Be sure to emphasize the importance of the expressive markings. Practice the third and fourth parts the same way. Then divide the class into four parts and clap the entire score together.

Now I want you to look at my part.

Put the piano score transparency on the overhead.

How does this part differ from the rhythm lines?

Discuss and demonstrate the two staffs, phrasing marks, and expressive symbols.

Now we are going to build a complex texture. First I want you to follow the piano score as I play it and decide whether I include all that the composer asked for.

Play the minuet expressively.

How did Bach vary the phrases in this piece?

Discuss the importance of articulation.

To make a thicker texture, we add more sound. So I will play the piano part again, and the first line of rhythm will play with me. The rest of the class is to clap their part very softly to help them.

Play the piece with one line. Discuss the effect and whether the result is a musical one. Then add the other lines in the same manner. If any part needs another practice, separate that line and have rest of class help by clapping the rhythm softly. End the activity with discussion of how any changes in texture occurred and the contribution of interpreting the symbols.

Note: *You now need to create the next two steps in the lesson.*

STEP THREE

STEP FOUR

STUDENT ASSIGNMENTS

1. Revise the evaluation form you developed for Assignment 1 in Chapter 9, and have a music teacher use it as you teach one of the scripts in Chapter 10. Write a reflection paper on the teaching and evaluation process.
2. Rewrite an earlier script in this text to include a section on teaching notation readiness for primary children.
3. Devise an evaluative activity for one of the teaching scripts in this chapter. Describe how you would record the achievement of each individual class member using your activity.

CHAPTER 11

Real Teachers in Real Worlds

Chapters 1 through 10 focused on developing your skills in engaging children in the musical behaviors of singing, listening, moving, playing and reading, and creating. You have learned to teach songs, develop listening lessons, design movement lessons, introduce instrumental playing, compose music with children, lead children gradually to read notation, and evaluate your students' learning. Although these skills are essential in your future teaching career, they alone will not guarantee your effectiveness as a teacher. You need to consider two other important aspects of teaching before you launch your career: planning and communication.

PLANNING

The experience of music does not happen for learners unless you have an organized and well-executed curriculum. Through all of your script and original lesson segment teaching this semester, you have had an opportunity to practice presenting musical behaviors, fine-tune your pacing and enthusiasm, and try different classroom management techniques. All these aspects of teaching are important in the presentation of lessons. However, as discussed extensively in Chapter 2, presentation of activities in music class is not the sum of music teaching. Each activity that engages children in a musical behavior needs to be related to prior and successive parts of a lesson as well as to a clear outline or framework. Similarly, each lesson needs to be related to prior and successive lessons. This cohesion comes about after you have developed a curriculum for all the grades you are teaching. Beginning teachers may want to start with curriculum documents developed by others, gradually making changes and adjustments depending upon their particular setting. However you approach this task, it is imperative that you structure your teaching content within a curriculum that defines your long- and short-term goals.

Your own college instructor and your cooperating teacher during student teaching may each require a framework different from the lesson plan format described in Chapter 10. You will find, however, that despite differences in vocabulary and format, all music lesson planning includes essentially the same content. No matter what the setting, you will always have to plan what you are going to teach, describe how you are going to teach it, determine what the children learned from your teaching, and then plan the next lesson.

COMMUNICATION

It's time to begin to refine your communication skills with a variety of constituencies, including cooperating teachers, administrators, fellow teachers, pupils, and parents. Communication includes listening and speaking and writing, and the more effectively you are able to express yourself, the better your message will be heard. Crucial to effective expression, however, is your thinking prior to communicating.

This chapter contains materials meant to stimulate your thinking and let you assume the role of music teacher in a variety of situations that require professional judgment. These situations are all from the real world of general music teaching. The remainder of the chapter includes three distinct types of content: case studies, role-playing encounters, and a concluding philosophical discussion supporting music's place in the public school curriculum.

The first section contains eleven short case studies based on typical events in the careers of student teachers and general music teachers. These case studies differ from the earlier case studies in this book in that *you* take the place of Miss Davis as the protagonist in each scenario. Your task will include finding the problems in each case and proposing solutions based on what you know as a student, a performer, and a colleague. You will gain invaluable experience from delving into these multilayered situations and discussing possible solutions, and this course may be your last opportunity to discuss situations such as these with music colleagues. One of the most valuable results of the task you are about to undertake is that you will gain a larger perspective on the wide variety in people's reactions and responses as your peers inform you about their solutions and reactions to the problems. Welcome to the world of real teachers in real classrooms!

RELATIONS WITH YOUR COOPERATING TEACHER

"You're Off to a Great Start, But . . ."

It is the fifth week of the term in your student teaching. You are sitting in the office of Dr. Devon, your university supervisor. He has just observed your teaching for the first time and is giving you feedback on what he saw. He says, "You are really doing a fine job! The children enjoy your class, and the content of your music lessons is age-appropriate and engages the children well. The students are singing so well, and your cooperating teacher tells me that their classes can't wait to come to music. There is one thing, though, that I'd like you to work on. You just don't have any affect. When you talk to the children, you don't have any change in facial expression. For example, when you tell them that their singing was good, your face doesn't match your words. I know you'll be able to fix this problem, so work on it before your next observation, OK?"

2. What will you say to Dr. Devon?
3. What will you do before your next observation?

"But They're Just Little Children"

It is the third week of student teaching. Ms. Brennan, your cooperating teacher, is going over this week's teaching with you. She says, "I'm concerned about the content of one of your classes. When I was watching your first grade lesson this week, I saw a lot of activity. You had the children singing a little bit, playing instruments a while, and moving some. They did a lot of group work to make up their own movement pieces and then performed them, and you spent time in some really fine class discussion. I think, however, that you should be spending a lot more time singing in your classes. After all, these are just little kids. They have such sweet singing voices, and they should use them more in music class. The other stuff is nice, but it's really too hard for them, don't you think?"

YOUR COOPERATIVE TASK
1. What can you say to Ms. Brennan to convince her that you are capable of choosing course content appropriate for young children?
2. How does it feel to be challenged in such a way?
3. What, if anything, will you do differently in your teaching? You really want to get a good grade in student teaching.

TEACHER-ADMINISTRATOR RELATIONS

"Oops, I Forgot To . . ."

As you are walking down the hall toward the teachers' lounge to eat lunch on Friday, the principal, Mr. James, comes to the door of his office and asks you if he can talk to you for a minute. You follow him into his office and sit down in front of his desk. "I was wondering when you see your fifth and sixth grade chorus next," he asks. You reply, "The next chorus rehearsal is on Tuesday from 12:00 to 12:30. That's our short rehearsal because the children have to come in from the playground in order to have the rehearsal at all, and I hate to have them give up all their play time. Is there a problem?" He replies, "Well, I don't think it is a problem. I know you are working hard with the chorus for the music night next Wednesday. But last night at the supermarket I had a short conversation with Mrs. Polk, the president of the PTA. She and her family have lived in this town all their lives, and she reminded me that she is really looking forward to your music night. She is especially anxious to hear the school song again. Have you taught it to your chorus?" You look at him in amazement and say, "I've never even *seen* the school song. What are you talking about?" He looks at you with a guilty look and says, "Oops, I forgot to give it to you in September. But the children need to sing it next Wednesday night. The parents will be upset if they don't hear it."

YOUR COOPERATIVE TASK
1. What will you say next?
2. What will you do before next Wednesday?
3. Brainstorm some creative ways to include the school song in the program without making your chorus appear to be unprepared.

"We Have a Problem"

When you get to school on this beautiful April morning, your find a note in your mailbox from Mrs. MacIntosh, the principal. The note says, "Would you let the secretary know when you are free today? We need to meet about next year's building plan." You quickly review your day's plans and walk over to the secretary. "Mac needs to see me today, and I'm free from 11:00 to 11:20. Will you check with her and see if that time is good?" At 11:00 you knock on the door frame and walk through the open door into the principal's office. She looks up and says, "Thanks for coming in this morning. I want to tell you want I learned at the superintendent's meeting yesterday before I announce it at the faculty meeting today. The enrollment numbers for this building next year have skyrocketed. We will have to add another section of first grade, and we decided in yesterday's meeting that we will use the music room for this new class." You look at her in dismay and reply, "When you hired me last year, you told me that I would always have a music room! I left a job where I went room to room with a cart and a portable keyboard. Isn't there any other solution to the space problem?" She looks at you sadly and says, "Well, there is the stage between the gym and the cafeteria that is not being used."

YOUR COOPERATIVE TASK
1. What should you say next?
2. What should you do about this problem?
3. Make a list of compelling arguments for keeping your music room, which you will use in another meeting with the principal.
4. What other approaches could you use to change this decision?

TEACHER-TEACHER RELATIONS

"Don't You Tell On Me!"

One elementary classroom teacher, Mrs. Radovich, consistently keeps students from attending your general music class if they do not finish their other work. You have spoken to her about this problem many times, and she has agreed that she will not do it anymore. You have begun to keep track of each instance when this occurs, and you discover that Mrs. Radovich is continuing to keep between one and three children from music each week. You see the children at this school for only forty minutes each week—and Mrs. Radovich has kept a few students out of music for more than a month. You decide to speak to the principal, and you take with you your carefully kept documentation of these instances. The principal agrees that something must be done and promises to speak to Mrs. Radovich. The following week, just before your lunch break, Mrs. Radovich storms into your classroom and says, "You have no business going to the principal about me! You should talk to *me* if you have a problem with the way I run my classroom!" You patiently explain that you did, in fact, discuss the problem with her many times but that it seemed to do no good. Mrs. Radovich screams, "Well, you have no business going to the principal about *me*! I've been at this school for twenty-seven years, and no one goes to the principal about *me*!"

YOUR COOPERATIVE TASK
1. What can you do or say next that will allow each of you to leave the scene gracefully?
2. Should you have done something else instead of going to the principal? If so, what?
3. Will you go into the lunchroom today, or will you avoid it? (Mrs. Radovich and her friends will all be there when you arrive.)

Late Every Time

It is Thursday afternoon, and just like every other Thursday this year, you are standing at your door waiting for the fourth grade class to come to music. The class is already five minutes late. Finally you hear the sound of laughing, excited children; the class is coming down the side hall from the gym.

The children burst around the corner and come to a stop at your door, but they are unable to quiet down. The teacher, Miss Grossman, says, "Gee, I'm really sorry we're late again, but we were having a great kickball game."

YOUR COOPERATIVE TASK
1. What should you say to Miss Grossman now?
2. What should you say to Miss Grossman after school?
3. What are some effective ways to deal with the continual lateness of this class?

TEACHER-STUDENT RELATIONS

Naughty Words

While rehearsing the sixth grade chorus, you encounter some opposition from Shawn, who is one of your best singers but one of the most volatile students in the school. During a particularly difficult woodshedding session, Shawn does not hear you give directions and doesn't know where you are starting. You have the group sing their starting pitches and give the signal to begin, but only half the students come in on the first beat. You are exasperated and say, "Let's see if we can get that right this time." Then Shawn loudly says, "Well, if you wouldn't make us sing this (expletive), we wouldn't have such a hard time getting it right!"

YOUR COOPERATIVE TASK
1. What will you do next?
2. What can you say to the rest of the group to take them past this situation and resume the rehearsal?
3. Will you involve the principal? Shawn's parents? The classroom teacher?

Children Are Not Always Responsible

It is the morning after your spring concert. On your way to your music room you pass by several sixth grade girls who were in the concert last night. "You did a great job last night, ladies. I was really proud of you." One of the girls is Linda, who was supposed to sing a solo but did not come to the concert. You stop and say, "Gee, Linda, what happened to you last night?" Linda looks at you and says, "Oh, I am so sorry. I got sick when I went home, and my mother wouldn't let me out of bed." You commiserate with Linda and tell her you are glad she is feeling better. As you continue to walk down the hall, one of the other sixth graders, Patricia, starts to walk with you toward the music room. She says, "Lisa did a really nice job at the last minute when she sang Linda's solo, didn't she!" You nod and keep walking. You can't talk to a sixth grader about how upset you were when you warmed up the chorus at 7:00 and Linda was not there to sing the solo she had auditioned for and had been so prepared to sing. Patricia looks at you and says, "You know, Linda went to the mall last night with her mother. She called me when I got home from the concert to tell me what they bought."

YOUR COOPERATIVE TASK
1. What will you say to Patricia?
2. What is the next thing you do to deal with this situation?
3. How do you emphasize the importance of responsibility and concert attendance?

Controversial Content

Mrs. Kiersky calls you and complains that her Kindergarten child is going around the house singing a song about "Baby Jesus and Mary." Mrs. Kiersky states that as a Jewish parent she does not think this song is appropriate for her child to learn in a public school. You explain that "Mary Had a Baby" is a traditional *spiritual* song and that all the Kindergartners are also learning Hanukkah songs for the winter concert, but this does not satisfy her. Although she offers that her husband is Catholic and that they are raising their children to be both Catholic and Jewish, Mrs. Kiersky demands that you remove this song from the program.

YOUR COOPERATIVE TASK
1. What will you say next?
2. What will you tell the principal?
3. Will you continue to let the Kindergartners sing this song in class? It is one of their favorite songs, and they have even made up a dance to go with it that shows the call and response sections.

Is a Solo Worth a Lawsuit?

It is after school on a Friday, and you are in your room waiting for Mrs. Pringle, who has sent a note asking for an appointment. She is the parent of a talented fifth grade boy, and you wonder if she is going to talk about having Adam audition for the nearby University Children's Chorus. You sent a note to her about this idea a month ago but never had a reply, and Adam has not mentioned the note at all. Mrs. Pringle comes into the room. Adam is walking behind her rather slowly. She turns around and snaps, "Hurry up, Adam—we haven't got all day!" You walk over to her and say, "It is really a pleasure to meet you, Mrs. Pringle. Adam is such a talented singer, and he is a joy to have in class and in chorus. Won't you sit down?" Mrs. Pringle looks at you with an unsmiling face and says, "That's just what I want to talk to you about. Adam tells me that the reason he didn't have a solo in the concert last week is because you don't like him and you are unfair." You look at her with complete surprise and begin to explain to her how the soloists were chosen. "Mrs. Pringle, after we decided that there would be three solos in this concert, the children who wanted to try out for these solos stood behind a screen and the chorus members voted who would sing each solo. Didn't Adam tell you this?" The mother looks at you in disbelief and says, "That is not what my son told me, and he does not lie! You'll hear from my lawyer very soon." She grabs Adam by the arm and storms out of your room.

YOUR COOPERATIVE TASK
1. What will you do next?
2. List the steps you might need to pursue regarding this problem.
3. How can your teacher's organization help you when a lawsuit is mentioned?

Same Child, Different Perceptions

It is late afternoon, and you have one more parent phone call to make before you leave. Your princi-pal has encouraged everyone on the staff to find as many positive moments to share with parents as possible, and you are really pleased that you can call Tilene's home today and describe how she organized the other children in her group, kept them on task, and encouraged each of them in a positive and mature way. You are especially pleased at how gentle and supportive she was with one group member who is mainstreamed into music. The teachers in this grade level have been working on cooperative behaviors, and you can tell from today's class that the children have developed a warm and caring attitude toward each other. You dial the number and say, "Hello, is this Delia Williams?" You explain who you are and describe the positive behaviors you observed today in your class. Tilene's mother says, "I don't think we're talking about the same child. This girl was supposed to stop at the store for milk on the way home and she forgot. She is the most irresponsible child I ever saw."

YOUR COOPERATIVE TASK
1. What will you say next?
2. What other steps can you take to communicate with this parent?
3. What other faculty members should be made aware of this conversation?

ROLE-PLAYING ENCOUNTERS

The following role-playing experiences are designed to provide an opportunity for you to become even more deeply involved in thinking about what it means to be a real teacher in the real world. These four encounters are based on actual situations that general music teachers have encountered during their school year. The situations, settings, and characters are described in general terms; prior to the actual role-playing session, your instructor will give each member of your group a separate role description.

For successful role playing, each member of the group must assimilate the information provided about his or her role and then act out the assigned part without stepping out of the fictional setting. We encourage you to think not only about your assigned role but about those your classmates are playing, as well as how all the roles and settings represent the real world of music teaching.

1. TIME: After school
   DATE: Spring of your first year in the district
   SETTING: Junior high band room
   PARTICIPANTS: Junior high band teacher; junior high choral/general music teacher; elementary and junior high string teacher; elementary band teacher; you
   TASK: Determine the concert calendar for the upcoming school year.
   MOTIVATION: The other teachers have always met on their own, but because you have asked to have your newly formed elementary chorus included on the concert schedule, you have been invited to participate in this annual scramble for dates.

2. TIME: 3 P.M.
   DATE: Second week of school
   SETTING: High school choral room
   PARTICIPANTS: All of the five elementary music teachers in the district
   TASK: Discuss and organize the first elementary honors chorus.
   MOTIVATION: One teacher has an outstanding choral program and wants to provide enrichment for her students.

3. TIME: 8:30 A.M.
   DATE: January in-service day
   SETTING: Junior high learning center
   PARTICIPANTS: All elementary teachers in the district
   TASK: Learn about and discuss portfolio evaluation, and then determine how to implement it across the elementary curriculum.
   MOTIVATION: The district has adopted portfolio evaluation as the method whereby all elementary students will be graded.

4. TIME: 11 A.M.
   DATE: Second week of January
   SETTING: Small conference room next to the principal's office
   PARTICIPANTS: Principal; school psychologist; classroom teacher; Daniel Moore's parents; music teacher
   TASK: Discuss Daniel's future placement.
   MOTIVATION: Daniel has been recommended for placement in a self-contained classroom for behaviorally disordered children.

WHY MUSIC IN THE SCHOOLS?

The case studies and role-playing exercises in this chapter have given you a taste of the many conflicting situations that confront the general music teacher. You may have been surprised by some of the situations in which you found yourself, and you may be amazed that an individual teacher has so many decisions to make. Because teaching is a context-specific profession, every teacher needs to arrive at solutions based on particular facts and events as they unfold. You have two sets of professional ammunition to take with you: your "people skills" and your philosophy.

People skills are an essential component of your professional education, and these skills will guide your judgments. For example, the skill with which you are able to "read" a parent who wants to talk with you will determine whether you sense that this is an urgent request or a routine chat about an upcoming music event. However, an even more important aspect of your professional preparation is your philosophy of music education. Your philosophical basis for teaching music is the single most important idea that you have formulated during your undergraduate work, and it is the most important idea that you will take with you to your first teaching job. Your personal philosophy of music education gives you your very reason for teaching music, and it will guide your responses to all of the dilemmas and problem situations you encounter in your career.

For example, if you believe that the best reasons for teaching music to children are social ones, you may have decided in role-playing encounter 3 that you will continue to give grades based on class participation and will simply stay out of the portfolio assessment argument completely. On the other hand, if your philosophy of music education is based on giving children the best possible access to musical understanding through a wide variety of real experiences, you may have argued for a portfolio evaluation technique that includes many musical behaviors as well as reflection on those activities. You may be able to state your philosophy simply as a few dearly held beliefs about why you want to be a music teacher, but developing a philosophy is still one of the most important aspects of your professional education. The following section restates the major ideas of this text and summarizes the authors' philosophy of music education.

EVERY CHILD DESERVES A MUSIC EDUCATION

In our democratic society, we educate our children so that they will encounter the facets of human knowledge and culture that we adults believe they will need in order to become productive and contributing members of our society. And as adult musicians, we believe that all children deserve an opportunity to experience the joy, wonder, and delight of musical experience. Because the process and the product of music can be difficult to describe and too often are not perceived as an important part of the curriculum, our subject needs continual defense and support as a part of schooling that is valuable for each child.

Every future music educator must be able to describe the content, process, and outcomes of a complete music education, using language that parents, administrators, fellow teachers, and school board members will understand. And this description *must* be grounded in music. What is it that you teach in music, and how can you describe all the facets of your curriculum to others? The development of an answer to this question may seem onerous and unnecessary now, as you sit in a college classroom, but when you walk into your first interview—even the interview that precedes your student teacher placement—you may be asked to articulate what you believe is important about what you teach.

Powerful and effective music teaching consists of organized and sequential encounters with good music in each of the various ways that music can be experienced. It is difficult to explain what "good" music is, but as a trained and practicing musician, you are able to distinguish the trivial from the profound and the easily accessible from that which takes more time and exploration to truly experience. Young children deserve the best musical diet possible, and an important part of your job will be to select this diet and verbalize why you have done so.

One of the most powerful ways that human beings have to express themselves is through the use of their vocal instrument. Almost every child you teach has the ability to improve this important form of musical expression, and singing is one way to encounter the depth of feeling contained in music. As you monitor each child's vocal growth and instruct children in correct vocal production, you are teaching an important musical skill or behavior. More important, however, is that you provide the means by which each child will be able to experience the wide range of feelings music stirs within us.

A reality of present-day society is that music surrounds us, often from the time we arise until we go to bed. How do we deal with this plethora of sound? And how do children deal with it? Teaching children to become perceptive listeners—human beings who can discriminate pulse, melody, meter, timbre, harmony, and so on—is an important part of music instruction in elementary schools. But mere perception is not enough, of course. Perception or recognition or naming are the initial steps you provide in music instruction, but reflection and discrimination and reaction are the ultimate and valued goals of your listening instruction. All children must have continual encounters in listening to music in ways that will enable them to become adult listeners who can experience the powerful feelings that music sets free within us.

As you deepen your understanding of what music means to human beings, you also need to recognize that not every child will have the same experience in the same way in each of your music lessons. Some children will feel music most strongly through singing, others through listening, and still others through the other musical behaviors of composing, moving, or playing instruments. Each of these behaviors fosters individual encounters with worthwhile musical experience. Therefore, your teaching must include all these important opportunities for individual children to interact with the content of music.

Administrators, parents, and your teaching colleagues perceive performance as the ultimate goal of music education. How you perceive your subject and how you educate these constituencies about the value of music education will be a very important part of your teaching career. If the other significant adults in your environment see and hear children only in polished performances, you tacitly communicate the belief that only a completely rehearsed musical product is of value and worth sharing. Public performance is certainly an important part of music making, but youngsters should not be expected to emulate professional entertainment. When you share children's music making with others, the emphasis should be on the process, the learning, the growth, and the potential of those you teach.

In this text, we have explained why we think music is a valid part of every child's education. In addition, we have provided you with the knowledge and skills necessary to practice the craft of teaching. We hope that your practice has enabled you to move to the role of teacher, one who reflects on what is happening to students as a result of instruction. When you reach this level of teaching practice, you can step back, enjoy what is happening as you teach, and savor the ability to share your love of music with others. We hope you will find that teaching general music is a joyous and delightful experience.

Appendix A:
Musical Concept Taxonomy

Rhythm

1. Awareness of beat and no beat
2. Beat subdivision (rhythm patterns)
3. Duration
4. Meter
5. Uneven beat subdivision (dotted, syncopated, fermata)

Melody

1. Register
2. Direction
3. Contour
4. Duration
5. Phrases
6. Tonal centers
7. Intervals
8. Sequence

Harmony

1. Presence/absence
2. Contrasts of texture (homophonic, polyphonic, monophonic)
3. Polyphonic (descants, canons, rounds)

Timbre

1. Difference between voices and instruments
2. Contrasts of high and low instruments
3. Contrasts of instrument families

Form

1. Phrases
2. Song sections
3. Introduction, coda
4. AB, ABA
5. Rondo, theme and variations, fugue

Dynamics (Expression)

Appendix B:
Additional Listening Selections

PULSE

AARON COPLAND, "Hoedown" from *Rodeo*
DUKE ELLINGTON, "Ain't Got Nothin But the Blues"
MICKEY HART, "Jewe" (Planet Drum RACS 0206)
WYNTON MARSALIS Septet, "And the Band Plays On"
MARIANNE MARTINEZ, "Allegro con Spirito" from *Sinfonia in C* (Baroquen Treasures, NCC60102)

RHYTHM PATTERN

LUDWIG VAN BEETHOVEN, Third movement from Symphony No. 7
CLAUDE DEBUSSY, "Golliwog's Cakewalk"
EDVARD GRIEG, "In the Hall of the Mountain King," from Peer Gynt Suite
SCOTT JOPLIN, "Maple Leaf Rag"
ANTONIO VIVALDI, "Winter" from *The Four Seasons*

DURATION

JOHANN SEBASTIAN BACH, "Passacaglia in C Minor"
HECTOR BERLIOZ, Fourth movement from *Symphonie Fantastique*
AARON COPLAND, "Circus Music" from *The Red Pony Suite*
FELIX MENDELSSOHN, "Nocturne" from *A Midsummer's Night Dream*
MAX REGER, *Sonata No. 4 in A Minor for Cello and Piano*, "Presto"

MELODIC DIRECTION

EDWARD ELGAR, "Fairies and Giants" from *Wand of Youth Suite No. 1*

ANDREW LLOYD WEBBER, *Requiem*, "Pie Jesu"
NICCOLO PAGANINI, "Caprice No. 5 in A Minor"
CAMILLE SAINT-SAËNS, "Kangaroos" from *Carnival of the Animals*
JACK TEAGARDEN, "High Society"

DYNAMICS

LUDWIG VAN BEETHOVEN, First movement of Symphony No. 8
HECTOR BERLIOZ, Fifth movement of *Symphonie Fantastique*
JOSEPH HAYDN, *Symphony No. 97*, "Movement IV: Presto Assai"
GUSTAV HOLST, *Suite in E Flat*, "March"
JOHANN STRAUSS, "Banditten Gallop"

TIMBRE

CLAUDE BOLLING, "Irlandaise"
GEORGE GERSHWIN, "Oh, Lord, I'm On My Way" from *Porgy and Bess*
CARL ORFF, "Movement 1" from *Carmina Burana*
GIUSEPPE VERDI, "Libiano ne Lieti Calea" from *La Traviata*
ANTON WEBERN, *Five Pieces, Op. 10, No. 1*

FORM

LEONARD BERNSTEIN, "Prelude, Fugue & Riffs"
PERCY GRAINGER, "Lost Lady Found" from *Lincolnshire Posy*
GEORGE FREDERICK HANDEL, "The Harmonious Blacksmith"
ZOLTAN KODÁLY, *Hary Janos Suite*, "The Viennese Musical Clock"
GLADYS YELVINGTON, "Piffle Rag" from *Pickles and Pepper and Other Rags by Women*
    (Northeastern 225)

TEXTURE

ANONYMOUS, *Recordings for a History of Western Music and Norton Anthology of Western
Music* (1980) NY: WW Norton.
    "Victimae Paschal: Laudes"
    "Senescente Mundano Filio"
    "Pucclete, Je Languis, Domino"
THE BEATLES, "When I'm Sixty-Four" from *Sgt. Pepper's Lonely Hearts Club Band*
JOSEPH HAYDN, "Kyrie" from *Lord Nelson Mass*
WOLFGANG AMADEUS MOZART, *Duo for Violin and Viola, K 424*, second movement
SUKAY, "Huayno" (Bolivian folk song from Flying Fish 90501)

Appendix C:
Additional Listening Resources

These two recording labels include the music of women composers from all historical periods:

Newport Classic

106 Putnam Street

Providence, RI 02909

Northeastern Records

P.O. Box 116

Boston, MA 02117

The book *Women Composers: The Lost Tradition Found* by Diane Peacock Jezic (1988, New York: Feminist Press) is another good source. Two companion tapes are available:

Leonarda Productions, Inc.

P.O. Box 1736

Cathedral Station

New York, NY

CATALOGUES

An extensive listing of world music sources, including recordings from Africa, the Caribbean, Europe, India, Indochina, the Middle East, and North America, is found in this source:

World Music Catalogue

West Music

1208 Fifth Street

P.O. Box 5521

Coralville, IA 52241

Phone: 1-800-397-9378

A wide array of listening and music video resources for children are available:

Music for Little People

P.O. Box 1460

Redway, CA 95560

Phone: 1-800-727-2233

Index